New Approaches in Ethics for the Caring Professions

Richard Hugman

palgrave
macmillan

First published in 2005 by
PALGRAVE MACMILLAN
Houndmills, Basingstoke, Hampshire RG21 6XS and
175 Fifth Avenue, New York, N.Y. 10010
Companies and representatives throughout the world.

PALGRAVE MACMILLAN is the global academic imprint of the Palgrave Macmillan division of St. Martin's Press, LLC and of Palgrave Macmillan Ltd. Macmillan® is a registered trademark in the United States, United Kingdom and other countries. Palgrave is a registered trademark in the European Union and other countries.

ISBN-13: 978–14039–1471–2
ISBN-10: 1–4039–1471–0

This book is printed on paper suitable for recycling and made from fully managed and sustained forest sources.

A catalogue record for this book is available from the British Library.

Library of Congress Cataloging-in-Publication Data

Hugman, Richard, 1954–
    Professional ethics : taking account of change for caring professions / Richard Hugman.
        p. cm.
    Includes bibliographical references and index.
    ISBN 1–4039–1471–0 (paper)
        1. Human services personnel – Professional ethics. 2. Medical personnel – Professional ethics. 3. Professional ethics. I. Title.

HV10.5.H84 2005
174—dc22   2005041950

10 9 8 7 6 5 4 3 2
14 13 12 11 10 09 08 07 06

Printed in Great Britain by Biddles Ltd., King's Lynn, Norfolk

For
Michael, Rosalind & Charlotte
Emma & Jennie
Shelley
Felicity & Lucinda
… the next generation

Contents

Preface

Interest in ethics, especially within the professions, has grown considerably in recent decades. There are several reasons for this, including the challenges that arise from the increasing complexities of contemporary society and from technological developments. Much of the existing literature examines professional ethics in terms of the traditions, such as deontology and utilitarianism, and to a lesser extent the virtues. However, moral philosophy, like the society of which it is part, has also been subject to constant debate and change. While the debates of applied ethics in the caring professions have dealt with the changes arising from social and technological developments, the same cannot be said about responses to changes in philosophy and social theory. This book, therefore, seeks to respond to significant developments in ethical thought and how these impact on the questions that are of concern to the caring professions. In particular, new approaches to ethics have emerged from feminist, ecological and postmodern ideas, as well as from recent directions in liberal philosophy. For the caring professions to grasp the ethical dimensions of social and technological changes it is important that attention is given to such wider developments in moral philosophy. That is the goal of this book.

In the following discussion the realities of professional practice are the core concern. Wherever possible I have sought to ground the exploration of ideas and principles in the type of situations for which a practical ethics is essential. The argument presented here leads towards a particular way of thinking about and engaging with ethics in practice. This orientation, as it becomes clear, is based on a commitment to the idea that ethics is too important only to be left to specialists – it is the responsibility of every member of the caring professions. My hope is that by enlarging the ethical vocabulary of the caring professions to include recent developments we will ensure that they are able to do 'good' work.

My own thinking about the ideas presented here has gained greatly from discussions with many colleagues, in particular in recent times with Diane Barnes, Wendy Bowles, Fran Crawford, Damian Grace, Sabina Leitmann and David Palmer. Thanks are due especially to Damian Grace and anonymous reviewers for perceptive comments about an earlier draft, as well as to Anne Copeman and David Palmer for research assistance. Any errors and omissions are my own responsibility. Catherine Gray and Beverley Tarquini at Palgrave Macmillan have provided invaluable guidance and support throughout the process of producing this book, for which I am very grateful. Finally, I would like to acknowledge all the students, too numerous to mention by name, with whom I have shared debates about many of the questions that are explored in the following pages.

Richard Hugman
Sydney 2004

CHAPTER 1

Contemporary Professional Ethics

Ethics and the caring professions

Ethics should be of concern to everyone. We can no more avoid facing moral issues than we can avoid breathing. It is impossible to think of human society without recognising the role that moral values and beliefs play in the way in which day-to-day life is conducted. Our ideas about what is good and what is right are woven into the fabric of thought and action so that, whether we are conscious of it or not, they affect our wishes and our choices. A practitioner in a caring profession may not stop to consider the question of 'good' or 'right' in every task they perform, as for much of the time the values and beliefs that underpin all aspects of our lives simply 'are'. Like many things that are necessary for society to operate, such as language, we take them for granted and would find it strange to be constantly engaged in critical reflection. Yet there are also times when the professional ought to give conscious attention to the reasons why one choice seems better or worse than another, whether about the way in which something is done or about the objective that is being sought. In these circumstances the person is engaging with ethics. Ethics, in this sense, is the 'conscious reflection on our moral beliefs' (Hinman, 2003, p. 5).

The purpose of this book is the conscious reflection on the moral values and beliefs associated with those occupations that are understood as 'caring professions'. This term is intended to encompass those occupations that, on the basis of a high level of training in specific knowledge and skills, undertake work in which the human person is both the object and the subject, whether physically, mentally, emotionally or spiritually. Included in this concept are allied health professions (including dietetics, occupational therapy, pharmacy, physiotherapy, podiatry and speech pathology), counselling, (clinical) psychology, nursing, medicine, religious ministry, social work, teaching and youth work. Indeed, it is a premise of the discussion that these are as much moral or ethical practices as they are knowledgeable and skillful in a technical or scientific sense. (More will be said in Chapter 3 about the notion of 'caring profession' and the way in which this idea shapes the approach to professional ethics that is taken in this discussion.)

This book looks at the ways in which ethics in these caring professions is the same as or distinct from ordinary, everyday ethics. It also explores the way in which the ethics of the caring professions relate to the wider ethical sphere within which professional work is undertaken. These are questions that have been identified as central to professional ethics, especially in contentious areas such as those that are the concern of the caring professions (Johnstone, 1994; Beauchamp & Childress, 2001).

More specifically, the main focus of this book is on recent developments in ethical thought more generally, both to understand how these changes might raise new questions for the caring professions and to consider the implications of contemporary ethics for practice in the caring professions. Professional ethics is often discussed as a special aspect of ethics. My starting point here is to ask to what extent this is the case and whether this is the most helpful way of considering ethics in professional work. How have debates about ethics in other areas progressed? What is the current thinking about issues such as compassion, care, virtue, respect, justice, benevolence, equity, utility, and so on? Have approaches to ethics in the caring professions kept pace with thinking elsewhere? To begin to answer these questions, we must look first at the ethical heritage of the caring professions.

The legacy of ethics in the caring professions

Ethics in the contemporary professions reflects the history of social thought. Bauman (1995) describes the development of ethics in western society in terms of a typology of the over-arching social and religious world-views that have prevailed in successive eras. His discussion portrays this sequence as having four main stages.

- First, the period of classical philosophy, in combination with religious polytheism – the Greek and Roman era, in which the foundations of western philosophical thought were established.

- Second, the medieval period, in which the ideas of the classical era were rethought within the social context of theocracy and monasticism – in this era moral thought continued to be religious in character, that is predominantly Christian, with Judaic threads (monotheism).
- Third, the period of modernity, the 'age of reason' in which scientific modes of thinking began to replace religious approaches in social thought – this is the era of classic liberal philosophy, in which ethics started to become the science of moral life, in the context of the rapid development of industrial society.
- Fourth, the present emergence of 'postmodernity', which is marked by fragmentation, plurality and diversity – in this era it appears that scepticism and uncertainty are leading to a rediscovery of earlier periods, plus attempts to synthesise competing ideas.

Each of these eras can be seen as having continued influence through those that follow; hence, all of these eras impact on current debates in different ways. As we shall see, the third and fourth, that is modernity and postmodernity, are the most overt in the development of formal professional ethics, because these define the historical periods in which the caring professions themselves have grown.

The classical era

Considerable regard is paid in discussion of professional ethics, especially in the health field, to the influence of the early Greek philosophers. For example, Glannon (2002, p. 1) traces medical or health ethics back to Hippocrates, whose physicians' 'oath' can be seen as the first declaration of professional ethics. This oath included statements of commitment to pursuing the good of patients and avoidance of doing harm, refraining from corrupt self-interest (including sexual exploitation), and maintaining confidentiality. For Hippocrates the virtuous physician was one who achieved moral balance by placing the interests of patients and the members of the surrounding society clearly within the meaning of health. The physician who attended to the physical health of a patient while causing harm to other aspects of well-being would lack integrity. Virtue as balance suggests the integration of all aspects of life.

The approach to moral thought that emphasises virtue or 'good character' as the basis for ethics predominated among the ancient Greek philosophers (Pellegrino & Thomasma, 1993, p. 4). Aristotle, in particular, is credited with the idea that a systematic method can be applied to the self-development of virtuous character, in which a person strives for balance between extremes (pp. 5–6). That is, it is possible to be 'too just' or 'too compassionate', for example, as much as it is possible to exercise these virtues too little. Furthermore, the Greek philosophers asserted that virtues can be taught and developed through practice; they are not just natural. The implication is that virtues are not simply the innate property of some individuals due, perhaps, to chance in the same way that physical characteristics might be, but can be seen as the result of a variety of external influences and subject to conscious choice. Thus, ethics concerned the active pursuit of the integration between right thought and right action. As Hinman (2003, p. 269) puts it, Aristotle's central ethical question was 'what kind of person should I be?' As we will see, this question and Aristotle's philosophy generally are of particular significance in recent philosophical developments.

The medieval era

Medieval western philosophy built on the traditions laid down in the classical era, and can be described in terms of a growing debate (over several centuries) between a view of the world derived from Plato and a 'rediscovery' (through translation) of Aristotle's ideas (Copleston, 1955, pp. 63–9). Because of the social dominance of the Christian church in matters of philosophy and other learning, the key figures of this period were monastic scholars. Thomas Aquinas is regarded by Pellegrino and Thomasma (1993) and by MacIntyre (1985) as the most influential of these theologian-philosophers, in this respect. However, as all intellectual and social life in the medieval period was dominated by the Christian Church, there was no formulation of distinct 'professional' ethics, with the exception of a continued reference to Hippocrates' oath. Yet even this was contextualised within the same general ethical teaching that applied to all members of Christian society.

Aquinas was not the only medieval thinker to be influenced by Aristotle's ideas. Another notable theologian-philosopher was William of Ockham, who, in his application of Aristotelian logic, laid foundations for later modernist developments in ethical thought through two propositions: first, the separation of human reason from divine revelation as the authority for moral values (Hinman, 2003, p. 88); second, 'Ockham's Razor', the idea that the simplest arguments should always be preferred, so that it is pointless to multiply or complicate hypotheses (Delanty, 1997, p. 15). Such arguments were key stages in the move towards a philosophy, including ethics, based on human reason operating through logical deduction. Indeed, it is this type of development in western thought that can be used to explain the emergence of modernism (and of industrial society) compared to other religious/cultural traditions (Tawney, 1938).

The modern era

Following the late medieval break between philosophy and theology, western science and philosophy of recent centuries have been built on faith, not in gods or God, but in the capacity of human reason, through the application of correct techniques, to determine truths that apply to all classes of subject (whether in the natural world or human society). This belief in the capacity of human reason as the basis for understanding the world is usually known as 'rationalism', the approach to knowing the world that seeks truth in objective observation is 'empiricism', while the idea of truths that apply to all subjects is termed 'universalism'. These tenets are the cornerstone of modernist thought, together with 'individualism' (valuing the individual person as the unit of moral consideration, as compared to the family or the community). Indeed, it may be argued that the resulting technologies provide abundant evidence that such faith was not entirely misplaced. Even the most profound sceptic expects everyday technology to work, and for there to be a rational empirical explanation when it does not. Indeed, the very professions with which this book is concerned are an integral part of these kinds of technical and intellectual developments, whether bio-medical, psychological or social.

Alongside such successes has been a concern to match the shift from a religious to a scientific understanding of the natural world, with a systematic grasp of comparable laws of human nature and society. Moral philosophy in the 'age of reason' has been subject to the same intellectual processes, and the quintessential attempt to produce 'ethical laws' to replace 'divine law' was the work of Kant (MacIntyre, 1985). Kant's work epitomises ethics founded in rationalism, in which abstract and universal principles define 'right conduct'. This approach, known as 'deontology' from the Greek δεον (deon), duty, is based on the assumption that ethical laws are duties. Such principles are defined in abstract terms; they are general and universal, applying equally and impartially to everyone in the same type of situation. This idea is most famously expressed in terms of a 'categorical imperative': 'I ought never to act except in such a way that I can also will that my maxim should become a universal law' (Kant, [1785] 1964, p. 67). In other words, whatever standards of good and right I claim for myself I must also claim for everyone else. Kant also argued that all moral agents should be respected solely on the grounds that they are in themselves moral agents. This idea is expressed as a 'practical imperative': 'act in such a way that you always treat humanity, whether in your own person or the person of any other, never simply as a means, but always at the same time as an end' ([1785] 1964, p. 91). In other words, to summarise, the principles on which you act should be applicable to everyone and you should not use people as a means to achieve ends that they do not share or are not relevant to them.

Furthermore, for Kant '[a]n act's moral worth depends on the reason for which it is done' (Hinman, 2003, p. 176). In other words, the good person must not only be following the right rules but also doing so for the right motives, of which duty opposed to self-interest is seen to be the best. Arising from this perspective has been a development of formalised codes of ethics (laws of right action) alongside the rational scientific practices that define each profession. Indeed, it is often the conjunction of distinct scientific bodies of knowledge and skills with a code of ethics that is taken as the defining feature of 'a profession' (Abbott & Meerabeau, 1998, pp. 2–5), a point that will be discussed further in Chapter 3.

Utilitarianism, the main rival to deontology in modernist ethics, also reflects the scientific spirit of the era but has very different premises. Originating in the work of Bentham ([1781] 1970), and developed by J. S. Mill ([1861] 1910), this approach to ethics looks not at principles and duty, but is founded on a rational calculation of the consequences that follow from an act. Utility, according to Bentham, is that which 'tends to produce benefit, advantage, pleasure, good, or happiness [and] to prevent the happening of mischief, pain, evil, or unhappiness' ([1781] 1970, p. 12). This approach is often summarised as the pursuit of 'the greatest happiness of the greatest number' (Freeman, 2000, p. 51), although it has always been faced with the problem of both defining and measuring 'happiness' despite the painstaking discussion offered by both Bentham and Mill concerning the inclusion of physical, psychological, emotional, cultural and spiritual aspects of experience in this concept (Sumner, 1996, pp. 147–56). Moreover, there are two versions of utilitarianism that have developed the original idea in different ways. 'Act utilitarianism' is the view that the good person should do that which will maximise utility. 'Rule utilitarianism' advocates action in accordance with the principles that ought to maximize utility for the society. As with deontology, utilitarianism is individualist, rationalist, empiricist and universalist.

Both deontology and utilitarianism emerged as formal ethical doctrines in the context of the industrialisation of western society. It is possible to see in both approaches, but particularly in deontology, the continuation of ideas that were already established, such as the idea that it is always right to tell the truth and wrong to lie, but with these ideas based on an appeal to the authority of scientific rationalism rather than divine inspiration or tradition. This period was also marked by the growing dominance of liberal humanism in political and social philosophy, with an emphasis on the pursuit of individual liberty. Thus both bodies of ethical thought were seeking to develop approaches that would encompass the idea of individual human rights, volition, responsibility and so on, while at the same time to locate the individual human subject within the social and political order.

For much of the time in which the caring professions have grown and assumed their contemporary forms, debates about ethics within the professions have tended to be characterised in terms of a tension between deontology and utilitarianism. This can been seen in allied health (Barnitt *et al.*, 1998), medicine (Downie & Calman, 1994), nursing (Burnard & Kendrick, 1998), psychology (Francis, 1999), social work (Clark, 2000) and teaching (Carr, 2000). However, the impact of wider changes in western social and cultural thought has caused an increased questioning of this bipolarity, opening up new possibilities in thinking about ethics and in looking again at older ideas. Not only is there a tension between the ideas of individual rights and of the maximization of utility, but also for professions that are focused on the needs of people the emphasis on reason over emotion or relationships can be seen as inadequate because it is impersonal. The first tension suggests that neither deontology nor utilitarianism on its own is sufficient as an account of professional ethics, while the second suggests that nor are they sufficient when taken together.

The 'postmodern' era

Although there are many different positions within 'postmodernism', the common idea that characterises this broad trend is the decline in the authority of 'meta-narratives' (Lyon, 1999). A 'meta-narrative', in this sense, is a theory that seeks to provide a universal, over-arching explanation of the social world. This includes the notion of 'human nature' as it applies to all people, including all the ideas that would follow from it, such as 'human rights' or 'human needs'. In contrast, postmodernism argues that such universal perspectives have lost any plausible meaning. In a social world marked by flexible, floating, plural, contingent and uncertain meaning universal explanations of what it is to be human appear, at best, to be the mistaken application of a partial and contextualised view of the world across people and situations to which it does not fit. For example, although the idea of 'human rights' may seem to apply to all people, what it actually means is culturally loaded in that the very notion derives from western polit-ical and social thought in a particular period. Postmodernist views tend to regard society as a network of meanings that are constructed by human beings through language, and so may only be understood through language. Society, and therefore meaning, is constantly shift-ing. Because of the primacy of language, society is to be 'read' like a written text and, as with a text, meaning is not fixed but changes with different readings. So any 'reading' or analysis of society is tentative and never final in its judgements (Sim, 1999, pp. 30–8).

In contrast to the emphasis placed by 'modernist' theories on the scientific objectivity of method in ethical thought, postmodernism replaces these with attention to language. It is also marked by philoso-phers and applied ethicists revisiting the thought of earlier periods, while looking at these ideas through contemporary lenses (much as had Aquinas and other medieval scholars, although with different conclusions). In particular there has been another 'rediscovery' of the ancient Greek tradition, especially the work of Aristotle and attention to virtues as the basis of ethics (MacIntyre, 1985; Foucault, 1997). A different direction has been taken by Bauman (1993), for whom the starting point of inquiry is the contemporary shifts in the social context within which the moral life is lived, especially in so far as these indicate a weakening of universal values and the emergence of a more plural and fragmented society. Ethics based on ecological perspectives also look at changes in society, notably in arguments about 'risk society' (Beck, 1992, 1999). This concept refers to the impossibility of achieving certainty in a highly technological age, because, just as science has extended human control over the natural world, through the unintended outcomes of technology it has also shown the limita-tions of human knowledge and understanding. For some ethicists this strengthens arguments for utilitarianism (Singer, 1975), while for others it connects with the feminist 'ethics of care' in caring for the whole of the natural order (Mies & Shiva, 1993) and for others again a more plural position is required (Smith, 1998).

Three particular strands of development in philosophy can be seen in the later part of the twentieth century. Drawing on the critical alternatives to liberalism, these three reflect an interest in subjectivity, emotion and experience. Attention to the first of these, virtue ethics, has grown rapidly in professional ethics in the 1990s. This can be seen particularly in writing about medicine (Pellegrino & Thomasma, 1993), nursing (Tadd, 1998) and social work (Rhodes, 1986). Second, arguments that emotion plays an important role in ethics are of interest because of the core notion of compassion. In some considerations of professional ethics, compassion is regarded as a virtue (Beauchamp & Childress, 2001), while in others it is seen as a distinct emotion that guides careful judgement about values (Brown, 1999; Fischer, 2001). Third, there is also growing attention to relational ethics, particularly the 'ethics of care' that stems from the writing of Gilligan (1982), and which is itself, in part, grounded in a particular idea of virtues. Originating in psychology, this concept has been applied widely to nursing (Bradshaw, 1996; Sevenhuijsen, 1998) and to education (Acker, 1995; Sumison, 2000), and to an extent also to allied health professions (Taylor, 1995), to medicine (MacLeod, 2001) and to social work (Parton, 2003).

Interest in virtue, compassion and care draws on the philosophical tradition that was established by Aristotle (Tronto, 1993; Blum, 1994). These aspects of ethics each, in different ways, address Aristotle's core question, 'what kind of person should I be?' that was noted above. They also, each, in some way draw on Aristotle's concept of 'phronesis', or practical wisdom, as an ideal professional characteristic (Scott, 2000) and his idea of living well (human flourishing, or 'eudaimonia') as the ideal goal of human action (van Hooft, 1995, p. 141). Van Hooft argues that it is these ideas that distinguish 'ethics' from 'morality', in so far as the former concerns 'that vague and undetermined set' of socially contextualised ways in which we might live well (an 'ethos') and the latter (as in Kant's philosophy) is about sets of universal and objective principles for human conduct (1995, pp. 141, 144). Although this distinction is widely recognised by philosophers, in everyday usage the two terms tend to be less distinct. So, in this discussion of professional ethics, following Hinman's definition quoted above, I will focus on ethics as conscious reflection on beliefs and values and morality as the set of beliefs and values about what constitutes good action.

Even if the full analysis of postmodernism is not accepted, there appears to be increasing attention to matters of subjectivity, particularity and experience that goes against the predominant strands of modernism that are reflected in a focus on duties, rules and principles. Yet, as Scott notes (2000, p. 124), because of the existing strong emphasis on liberalism in ethics each of these developments has only recently begun to make an impact on the study and teaching of ethics in the caring professions (also see: Gallagher, 1999). So, in order to examine recent changes and challenges in ethics for the caring professions, emotion and compassion, the 'ethics of care' and virtues in conditions of postmodernity will be explored further, in Chapters 4, 5 and 7 respectively. Following from the discussion of 'care' in Chapter 5, Chapter 6 will take a slightly different direction in an examination of the 'ethics of ecology' as a concern with care for the non-human natural world as well as the place of humanity within it.

Main themes in contemporary professional ethics

Although the liberal thought of the modern era has provided the ethical foundation for the caring professions, recent discussion has tended to avoid employing 'pure' forms of deontological or utilitarian theories. Starting from a high level of philosophical thought and then seeking to 'apply' abstract ideas to concrete situations is to mistake the appropriate purposes of different theoretical levels. So, while deontological or utilitarian ideas may be useful as ways of thinking, they cannot be simply imposed onto practical situations as they stand. Attempts to construct 'deontological' or 'utilitarian' premises from which all practical ethical debates and dilemmas can be viewed leads only to an oversimplification of the complex circumstances in which caring professionals practise.

As a consequence of this limitation of 'pure' theories, the predominant approach of practical ethics in the caring professions has become that of 'principlism' (Gallagher, 1999). This simply means that ethics is derived from basic principles. Principlism begins from the relationship between action and core values. Of course, as we shall see, these values may themselves be expressed in the terms of the two pillars of classic liberalism, but used in this way such ideas represent styles of thinking rather than abstract and binding rules of human action. Principlism is a pluralist approach that brings together ideas about duty, consequences, character, relationship, emotion and so on (Beauchamp & Childress, 2001).

Lewins' (1996) review of key texts in health ethics shows that the same core principles occur repeatedly. These are: respect for the autonomy of the individual person; non-maleficence; beneficence; justice (p. 34). Concepts such as veracity, fidelity, privacy and confidentiality also appear frequently as subsidiary principles. Of all of these principles, 'respect for the autonomy of the individual person' is predominant, if its derivations and variants are taken into account (p. 12). (Downie & Calman (1994), whose work is not part of Lewins' analysis, provide a philosophical defence of this position.) Indeed, the same principles also occur widely in the formal ethical statements and codes of caring professions, as I will examine in more detail in Chapter 9.

Arguably one of the most influential texts in bio-medical and health ethics is the work of Beauchamp and Childress (2001). They advocate principlism as a realistic position that avoids problems inherent in a strict adherence to either deontology or utilitarianism. Furthermore, while two of their principles draw on ideas of obligation to generalised concepts, other principles draw on notions of virtue. They arrive at this view by noting the difference between moral norms, that is general 'rules' of what is good, and descriptive statements of what is good. Their application of principlism, therefore, combines attention to both concepts and practices. This leads them to say, contrary to the idea of a single foundational principle, that there can be ethical dilemmas in which it is very hard for someone to choose between competing and even contradictory ideas that all have the same moral weight. This position is a type of 'ethical pluralism' in that it recognises that no one value or approach is always paramount over all others (Kekes, 1993).

For Beauchamp and Childress (2001), some of the categories they use to delineate professional ethics are liberal principles, namely respect for the autonomy of the individual person and justice. Other categories, however, are drawn from the tradition of virtues, namely non-maleficence (not doing harm) and beneficence (doing good). In other words, for instance, they would distinguish between seeking justice as acting on a principle and being beneficent as exercising a virtue. Both, however, are part of the framework of professional ethics and can be specified in general terms as applying to everyone who is part of a profession. They go further, and suggest that consequences ('ends') may also be an important consideration:

> ... in contrast to radical forms of character [that is, virtue] ethics, we do not hold that the merit in an action resides in motive or character alone. The action must be appropriately gauged to bring about

the desired results and must conform to the relevant principles and rules. (Beauchamp & Childress, 2001, p. 29)

The result is that it is no simple matter to infer what 'ought' to be done with respect to 'being' and 'doing' 'good' either from notions of virtue or from principles alone (or, indeed, from calculation of utility or rules derived from duties). Rather, what is required is the capacity to gauge the balance between different ethical demands in situations where all the evidence that ideally would be required to make the 'best' decision may not be available, and where a 'blend' of 'principles, rules, virtues, passions, analogies, paradigms, narratives and parables' is necessary to achieve practice wisdom (Beauchamp & Childress, 2001, p. 408).

An example of this can be seen in the following situation (which is hypothetical, but derived from the present author's practice experience).

A girl aged 15 discloses to a teacher that over the last three years she has regularly smoked marijuana and had sex with a man who is now aged in his early twenties. She has just heard that he is being treated for a sexually transmitted disease and is concerned that she may have been infected. So she wants the teacher to help her to see a doctor who is not her own family's general practitioner; she also does not want her parents to know.

This is a situation that may face not only teachers, but also other caring professionals, whether based in a school setting or practising elsewhere. The dilemmas inherent in such a situation come from the contradictions between principles and values that underpin professional ethics as widely understood.

First, there is a dilemma arising from a contradiction between the teacher's duty to uphold the law and respect for the autonomy of the individual person in terms of self-determination, privacy and confidentiality. The law in most western countries defines a minimum age at which sexual acts may be regarded as 'consensual' and below which such acts must be regarded as coercive or exploitative. As this relationship appears to have begun when the girl was aged 12 it is the case that in most countries this situation will be seen as breaking the law. In many countries there will be a mandatory requirement on the teacher to notify other agencies who are empowered to take legal action in respect of the young man. However, the girl has trusted the teacher in an expectation of confidentiality. While in many countries it is well established in law that professional confidentiality is not absolute but must be weighed against probable harm (Bersoff, 1995), there is also the practical aspect of how this might affect the girl's response to other help that she clearly needs. For instance, the teacher's experience of the girl may suggest that she will withdraw her co-operation from a medical consultation if such action is taken, which clearly would be against the interests of the girl's well-being. Thus the teacher may have to struggle between duty, respect for autonomy, beneficence and non-maleficence.

Second, there is a range of subsidiary issues that the teacher may have to face. Can a good resolution be reached without colluding with the student? Or without deceiving the student? Is there the same obligation of respect for the autonomy of a minor as there would be for an adult? (For example, on a Kantian basis we might wish to consider whether children are to be regarded as 'rational beings' in the same sense as are adults – laws in many countries do make judgements of children's moral capacities in precisely this sort of manner.) Would or should it make a difference, and if so what, if it were suggested that the nature of the potential 'infection' was HIV or Hepatitis C as opposed to gonorrhoea or syphilis? What are the implications if the student and the teacher are from different ethnic or cultural backgrounds? What are the school's policies on such matters, and to what extent should they have a bearing on decision making?

It is not the purpose of this discussion to provide a 'model answer' to this hypothetical situation. Indeed, the point of arguments such as that of Beauchamp and Childress is that 'moral diversity and moral disagreement' may be inevitable because of different views about facts, norms, capacity and so on (2001, p. 22). What would be seen as the 'right' response by the school administration or a child protection agency may be at odds with some teachers or youth workers, for example, because of differing orientations to their relationship with the student, differing views of the important values in the professional role, and so on.

This is not the same as arguing for 'moral relativism', in which any moral value is equally plausible and acceptable as any other. Rather, it is to acknowledge that discussions of ethics from a particular theoretical perspective may in themselves disagree – after all, some of the theories that have been outlined in this chapter contain mutually exclusive ideas (Rachels, 1998). Veatch (1997), for example, takes a very different line to Beauchamp and Childress on the relationship between principles and virtues, seeing the latter as secondarily derived from the former, and thus as the expression of principles in practice. So professional practitioners are left with the question of which authority they should rely on. Furthermore, theoretical discussions may tend to allow a degree of clarity or certainty that is missing from the world of practice, in which what people think should happen and what they do may be quite different. Lewins (1996) makes the same point quite forcibly, when he argues that it is actual behaviour that should be the most important concern of ethics. Nonetheless, principlism has been a major feature of ethical discussions in the caring professions (for example: Barrowclough & Fleming, 1991; Barnitt, 1993; Tadd, 1998; Campbell *et al.*, 2001).

It is this very uncertainty from which the concern with 'ethical issues' in the caring professions originates (Fry & Veatch, 2000). Many of the debates about professional ethics have not started with the question of theories or principles, but by beginning with concrete concerns from practice and teasing out the ways in which ethical solutions to the 'issue' will lead to a way of disentangling the principles and theories in the messy everyday world. In this book, I have decided not to follow the 'ethical issues' approach as a way of organising the discussion, because my primary concern is to examine contemporary developments in ethics and consider how these might relate to professional concerns. So, throughout the following chapters examples of ethical issues in practice, or which relate to the context of professional practices, will be used to illustrate the points being discussed.

Principlism, while it has become predominant in applied ethics in the caring professions, is not the only way of addressing the plurality of approaches in practical ethics. As I have outlined in this chapter, the task now is to consider more recent developments in ethics. These have developed from a diverse range of critical reflection on contemporary society, including feminism, ecology and postmodernism. The ethics that have emerged from such changes in social thought are seen especially in the ethics of compassion and a concern with the rationality of emotions, the 'ethics of care', ecological ethics, and postmodern discussions of virtues and the ethics of the self. It is on these developments that much of the attention of this book is focused.

Conclusion

The historical development of ethics forms a heritage in which ideas from different eras, and hence diverse social circumstances, continue to varying degrees to play a part in contemporary thinking. While the predominant influence on contemporary professional ethics is the liberal modern period, the shift towards 'postmodernity' has seen a renewal of interest in ideas that derive from earlier eras, including the concept of virtue and other ideas that spring from it. We have also noted that professional ethics is not simply a matter of 'applying' discrete philosophical approaches to professional work. Moreover, competing ideas cannot always be easily reconciled, and this leaves the practitioner with the need to make choices about how to integrate actions in specific situations with more general statements of theory or principle, including professional codes of ethics.

Four broad issues emerge from the discussion so far, which are illustrated in the case situation presented above. First, should professional ethics be understood as universal or as particular? Some theories and principles only make sense if they apply to all people and all circumstances, but this may be challenged if the underlying values are seen to be specific to a particular perspective or social group. Second, is professional ethics binding on professional practice or is it for guidance? The idea of a code of ethics suggests that it is binding, but in relation to specific circumstances some professionals might wish to act contrary to a code *on ethical grounds*. Third, we need to consider whether professional ethics should be made explicit in practice or if it can remain implicit. Fourth, consideration must be given to whether professional ethics is the properties of individual practitioners or if it is social. In the next chapter each of these questions will be addressed in turn.

CHAPTER 2

Key Debates About Ethics

In the previous chapter, the historical background and predominant contemporary approaches to professional ethics were outlined and discussed. Four broad questions emerged from that analysis and in this chapter will be considered as key debates in understanding ethics in theory and in practice. These debates are:

- To what extent is professional ethics to be understood as universal or as particular?
- Should professional ethics be seen as binding or guiding professional practice?
- Is professional ethics explicit or implicit in practice?
- To what extent is professional ethics to be regarded as the property of individual practitioners or as social in nature?

Universal or particular?

Fairness

The concept of fairness and the related values of impartiality and justice are of central concern in liberal modern ethics (Freeman, 2000, pp. 55 ff.). As Hinman (2003, pp. 182 ff.) points out, Kant's 'categorical imperative' can be seen as a statement that implies fairness as a moral good, because it asserts that what applies for one person should apply for everyone in similar circumstances. Impartiality is a cornerstone of Kant's moral philosophy. So the only way in which a deontological approach can deal with exceptions is to apply them to context or situation rather than to a person. One example that Hinman gives is that of whether it is ethically acceptable to break the law, to which the answer is 'yes, *if* certain specifiable conditions are met'. His example is that of breaking speed laws in order to get someone who needs urgent medical attention to a hospital. Such a view is clearly fair, as well as 'just' in a legal sense, because it is not seeking to make an exception of the individual, as in 'I can break the speed laws but no-one else can', but rather to assert a principle that would be applicable to anyone who needed to respond to a medical emergency. The law is upheld as right and at the same time the exception is right because of its special circumstances.

Utilitarianism is also concerned with fairness, but from an entirely different perspective. As Clark (2000, p. 73) notes, within this approach fairness is achieved when utility is maximised (the sum of the greatest happiness with the least misery). An example of this would be in the example of organ transplantation. There are rarely enough organs available for those patients who are judged clinically to be able to benefit from this procedure, so it is necessary for decisions to be made about who should be a recipient. This type of rationing calculation is utilitarian, in that it seeks to balance the best possible outcome with the least negative consequences. As with the deontological example given above, the point is that the basis for calculation is arrived at independently of considering the individual identity of people whose lives will be affected by any decisions. However, where the resources to be rationed are determined by political processes, as in public health funding, the problem of fairness becomes more acute, as those with personal wealth can make market choices while those without such resources have options determined for them. Nevertheless, a utilitarian approach can address fairness at the structural level, in this example by being applied to issues of taxation to pay for universal health care (see Barry, 1998, on this point). This issue will be examined in more detail in Chapter 6.

In response to the example of breaking speed laws, the utilitarian position would reach the same outcome as the deontological position, although for different reasons. However, in relation to establishing criteria for health rationing, deontological arguments would not necessarily be as likely to reach similar conclusions as those from a utilitarian standpoint. So, on issues of fairness, it appears that while both approaches can be used to examine the same ethical issues, there are issues on which their differences are much more apparent than on others. It is this juxtaposition that leads Beauchamp and Childress (2001, p. 402) to assert that neither of the two major approaches of liberal ethics can be applied to the caring professions in a pure form, but that they must be operationalised through principles. Both deontology and utilitarianism in a general sense encompass ideas of fairness and impartiality, in that both systems of thought contain ways of deciding what is 'fair' because they both provide a means for focusing on the issues and not on other factors (such as the relationship of the person with authority or power to the persons about whom decisions are to be made). At the same time, the actual approaches may lead to markedly different conclusions in concrete instances. Thus, while each seeks to be universal, there is no one common standard by which the same conclusions about what is universally just or fair might be reached.

Human nature and culture

Contemporary debates between universal and particular views of ethics often have their origin in arguments about the balance between human nature and culture as the foundations of identity and meaning as well as the source of human needs that are the concern of the caring professions (Doyal & Gough, 1991; Kekes, 1993). On the one side is the view that what it is to be human is so shaped by nature that cultural phenomena may be regarded as secondary or as a surface gloss. Needs for food, shelter, sex and so on can be seen as universal, in that they occur, and have always occurred, in all human societies. This position may go further and suggest that other (social) phenomena are also found universally, such as 'religious belief' and concepts of 'family' (what Maslow, 1970, called 'higher level needs'). From this perspective, the different form in which these needs may be met, and consequent ideas about what 'right' or 'wrong' conduct, follow from and give local expression to the same universal human needs. On the other side of the debate is the position that culture not only shapes but actually creates needs and the drive to meet those needs. From this perspective the influence of culture is so powerful that it is not just the expression but the actual needs themselves that vary between localities. Even the 'need' for food, shelter, sex and so on are not the same in all times and places, according to this position. Although they may have a biological component, it is shaped to such an extent by social forces that these phenomena are better understood an artifact of culture.

From the former position, any professional ethics must be based on common values that have a shared basis in what it is to be human. The dominant idea of respect for autonomy, and principles of beneficence, non-maleficence and justice can be seen as having a core meaning that transcends particular cultural expressions. For example, Browne (1995), a European Canadian nurse working with Inuit people in northern Canada observed that in making sense of her relationship with her patients, respect for their autonomy and dignity was a key principle in achieving good practice. Browne argues that she was not simply imposing western values onto non-western people, but finding a common ethical basis for the provision of nursing care. Her descriptions of good nursing in this context, such as ensuring privacy and personal dignity in physical examinations, providing clear explanations of health information and so on all parallel descriptions of practice in western contexts. Yet, it is important to note that it was the Inuit people with whom she was working who saw her approach as 'respectful'; this is not simply Browne's self-evaluation. The point is that the meaning of respect was tangible from different cultural perspectives. Moreover, this shared meaning enabled both the professional nurse and her patients to experience their interaction as 'good'.

In contrast, Azmi (1997) advances an argument that cultural differences are at the core of meaning and ethics. Also writing from Canadian experience, Azmi examines the meaning of health and social welfare interventions from the perspective of a traditional Islamic community in Toronto. He concludes that the difference of world-view between holders of traditional Islamic faith and western secular professionals is such that they are implacably opposed, with the former seeing itself as separated and different from the surrounding culture, while the latter regards itself as universal. Azmi's focus is on social issues, particularly domestic violence, for which he argues the traditional religious perspective has an explanation and response that is entirely different from that of the caring professions. For Azmi, the withdrawal of claims by western secular professions to universal expertise is the only plausible outcome; the alternative is a position of implicit imperialism, in which the caring professions reveal a 'missionary' goal to convert the traditional community to modernism. The good professional stays away and leaves people to find their own ways of addressing their needs. Given the commitment of the caring professions to informed consent such an argument only becomes contentious when practices are sanctioned by law, as in child protection investigations, for example.

One apparent difference between the situations described by Browne (1995) and Azmi (1997) is that of physical health and social welfare concerns. This raises the question of whether the distinction between universal and particular values can be seen in terms of physical and social needs respectively. However, the situation described by

Browne not only includes the actual physical examinations and treatments that she was administering, but also social aspects of her actions as a professional nurse, and the meanings ascribed to the whole process by Inuit patients. Similarly, Azmi notes that the religious world-view encompasses the care of the sick as well as people with social welfare needs. We may conclude that the debate between the universal and the particular is not simply that of the difference between physical and social needs.

A further example of a debate about universal and particular views of values can be seen in the arguments for an 'ethics of care' (which will be discussed in detail in Chapter 5). Because this approach comes from the feminist critique of psychological theories of moral development, and is based on Gilligan's (1982) research which showed that young women tend to deal with ethical issues differently to young men, it raises the question of the extent to which moral values and ethical ideas can apply equally to women and men or whether the gendered differences observed by Gilligan point to discrete and particular ethical realms on the basis of sex. As we will see, the debates that have followed this research have included claims that this is, indeed, the case, and that women's ethical sense is superior because it values people as opposed to principles (for example: Noddings, 1984). Other feminists, however, have argued that an ethics of care is not exclusive to women nor does it reject principles such as justice (for example: Tronto, 1993).

The model of 'ethical pluralism' proposed by Kekes (1993) provides a robust rejoinder to this debate. Pluralism here means a position in which no one value is held to be paramount, but in which not all values are equally acceptable. Pluralism thus rejects both absolutism and relativism. The basis by which pluralism enables ethical judgements to be reached is through the distinction between primary and secondary values or goods. The former are understood at a high level of generality, such as 'life', 'health' and so on, while the latter are more specific, concerning culturally specific goods. An example would be that all human beings require drink and food to survive and then to be healthy – this is a primary good. However, what constitutes a 'good meal' will vary according to context – this is a secondary good. The ethical pluralist would, therefore, find no difficulty in saying that in cases concerning primary values claims to cultural or gendered standpoints are not plausible. Thus, from this perspective, Azmi's position could not be used to defend the practice of domestic violence or to argue for taking away access to modern health services for traditional Muslims in Toronto (and I am not suggesting that Azmi does so). What is at issue is the way in which caring professions might best respond, which is a secondary good. Similarly, Tronto's inclusive position on the ethics of care and its relationship to gender meets the criteria of ethical pluralism in these terms as it separates primary and secondary levels of value.

The debate about fairness and the debate about culture demonstrate that the way in which ethical positions deal with the tension between universality and particularity will be based in both the ethical approaches brought to bear on them and the wider notions of human nature and of the society in which ethical relationships are enacted.

Binding or guiding?

The second issue that faces contemporary professional ethics is the question of whether ethics should constitute 'laws' or should be an expressions of a 'value base' for an occupation. To address this issue, let us briefly consider the following hypothetical case situation.

Jane has just been diagnosed as having an advanced form of cancer for which the prognosis is poor. Her consultant oncologist considers an operation to be extremely hazardous and both chemotherapy and radio-therapy are likely to be futile. However, he also thinks that Jane will enjoy the months of life that she most probably has remaining if she is not given the prognosis in detail, so he instructs the team caring for Jane that she must not be told. In contrast, the junior doctors, the nurses and the social worker consider that Jane has a right to know both the diagnosis and the prognosis, so that she can make informed decisions about treatment options and also how she will spend the remainder of her life with her partner and family.

What is the basis for choosing between these ethical positions, and are there limitations on professionals in choosing to withhold or to share information?

Ethics as law

The idea of ethics as 'moral law' is clearly articulated by Kant (Hinman, 2003, p. 176). Indeed, the 'categorical imperative' (see Chapter 1) contains the phrase '... that the maxim behind your action can be willed as a universal *law'* (emphasis added). We should note the expression 'universal' in this imperative. Kant intended that any rule or principle that a person wished to apply should not only be for their own benefit but should be applied consistently to all persons. At the same time, it should also be observed, this is an ethics that seeks to identify *duties* of right action, which having been articulated are intended to be binding on the person who advances them as well as others. For Kant, the notions of law, universality and autonomy are inextricably connected. As Freeman (2000, p. 72) argues, making one's actions 'conform to universal laws as if they were laws of nature' and regarding all rational beings as 'ends in themselves', leads to the categorical imperative. In other words, a person who asserts a position as an ethical law is not simply being subject to a law, but by making the assertion is at the same time making the law and so is subject to their own self. Autonomy is, in this way, the source of reasoned ethical authority, not compromised by it; the rules of ethical conduct must be binding, as if they were laws, and universal, in order for ethics to be reasoned and not arbitrary, subjective, self-interested or capricious.

For example, let us consider whether it is acceptable for a professional practitioner ever to lie to a client. In the example presented above, may Jane be given the impression that she is likely to recover in order to give her hope? This is an issue that is widely discussed (for opposing views see: Higgs, 1998; Jackson, 2002). From a position of ethics as law the answer must be 'no'. The reasoning is that if we say that it is acceptable for the practitioner to lie, then we are permitting the action of lies in general, a position that is self-defeating, as illustrated in the conundrum of 'I never tell the truth' (Hinman, 2003, p. 182). It is not a matter of the consequences, but that the principle of the acceptability of lying is inconsistent.

But what of a situation in which to tell the truth would cause harm? Jane's capacity to enjoy life despite the cancer may be undermined by knowing exactly how bleak the prognosis is. So, considered in terms of consequences there may be situations in which truth-telling may appear to be counter-productive. In the medical field there is a widespread debate about whether disclosing a poor prognosis can worsen a person's condition, through shock or giving up hope (Veatch, 2002). Against this, it is argued that although the motive behind such paternalism is benign (to improve the patient's chances, or to spare them unnecessary anguish), the effect of not being truthful lacks integrity. Higgs (1998) very forcefully makes the point that by not being truthful a clinician is undermining the person's autonomy and hence not treating them with respect. He also cites case examples of situations in which the impact of uncovering the lack of truth led to worse clinical and social outcomes for individuals. However, Higgs' argument does not rest in the consequences, but in that integrity and veracity are not relative. This is so even though many issues in health are probabilistic rather than certain. Indeed, Higgs argues that in so far as this is the reality of practice, the issue is one of 'truthfulness' rather than 'technical certainty' (p. 434). This is a different view of an ethical law, transposing 'never lie' into 'never be untruthful'. The intent that as a principle it is universal and binding, however, is not changed.

Ethics as guidance

In contrast, it is possible to see ethics as guidance, rather than laws, in which the exercise of reason leads people to establish what is 'good' or 'right' under specific circumstances. Fairness, according to all forms of utilitarianism, is achieved by the maximisation of utility. If they are to be consistent, these principles cannot be used to create universal laws that must apply in all circumstances. It is possible to hypothesise situations in which following such a law would produce an increase in misery, because of the specifics of those situations.

In the example of the oncologist lying to Jane, the position of benign paternalism is based on a belief that the concrete misery caused by telling the truth about a serious medical condition can be greater than the more abstract ideal of telling the person the truth about their condition (Jackson, 2002). As has just been noted above, prognosis is never completely certain, even where probabilities approach one hundred per cent. There is a risk that disclosure may cause harm, through the patient's reaction, and so increase misery disproportionate to the utility of respecting autonomy. There are also cultural factors to consider. Autonomy as it is understood in western culture may not be as valued in other cultures. Cross-cultural research into expectations about 'sharing bad news' has suggested that although there is now an expectation in western culture that such information be shared truthfully with the individual patient, in other cultures the idea of sparing the person further suffering may be more highly valued (Blackhall *et al.*, 1995; Carrese & Rhodes, 1995). In some cultural groups it is family members who expect to be told the truth and to determine how much the person with the condition is told, although individuals may be asked to confirm their own preferences in this regard before diagnosis.

Ethics as guidance thus opposes ethics as law. In the case of truth-telling in professional practice, ethics as guidance starts from the position that 'truth' is to be understood in context, so the role of ethics is to help the professional to make judgements about how much and in what way the truth might be told, or withheld. For the position of ethics as law, the starting point is that of the categorical imperative to tell the truth. In the illustrative case above, only if Jane had explicitly said to the treating team that she did not want to be told would it be acceptable for the truth to be withheld. Even then, they would still have to consider how this could be done without actually making false statements.

Moral limits on the autonomy of professionals

While any member of a caring profession is continually faced with the need to integrate ethics in their practice, this is not the same as having complete autonomy in the sense of being free to select whatever they personally prefer to be a universal law. To take an example that is often discussed, a therapist is not free to decide that it is acceptable to have sex with clients, even though the therapist may reason that such actions are acceptable for all therapists (Strasburger *et al.*, 1995). Professions are social institutions that, among other things, formulate values that are held to apply to all members. They are ethical communities. By joining the community the individual practitioner is autonomously assenting to the limitation of their autonomy in their duty to all their peers, individually and collectively. In this context, professional codes of ethics proscribe certain actions, including not only having sex with people who use one's services, but also regarding veracity, privacy, confidentiality, honesty in financial and other material dealings with service users, and so on.

Downie and Calman (1994, p. 82) note that when a caring professional acts, an individual person acts but at the same time they are not acting as an individual but as a member of their profession. Yet, as they subsequently observe (pp. 267–9), the tendency for professions to operate on the basis of ethics as law in generating codes makes large assumptions which are of particular interest for this discussion. The first is the premise that ethics can be so clear cut as to be formulated as rules which will not be ambiguous or require nuanced interpretation in differing situations. The second is the premise that professionals can be 'given' their ethics, 'even literally given them in the form of a hand-book' (p. 268), when people also bring values with them as they join a profession. The third is that codes assume a consensus, which may not be reasonable. The fourth is that the professional has an exclusive relationship with service users, which ignores competing claims from other service users and the wider society. Each of these points suggest that the use of ethics as laws or ethics as guidance relates to the social role of the caring professions as a whole, and this point is pursued in more depth in the next chapter. Downie and Calman's argument also raises the question of whether ethics is the responsibility of each individual professional, or whether it can be handed over to certain members of the community, and it is to this question that the discussion now turns.

Explicit or implicit?

Ethics as a special category of expertise

Downie and Calman (1994, p. 16) argue that in so far as morality is 'all-pervasive' it not only concerns more dramatic issues, such as life and death decisions, but pervades every aspect of professional work. Even the question of whether standards of practice are lowered because a person feels tired is an ethical issue. So, all of life is infused with morality in this sense, and there is no part of practice or the identity of the individual professional that is not part of the ethical dimension of the wider social world. If Downie and Calman are correct, why should we need to address professional ethics in an explicit way? Why cannot the implicit ethics of the everyday world be left to operate in its normal fashion? The answer that they give is that although the ethics of the everyday world operates in professional contexts, it does so in ways that are at the same time both based on 'common sense' and consti-tuted as a special category of knowledge (Banks, 2004).

Nurses, social workers, and often teachers, are familiar with the sense that their work is seen as something that anyone could do, and that, indeed, some people do in other, usually domestic, roles (Hugman, 1991, p. 12). This is particularly the case when the primary service recipient is a child or an older person. However, the point is that when such tasks are performed by members of the caring professions *as professionals* there are issues of power, authority and responsibility that are not the same if done by a relative or friend. Quite specifically, the formality of the relationships between professional carer and cared-for means that the implicit nature of everyday ethics is not sufficient, although it may be a necessary ingredient. Furthermore, as Beauchamp and Childress (2001) repeatedly observe, even when closer bonds develop between professionals and those for whom they care, there remains a central characteristic of the relationship that it is between people who are 'strangers', either literally prior to forming the relationship around the needs of one person and the profession of the other, or where a degree of strangeness in the form of difference is introduced, as when someone might consult a friend in the latter's capacity as a member of a profession.

In order to be able to conceptualise and respond to the ethical demands of the specialised professional role, members of the caring professions also need to be able to deal explicitly with ethics of both the everyday and the specific kind. There are, therefore, grounds for arguing that, while the ethical challenges that may be faced in the professional role are of a similar kind as those faced in everyday contexts (respect, justice, veracity, confidentiality and so on), the situational and role differences mean that there is more to professional than there is to everyday ethics. Clark (2000, p. 174) calls this an 'intermediate position', between the view that there is no distinct professional ethics on the one hand and that professional ethics is entirely distinct and separate from everyday ethics on the other. Yet, in as much as the performance of the professional role requires a special expertise beyond that of everyday life, then the ethical component of that role is as much a part of that expertise as is the technical knowledge and skills that may be identified as the core of the profession (Fry & Johnstone, 2002). If this expertise is to be addressed appropriately then it must be made explicit.

Ethics as the business of every professional

Not many members of the caring professions would regard themselves as trained moral philosophers. Does this mean that they are able to leave matters of ethics to those of their colleagues who do have such training? If professional ethics constitutes an expertise, as has just been argued, then would it not be reasonable to treat it like any other aspect of professional expertise, that may be established as a branch of a profession so that not every competent member is required to have the same knowledge and skills as the specialist? However, an affirmative answer to these questions would be in clear contradiction with the intermediate position outlined above, that professional ethics is an extension of rather than a separate entity to everyday ethics. Just as in the rest of life moral responsibilities cannot be delegated to others, nor in professional life could such a claim be plausible. Because each member of a profession is a moral person in their own right this must apply also to a professional identity.

Yet the ethics of everyday life often remains implicit, in so far as people may not be required to give a reasoned account of principles even though they will often be able to make decisions between 'good' and 'bad' or 'right' and 'wrong'. Johnstone (1994, p. 194) cautions, from case examples, that while many practitioners intuitively act in accordance with ethical principles, not everyone does so. Coulehan and Williams (2001), reviewing medical training, note that this differing intuition may be related to the wider sense of ethical values, such as compassion and altruism. Yet it is often possible for practitioners to take greater personal responsibility if they have a more conscious understanding of the ethical dimension of their work. So in making ethics explicit and making it every professional person's business it is not a matter of helping them to 'be ethical', but rather of equipping them with sufficient knowledge and skills to be able to engage with the application of ethics in the specialist tasks that constitute professional work. The argument that ethics in professional contexts is both everyday *and* special leads to the conclusion that, although the capacity to think ethically applies in general to members of society, the capacity to analyse the ethical component of a situation logically from a professional perspective is a specialised skill that can be taught. Thus ethics in the professional context is made explicit and along with this the responsibility of each member of a profession to be able to articulate professional ethics is also made explicit. Ethical specialists may have a role in this task, whether as educators or consultants, but they cannot take on the ethical responsibilities of an entire profession.

Individual or social?

Ethics as personal choice and as social norms

As we have noted, when the caring professional acts, although it is an individual acting, the person does so as a representative of the particular profession. This means that the formal code of ethics, whether this is seen as law or as guidance, or as both, has to be brought together with the values of the individual professional. It has already been noted (1) that each member of a caring profession enters that role with their wider everyday ethical framework, yet at the same time (2) formal codes of professional ethics are constructed as requirements and not as options. The question facing each individual professional is what she or he will do if confronted with a professional requirement to act in a way that is contrary to her or his individual values (Banks, 2001). This can be seen in the many discussions of ethical issues in health and social care, such as abortion, withdrawing life-support, IVF, compulsory admissions to mental hospitals and forcible removal of children from their parents (for example: Johnstone, 1994; Clarke, 2000).

Banks (2001, pp. 139–44) summarises the main debate in this respect. On the one hand is the view that in becoming a member of a caring profession, an individual takes on membership of the profession as part of their personal identity. This position does not accept the separation of personal and professional values, but considers that they should be integrated. This is not just an argument that all members of a society should be considered as ethical, as discussed above, but that membership of a caring profession requires a special type of person, one whose values are integral to those of the profession. On the other hand is the view that the professional role and personal identity should be separated. This position asserts that when acting as a member of a caring profession it is incumbent on an individual to follow the ethics of the profession and not to pursue his or her own moral agenda.

Banks (2001, p. 144) concludes that neither of these positions is plausible. The first demands of the caring professions a moral standard and a way of life in which individuals are free to serve each person they encounter unconditionally. However, all members of the caring professions clearly operate within constraints, of time, personal resources, other relationships and so on. In contrast, the second position appears almost cynical, in that it demands that individual professionals act according to external rules with no thought for their own values. However, as we will see in the next chapter, this begs the very question of professionalism. It also confronts contemporary ethics in total, in that when such values conflict, the choice of how to deal with this cannot be shrugged off by the practitioner. So Banks proposes that the way in which we should examine the fit between personal morality and public ethics is through a framework that the *person* takes on the role of the *profession* that in turn requires the performance of a *job or tasks*, all of which is set in the context of *social norms*.

Ethics as part of practice

In as much as ethics is both personal and professional, and cannot be separated, this also means that ethics cannot be separated from practice. So, from this point we may conclude that a concern with ethics is not about adding something to technical problems of knowledge and skill, but rather is about drawing out an inherent facet of practice. It is about making explicit that which is implicit. This is not to suggest that ethics should be seen simply as 'another tool', because that would imply that it is something to be 'applied' at an appropriate moment, whereas the argument that we have been following leads to a position in which ethics is better understood as a dynamic aspect of practice, of the interaction of individual practitioners with the profession, with their tasks and with the wider social norms, including laws. At the same time, just as the application of knowledge and skill is situational, so too is ethics. Just as when driving a car we do not consciously think about every single act, so too in professional practice we may not stop and consider every aspect as if anew. However, if called to account for why we chose this rather than that action, can we articulate a reasoned explanation that, if necessary, not only encompasses the elements of knowledge and skill but also ethics? Thus members of the caring professions must be able both to give reasons for ethical choices and to be able to explain these in ethical terms.

Conclusion

This chapter has examined four key debates about professional ethics, looking at whether they are universal or particular, binding or guiding, explicit or implicit, and individual or social. Each of these questions is central to understanding contemporary ethics in the caring professions. We have considered that on the issue of fairness the predominant liberal ethical theories have tended to suggest that there is a universal element; however, when human culture is examined, there are conflicting ideas that are not so easily reconciled. Similarly, in looking at whether professional ethics is binding on action or serves to guide choices in action, we saw that liberal ethics tends to support the notion of ethical laws. However, the realities of practice mean that individual professionals have to exercise discretion and make choices, in which ethics cannot specify only one 'good' or 'right' action, and hence must be guiding and not binding. With regard to the question of whether ethics is explicit or implicit, we saw that although ethics may be implicit in some situations, there are others in which it must be explicit. In the context of the caring professions, therefore, it is important that the capacity to make ethics explicit is part of the capacities of every professional as well as the responsibility of the professions as communities. This leads to the conclusion that ethics is *both* individual *and* social. It is not possible to separate these aspects; indeed, it is more helpful to think of ethics in terms of the interaction between individual morality and social norms.

These debates constitute key themes in an examination of recent ethical theories and how such theories might be addressed from the perspective of professional ethics. Yet they are not the whole story. The other part of the picture is that which concerns the caring professions as the context in which our interest in ethics is located. So in the next chapter we look in more depth at the social terrain of the caring professions and the relevance of ethics within that context.

CHAPTER 3

Why Professional Ethics?

Professions as social terrain

Any discussion of ethics in the caring professions must address the question of the nature of 'profession' in order to give scope to the ensuing analysis. Understanding the social phenomenon of professions and professionalisation has been of interest for a long time and has attracted controversy and debate (Freidson, 1994). The purpose of this discussion is to look specifically at ethics within the caring professions rather than to explore the idea of 'profession' in a more general sense. Nevertheless, some preliminary comments are necessary, to ground our review of the reasons why a concern with ethics in the caring professions is important by briefly reviewing current thinking about their social terrain.

There is considerable agreement that the idea of 'profession', the attributes of 'professionalism' and the processes of 'professionalisation' refer to occupations that have developed claims to particular types of status, power and authority and a basis for asserting these claims within the wider society (Macdonald, 1995). Some analysis has looked at professions as occupations that possess certain characteristics or traits (Greenwood, 1957). This view predominated through much of the twentieth century. The traits which were identified include systematic knowledge gained through formal education, discrete skills, a corporate body, autonomy sanctioned by the community, and a code of ethics (Etzioni, 1969). In many ways the trait approach approximates to a 'common-sense' idea of a profession, what Freidson (1994) calls the 'folk concept' of the professions.

More recently, the trait approach has been criticised from the perspective that historically professions were occupations that had developed around the exercise of social power (Johnson, 1972; Wilding, 1982). This analysis showed that the type and degree of autonomy exercised by an occupation is as much a matter of state regulation as it

is of community sanction, or that knowledge and skills are often contested rather than 'naturally' resting with one occupation or another.
In this analysis a code of ethics is seen not as a 'natural trait' of professionalism, but a bargaining counter in the struggle to gain professional
status through state regulation (Wilding, 1982, p. 77). Subsequently
this idea has been further developed by arguments that professions are
occupations that have grown out of particular power relationships that
permeate society, notably gender (Witz, 1992), 'race' and ethnicity
(Potgieter & de la Ray, 1997; Watson, 1999; Mujawamariya, 2001) and
socio-economic class (Perkin, 1989). So, to understand an occupation
as a profession is to locate it within a set of social structures and social
relations.

The key element of professions is thus seen to be the control they
exert over particular types of work (Johnson, 1972). This may be understood in terms of 'occupational autonomy'. However, Freidson (1994)
questions the extent to which occupational autonomy ever was such a
defining aspect of professionalism. Apart from the implicit slippage of
attention from social action (what occupations actually do) back to
traits (what occupations are), he points to the historical features of
professions as providing service (or services) to others, whether these
are fellow citizens, fee-paying customers or the state (compare with:
Johnson, 1972; Koehn, 1994). For Freidson, the implications of this are
that the work of the professions requires a degree of trust, from service
users and employers alike, that goes beyond the normal degrees of trust
that would be necessary in any other social situation; this he calls a
'*double* fiduciary relationship' (1994, p. 209; emphasis original).
Professionalism, therefore, is not a matter of autonomy in the sense of
a 'zero sum', but rather of delegated or negotiated authority.

Such an understanding of professionalism responds to the issues
raised by critical analysis, notably concerning issues of the exercise of
social power, especially its abuse, by pointing to the importance of a
detailed attention to the ethics of professions, in the sense of the way in
which goals and techniques (ends ands means) are integrated, open
and accountable. Johnstone's (1994, pp. 12–19) detailed discussion of
scandals in the New Zealand health system provides an example of such
abuses of power. From 1958 to the late 1980s, at various New Zealand
hospitals, medical research had been done that involved withholding
treatment, undertaking invasive unnecessary procedures without consent (for instance on women who were already anaesthetised for an
unrelated treatment), and taking foetal tissue without parental consent.
In the UK, more recently, the taking and storage of foetal tissue for

research was also undertaken without parental consent (Redfern, 2001). Nurses and other professions are implicated along with the medical practitioners and researchers who were involved. As Johnstone observes (1994, p. 17), such abuses are possible because of the social structures and social relations of the caring professions and the contexts in which they work. Similarly, abuses of power have been observed in many other professional contexts, such as child welfare, mental health and community health (Payne & Littlechild, 2000). There are also many examples of caring professionals who practise ethically and act on the basis of supporting or defending service users' rights and interests, sometimes at the risk of their own careers (a point to be pursued below) (Baldwin & Barker, 1991; Kushner & Thomasma, 2001).

Although formal statements of ethics can be employed as 'bids for status and privilege' they can also be utilised by service users and others as a means of holding professionals accountable, both individually and collectively, for their actions. In this way ethics can be a basis for the exercise of social power in ways that challenge abuse. This is not without difficulties, because of the other aspects of the social terrain of the caring professions, such as controls over access to knowledge and skills. However, in as much as the caring professions rely on their ethical identity for the authority to do their work, this provides a point at which concerned members of the professions themselves as well as service users and other members of the wider society can apply arguments for change. The loss of confidence in health contexts resulting from the scandals in New Zealand and the UK has an impact for many individual professionals as well as for the wider social standing of professions as a whole (Johnstone, 1994). We will return to this issue in Chapters 9 and 10.

Another part of the social terrain of the caring professions is the demarcation of 'caring' from other professions. There is a distinction to be drawn here between 'caring about', that is in being concerned for the well-being of another, and 'caring for', which refers to the performance of tasks that contribute to the well-being of the other. This distinction was made by Peabody, an American physician, in 1927 (cited in Kushner & Thomasma, 2001, p. 14), and more recently has been developed by feminist analysis (Ungerson, 1990). The point of the feminist argument is that the work of caring includes, at its most basic, feeding, bathing, dressing, administering medicines, ordering the domestic environment, managing personal everyday affairs and so on. These tasks are not accorded the same status, power and authority as are highly technical knowledge and skills that, although they are employed in the service of 'caring about' the service user, do not engage the professional with the everyday needs of the people about whose well-being they are concerned as do the tasks of 'caring for'. This may lead to a view of the caring professions as those which encompass *both* senses of 'caring' (Hugman, 1991).

The range of professions that have been identified in Chapter 1 as the focus of this book is wide. These are allied health professions, counselling, clinical psychology, nursing, medicine, religious ministry, social work, teaching and youth work. Not only does the form and extent of professionalisation differ between these occupations, but the extent to which each of these conform to the definition of 'caring' is variable. However, all these occupations are included in the present discussion for three reasons. First, it is the case that in many situations members of all of these groups may have to act in both senses of 'caring' if they are to fulfil their ethical commitments. Medicine is perhaps the most contentious profession to include here, as only rarely does it involve the performance of the tasks of 'caring for' in the sense that has been defined here. This point will be pursued in Chapter 5.

Second, whether they 'care about' or 'care about and care for', these professions are all focused on the human person and their core practices impact directly on the human person. This is so whether 'the person' is understood in terms of physical, emotional, intellectual, psychological, or spiritual aspects, or as a holistic combination of all of these aspects. For this reason, in some discussion these occupations also may be referred to collectively as 'human services' (McDonald, 1999).

Third, with respect to ethical problems that are faced and the role of ethics within the construction of professionalism, these occupations share many of the same issues with each other, precisely because they are all focused on the human person. They also all draw on the same stock of ethical theory and norms to deal with these issues. Again, this may be expected as they share the same heritage that has been discussed above and in the preceding chapters. Also, they may work together. So, all of these occupations can be seen to connect through the questions of the nature of caring, their focus and impact on the human person and the consequent ethical issues.

The content of caring professions

Every aspect of the practices of the caring professions has the potential to affect the recipients of their services in profound ways. The work of the caring professions is very important and at the same time inherently risky for both the service user and the professional practitioner. This is not to suggest that the risks are the same for both parties; clearly, the service user faces greater risks than does the professional. Such risks may be those relating to quality of life, in that the service user may experience life as worse rather than better as result of receiving a professional intervention. For example, custody of one's children may be lost, or one's health might deteriorate rather than improving. At the most extreme, the service user may face death as a consequence of a professional intervention such as an invasive medical or nursing procedure. For the professional, there is a risk that a failure to act well, in all senses, may lead to causing harm to service users, both materially and in the moral sense of the abuse of power and authority.

The literatures on specific professions contain many concrete examples of the ways in which the practices of caring professionals may affect the lives of service users (Payne & Littlechild, 2000; Parsons, 2001). These divide broadly between those examples that represent a general class of actions and those that are concerned with the individual acts of professional practitioners in relation to specific service users. An instance of the former is Beauchamp and Childress' (2001, pp. 204–6) discussion of the ethics of breast implants. The issues in this case relate to the safety of both the procedure and the prosthesis used, but the *ethical* points centre on the disclosure of information and the extent to which women are enabled, or not, to make informed decisions concerning their own health. The key question is whether the practices of allied health professions, medicine and nursing in these situations in general are respectful of individual persons, beneficent, non-maleficent and just. Where high fees or profits are involved, or access to health care is controlled by third party insurance arrangements, ensuring that the patient's interests are paramount is an ethic that may not always be achieved. In the social welfare field in Australia, the routine removal of children of 'mixed-race' parentage from Aboriginal mothers for over half the twentieth century (HREOC, 1997; Kidd, 2000) is another instance of an ethical 'class of actions'. From the perspective of those professions that now undertake child protection work these actions now appear to have been disrespectful of persons, not beneficent but maleficent, and unjust. Thus, in Australia, to some extent all the caring professions are now faced with accountability for the ethical consequences of past practices.

Many caring professionals will think of 'ethics' as being about individual acts in relation to specific service users. After all, it could be said, a person has responsibility for that which they can control or affect. In professional practice this is, usually, the direct interaction between the professional and direct service users. It may also include indirect effects of decisions made, advice or instructions given to colleagues, or policies that are supported. For example, in Australia older people who are seeking help from the public health and human services system may have their needs assessed by a multi-disciplinary 'aged care assessment team' (Gibson, 1998). At the level of everyday practice, individual members of these teams may not feel as if they exercise much influence over the policies of aged care, but they do have extensive choices about the ways in which their roles are performed. Listening carefully to the older person and to family carers, providing information clearly and fully, speaking respectfully to and about people, sharing decisions openly, providing honest ideas about service options and their limitations, and using ideas and skills that are known to be the best currently available are all aspects of 'good' practice.

What is being identified here is that there is a relationship between ethics and the technical dimensions of professional work. This raises the question of whether ethics should be concerned with the application of techniques or whether techniques themselves have an inherently moral dimension. The answer will depend on the context and the type of practice to which the question is referring. This is not to argue for ethical relativism, but to recognise that although all practice is imbued with values, there may be some techniques that are morally neutral in themselves. Examples might include giving injections and undertaking an assessment interview. As has already been argued, the *way* in which these are done can be separated ethically from the *purpose* of doing them. A technically competent injection of antibiotics for an appropriately indicated patient can still be done 'badly', even though the purpose is morally supportable, if it is done without consent. How an injection is done becomes of different relevance if the purpose of the injection is the execution of a convicted criminal, where individual practitioners may differ in their views of the moral context (although it should be noted that nurses' participation in executions is deemed ethically unacceptable by the International Council of Nurses – Fry & Johnstone, 2002, p. 119). It is different yet again if its purpose is experimentation on someone who has not given consent, when it is going to be considered 'bad practice' no matter how 'competently' it is done. Similarly, undertaking a good assessment interview may involve issues of technique, but it matters greatly how the use of technique relates to the purposes of the assessment.

Koehn (1994) takes a different approach, arguing that expertise of itself is a dubious ground on which to base professional ethics. Her argument is that expertise concentrates on the technicality of a person's problems and not on the person, separating responsibility to a body of knowledge and skills from responsibility to clients. The client 'disappears' from the content of the caring professions or at least is 'displaced' from its 'moral centre' (p. 27), because the content of the profession becomes the professional knowledge and skills and not clients and their needs. Practitioners become experts in conditions, viruses, therapies, academic subjects and so on – the practitioner is a *sports* physiotherapist, or a *pediatric* nurse, or an *aged-care* social worker, or a *physics* teacher. Pellegrino and Thomasma (1993, p. 155) make a similar point when they note that '[p]rofessional knowledge does not exist for its own sake' but to meet the needs of service users.

Koehn's argument is complex, drawing widely on ethics across the different historical eras that were discussed in Chapter 1. What Koehn is contending is that the content of the caring professions should be the disciplined application of knowledge and skills to the needs expressed by people who require service from professionals, not 'expertise' as such. Seen in this way, the ethical content of caring professions can be regarded as the commitment to make competence available to those who use their services. Freidson (1994, p. 10) similarly argues that professionalism consists not in *types* of knowledge and skill, but in a 'dedication to the committed practice of a complex craft that is of value to others'. However, as Banks notes (2001, p. 87), some problems remain with the equation of professionalism and an ethic of service. This position may be 'unrealistic' because the empirical evidence often contradicts the idea that caring professions have 'a distinctive dedication which takes precedence over individual and collective material interests' (Freidson, 1994, p. 123). Such arguments may be appealing from a moral perspective because they provide both a statement of ideal and at the same time the basis for a sustained critique of the reality. However, they need to be located in the focus and social relations of the caring professions if they are not to risk becoming either an ideological gloss or merely a simplistic attack.

The focus of caring professions

A further issue arises from recognition that professional practice is contextualised, which concerns the way that the caring professions are located within the wider material and cultural life of societies, especially moral norms and values. In other words, the focus of the professions is very much a part of wider questions about the values of the society in which the professions exist (Hugman, 1998). The goals of the caring professions are not separable from the values that are prevalent in their social context. Having noted that the objectives of professional practice are an important component of ethics, a further problem is raised, therefore, concerning how the objectives of professional practice are defined and by whom.

The critical analysis of professionalisation, from Johnson (1972) onwards, has emphasised that professions are created by human action. It follows from this that the purposes of the caring professions, that is the goals or objectives to which they are directed, must also be seen as the products of human action. This observation may seem rather obvious, but the point is that just as goals or objectives are created, so too can they be rethought, contested, disputed, adapted, modified or abandoned. Just as the knowledge and skills of the caring professions are always developing, so too are their purposes always subject to change. Moreover, to the extent that we understand society as comprising different, often competing, interests, it would also follow that the goals or objectives of the caring professions may reflect the interests of certain sections of the society and not all its members.

A basic objection may be mounted to this premise. If as a statement of purpose for the caring professions we take 'the promotion of health, well-being, education or spirituality', it could be expected that there would be very wide social support. However, the problem with this objection is that the definition of 'health', 'well-being', 'education' or 'spirituality' must remain very wide. As soon as these concepts are operationalised there are many differences of view that can be held about what would constitute each broad objective. By 'health' should we mean the absence of certain basic life-threatening diseases and conditions, or should 'health' be seen as the full optimum state of the physical organism (Doyal & Gough, 1991)? By 'well-being' should we mean the absence of distress about basic life necessities (food, shelter and so on), or is this a question of maximum personal fulfilment (Maslow, 1970)? By 'education' do we mean the achievement of basic knowledge, such as functional literacy, or should this be defined in terms of the highest possible levels of scholastic attainment (Carr, 2000)? In terms of 'spirituality' do we mean an awareness of life outside one's own self or does this concern the capacity to engage with metaphysical and theological questions – do we even acknowledge that caring professions, other than religious ministry, might include spirituality in their focus (Roberts, 1999; Lindsay, 2002)? As soon as these questions begin to be faced then the possibility of many different, even opposing, positions on the focus of the caring professions become possible.

In so far as professionals exercise social power and authority, through their control over knowledge and skills about the human person, they have considerable responsibility for how the objectives of their work are related to wider social values. Indeed, this responsibility is the core of professional ethics. Caring professionals have the capacity to affect the lives of everyone in their societies as well as other aspects of the world around them. So a commitment to a focus on minimum rather than maximum definitions of 'health', 'well-being', 'intellectual accomplishment' or 'spirituality', for example, would have considerable implications. From the perspective of the key common principles in western health ethics (see Chapter 2), it matters greatly whether respect for the autonomy and dignity of persons, beneficence, non-maleficence and justice can be achieved through a focus on basic minimum goals or if they can only be realised through the pursuit of maximal objectives.

The choices that caring professionals make in this regard are not simply matters of personal preference. Although personal views must play a part at the level of individual action, choices are also formed through wider social values and in the context of material factors of the situation in which caring professionals are working. For example, an allied health therapist may be faced with a decision about how much time can be spent with any one patient, where increased time spent with a particular patient could greatly increase their improved functioning but at the cost of no service being given to others. This type of choice, faced by caring professionals in many settings, encapsulates social values in both the amount of resources allocated to services (in this case, allied health) and the priority that may be given to particular types of need. Nurses and others may also be used to balancing such demands ethically through a pragmatic sense of 'what can be achieved', whether or not this is explicit. However, at the same time there is often a countervailing sense that this is, in some ways, failing to live up to the values of the respective profession (Cherniss, 1995; Chilton, 1998). Similarly, teachers responding to different needs and abilities in a class room, or ministers of religion responding to different members of a congregation, may face the challenge of making ethical decisions about what they actually do. Such choices are grounded in both personal and social values. Where these clash, some individuals may choose to leave the profession rather than work with the resulting sense of compromise (Williams *et al.*, 1992).

The focus of the caring professions and its ethical implications concerns not only questions of *what* but also of *who*. That is, as well as considering the value base of the type of actions that are undertaken, the practices of the caring professions also have subjects, the users of their services. In making choices about the objectives of their work, or responding to the priorities that are set by wider social values, professionals must also respond to people. Their practices thus establish or 'construct' an identity of the service user, not only in the sense of 'a person with this or that problem' but also in a moral sense of being a person who has rights and responsibilities. Formally, from the oath of Hippocrates to contemporary codes, the ethics of the caring professions places an absolute value on *every* person for whom the professional provides assistance (Banks, 2001). However, expressing such values is difficult when choices must be made, such as in prioritising time and material resources. This difficulty is increased when some other aspect of the service user's life raises questions about the way in which their needs and the possibility of professional assistance have arisen.

A well established example of this, which will be familiar in allied health, medicine and nursing, is that of the person whose severe health problems are the consequence of life choices, such as diet, exercise (or the lack of it), smoking tobacco, drinking alcohol or using other recreational drugs and so on. Sometimes people negate the benefits of treatment by resuming harmful behaviours. Social workers, teachers and ministers of religion will also be familiar with individuals and families whose life choices appear to create the very problems that they bring to the professional, or which disrupt the service that is already being provided. Yet in all such circumstances, the option of refusing to provide further assistance is contentious. Some professionals do not regard this as an acceptable choice in any situation, while others may argue that it is inappropriate to continue to provide a service when the user's actions are creating the problem, either because it is colluding with a refusal to address the causes of problems, and thus is dishonest, or because it misuses scarce resources that could be provided to other people who are more likely to benefit fully. Of course, each of these solutions rests on a different set of ethical premises, so that discussions of these questions within specific professions tend to focus on the possible choices open to practitioners (Beauchamp & Childress, 2001; Fry & Johnstone, 2002). (This example will be revisited in later chapters.)

It is also the case that the morality of services is created not only by the actions of professional practitioners but also through social policies, such as those concerning education, health, housing and personal welfare. Specifically, decisions about the quantity and type of services that will be available are not made by individual practitioners, although it is practitioners who allocate services at the level of individual service users. Fry and Johnstone (2002, p. 126) note that nurses may face the question of whether to consider costs in allocating care among individual patients. Should nurses accept limiting the use of a very effective procedure because it is expensive, relative to a cheaper but less effective procedure? Their answer is that nurses should be guided by policies and not expect to make decisions in isolation from the wider social values expressed in policies. Similarly, we can note that all the professions with which this discussion is concerned face such questions because they are all conducted within the constraints of resources. Providing services on a private, fee-paying basis may reduce this problem as under this circumstance the decision about costs rests with the service user. Yet Beauchamp and Childress (2001, p. 240) describe as 'morally shameful' the situation in the USA where public policy and private insurance practices mean that many people cannot get essential health treatment, and this is a pattern that is becoming more prevalent in Australia, Canada, New Zealand, the UK and other European states, as such countries adopt the policies of privatised responsibility (Tope & Smail, 1998; von Dietze & Orb, 2000).

Social policies create the range of possibilities for practice and may even place specific requirements on practitioners. At the same time, members of the caring professions are themselves involved in the policy process, either directly or through research that informs the process. As individuals, the ethical responses of professionals relate to the roles that a person might actually perform in the formation of social policy, but this would also include membership of a professional association and the opportunity to influence policy through such a body as well as the particular role of policy maker or researcher. Thus professional practitioners are not separated from the social policy process, although as individuals they may feel that they have relatively little power over policies while policies create powerful constraints over them, especially when their personal values conflict with the values expressed by policy. In such situations, the focus of caring professions, both in terms of what practices are undertaken and with whom they are done, may be experienced as in conflict with the prevailing values of the wider society.

The social relations of caring professions

Because the caring professions intervene in people's lives through having a direct impact, in some way, on the human person, it is important that they operate through relationships of trust.

> Trust is confident belief in and reliance upon the moral character and competence of another person. Trust entails a confidence that another will act with the right motives and in accordance with appropriate moral norms. (Beauchamp & Childress, 2001, p. 34)

That professionals have, indeed often control, access to knowledge and skills creates the need for trust, as the service user often has limited ways of being able to ascertain if the person from whom they have sought assistance is acting in the service user's best interests. There are two main reasons why trust in caring professionals is said to have declined in the latter part of the twentieth century. The first is that professionals have been alleged to abuse the powers that they have over fellow citizens; the second is that attempts to create systems that limit the costs of services, especially in health, have created incentives for some professionals to make decisions based on their own incomes rather than service users' benefit.

Instances of abuse of professional powers by different caring professions have already been mentioned above. In part this can be seen as a consequence of shifts in general social attitudes, as critical histories suggest that it is not so much the actual practices of professionals but rather the social responses that have changed (Penhale, 1999). Examples include the incarceration of people with mental health problems and severe learning disabilities, sometimes followed by further abuse within closed institutions, prejudicial responses to family crises, the performance of unnecessary medical procedures in order to pursue research interests, sometimes without consent, and so on (Johnstone, 1994; Stanley *et al.*, 1999; Payne & Littlechild, 2000). The individually courageous actions of some professionals to protect and empower service users appear often to have had little or no ameliorating effect on the reduction of trust arising from abuses.

The issue of 'over-servicing' to benefit the professional personally, usually financially, is a different area in which trust is eroded (Lamont, 2001). Lamont divides such situations into two distinct groups: those who undertake practices that may be beneficial, or at least not harmful, which he terms 'benign' and those who undertake practices that are actually harmful, which he calls 'sinister' (p. 32). In both such types of 'over-servicing' Lamont is suggesting that the reason may be the same, namely to augment the income of the professional, although he adds that in medicine (the profession he is discussing specifically) there may be other reasons for 'benign over-servicing', most obviously that of defensive practice. Lamont contends that it is the sinister over-provision of services that causes a loss of trust, while benign forms may even be welcomed by many service users (p. 33).

There are both similarities and differences between these two ways in which trust may have been eroded. First, there is a strong similarity between the historical misuse of professional power and authority and 'sinister over-servicing', in that in both cases professionals are seen to act on the basis of their own interests, whether these are ideological or financial. Where professionals are seen to have acted in these ways, or to have failed to take action against colleagues who were believed to have been doing so, then the loss of trust takes the form of public campaigns and lawsuits. The difference between these ways in which trust has been lost relates to the financial motivation for the professionals' actions and the ways in which professions have responded to try to deal with each of these types of abuse. Lamont (2001, p. 25) cites arguments that the current procedures for self-regulation of professionals' behaviour have had a negative effect, in that they have protected poor and unethical practitioners. As a consequence, both service users and professionals appear now to prefer contractual relationships to ones based on trust. As Beauchamp and Childress (2001, p. 35) point out, as long ago as Aristotle it was recognised that trust is a central aspect of voluntary and intimate relationships, while contracts are the bonds of relationships with strangers. The shift from trust to contract is, therefore, both a symptom and a catalyst in the depersonalisation of relationships between caring professions and service users.

Koehn (1994, pp. 39 ff.) provides a different perspective on the social relations of service user and professional, asking whether the good professional can be tied through contract in advance of engaging with their intervention in the same way as, for example, someone who is providing the supply of domestic consumer goods. The professional's work depends on communication with the service user, which may shift as part of the relationship through which the professional service is provided. Moreover, there is a power imbalance between professionals and service users in which contracts may work for the benefit of the professionals. As a consequence, Koehn asserts, contractualism leads to relations of mistrust rather than the opposite, as both parties focus on the terms of the contract rather than negotiating the service relationship. For Koehn, therefore, the prevalence of a legalistic approach to the social relations between service users and professionals not only signals the end of trust but actually works against trust developing.

Against this, contracts may be seen as offering protection to service users. The service users' rights movements have tended to favour the sort of enforceable accountability that contractual relationships provide. The critics of the caring professions, or at least of abuses perpetrated by members of these professions, argue that the problem does not lie in the possession of knowledge and skills as such, but in the ways in which professionals can avoid accountability (Payne & Littlechild, 2000). Proponents of strengthening professional accountability suggest various ways in which the social relations of the caring professions might be changed to ensure that practice is undertaken *with* rather than *for* (or even *on*) service users. These include the greater participation by service users in the definition of content and focus, as well as reinforcing ethical sanctions and the means for relatively less powerful individuals to seek their enforcement. This position leads to the conclusion that trust may be possible, but it has to be through a more open, accountable and responsive way of understanding the social relations of the caring professions. Contracts may play a part in achieving some power for service users.

The 'social mandate' of caring professions

The work of the caring professions must be sanctioned by societies in some way, whether this is through law, individual consumer choice or bureaucratic decision (Freidson, 1994). Hence it is possible to think in terms of the caring professions having a 'social mandate' to undertake a particular range of tasks, based on an expectation that certain consequences will follow. In this sense, caring professions are a particular expression of the moral life of a society, as their formation around practices, objectives and social relations institutionalises certain social values (Koehn, 1994, p. 153). These values concern 'health', 'wellbeing', 'education' and 'spiritual fulfilment' as social goods, in pursuit of which the caring professions are endowed with a central role. That role is the committed application of their knowledge and skills (that which they 'profess' – see Koehn, 1994, p. 20) to the achievement of these social goods. Its ethic lies in the notion of commitment, in 'caring about' and 'caring for'.

However, as we have already noted above, the specific claims of any one occupation are always contested. Moreover, from a critical perspective, the 'social mandate' of the caring professions in its entirety is open to debate. This view rests on an understanding of society as divided structurally, so that the interests of various groups and the power to pursue those interests differ according to factors such as socio-economic class, sex, 'race' and ethnicity, age, sexuality, physical or intellectual ability and so on (Dominelli, 2002). Both academic analysis and the development of the service users' rights movement have challenged the 'social mandate' of the caring professions either as flawed or as a mask for powerful groups to obscure the imposition of their values on those who are less powerful (Abbot & Meerabeau, 1998, pp. 5–7).

As I have argued elsewhere, the evidence supporting a critical view of the 'social mandate' of the caring professions is compelling (Hugman, 1991, 1998). However, to state this is not simply to accuse the caring professions of bad faith. Both individually and collectively, many members of the caring professions (perhaps we can even say most) are committed to 'good' practice and 'right' conduct. However, there are two reasons why this in itself may not appear to be sufficient. First, as we have seen, there are different ways of deciding on what is 'good' and what is 'right'. Formal, collective agreements on these matters may, therefore, be compromises between several ideal positions. Second, practical definitions of what is 'good' and what is 'right' are socially contextualised, even when broad agreement can be reached at an abstract level. Consequently, formal ethical statements can be interpreted to reflect the interests of particular groups, over and against other groups, whether these are within a profession or between a profession and other social groups. What is still needed is a way of enabling caring professions to live up to their ethics, including the capacity to be accountable, to encompass difference and to be more comfortable with the idea that ethics is about understanding responsibility and commitment and not about limiting liability.

Further evidence for the contested nature of the 'social mandate' of the caring professions is provided by two concrete instances of professionals using their role as professionals to act as social critics. In these examples, differences in perspective can be observed, one at the level of individual practice, the other at the level of collective action. At the individual level, the phenomenon of 'whistle-blowing' represents a situation in which the caring professional acts as a critic of their immediate social surroundings. Manthorpe and Stanley (1999, pp. 226–9) note that 'whistle-blowing' is ethically complex, as to the professional who perceives that others have acted abusively it may be a matter of duty to vulnerable service users, whereas to those who are accused it may be a breach of duty to colleagues (loyalty). Where allegations are not accepted by the wider society the individual professional may pay a high price, losing both their job and the respect of others. Yet even where the allegations are substantiated, the individual may still be judged by colleagues to have acted outside the ethical boundaries of the profession (Baldwin & Barker, 1991). Johnstone (1994, pp. 48–50) observes that this is a matter of 'etiquette' not of ethics, and, like Manthorpe and Stanley (1999) and Baldwin and Barker (1991), is critical of colleagues who do not act in situations of abuse, even though all understand the significant social forces that act to inhibit such actions.

Caring professions may also be judged to have over-stepped their 'social mandate' when, collectively, they express criticism of institutional or governmental policy (Clarke, 1998, p. 248). The professional literature argues for the appropriateness of the caring professions' active involvement in policy formation, whether or not this is through involvement in formal processes, implying recognition by others of the competence to put forward ideas, or through advocacy and lobbying, which is the self-assertion of the right to participate (Chilton, 1998; Fry & Johnstone, 2002, p. 178). The profession in question is still acting within the notion of a 'social mandate', but there are times when advocating for or against policies is attacked as exceeding the legitimate role. Rorty (1999, p. 234) offers a version of this view when he distinguishes between statements made '... in my capacity as a professor of philosophy [and those made] as a concerned citizen of a country in decline [the USA]'. Institutional managers and governments have a different reason to challenge the use of professional expertise in policy advocacy as exceeding the 'social mandate', in that they may perceive this as a challenge to their authority to set broad objectives towards which the professionals are expected to work (Clarke, 1998, pp. 238–9).

There are strong arguments for the view that members of the caring professions have an ethical responsibility to use their knowledge and skills first and foremost for the benefit of service users and fellow citizens. On the basis of both deontological and utilitarian theories, or of principlism, professionals who do not act when they are confronted by bad practice become complicit in that bad practice, and the profession that does not research and publish statements on policies that they consider to be good or bad would similarly be abrogating their moral obligations. While Rorty's point (above) may be that on matters of politics his voice ought not to count any more than any other citizen, as a philosopher he does have a professional view that will be valued as such by others and which will facilitate his access to an audience that is not open to all others. The point that professionals do have a competence in matters that concern people that is different from ordinary skills and knowledge may be more obvious in relation to obligations to individual service users (as in Koehn, 1994, p. 21). Yet, in so far as we allow that health, well-being, intellectual accomplishment and spiritual fulfilment have social dimensions, then the moral obligations of the caring professions to that which they profess do extend to matters of policy as well as applying to individual instances of need. That the 'social mandate' may be contested, even at times contradictory, does not release the caring professions from keeping open the question about those instances in which advocacy and lobbying on issues of policy are part of their professional responsibilities.

Conclusion

In this chapter the caring professions have been examined in terms of their content, focus, social relations and the 'social mandate' within which they operate. The discussion has looked particularly at these aspects as they relate, respectively, to issues of competence and expertise, objectives, status and trust, and responsibility. In each of these areas, it has been observed that there are debates between different positions, each of which rests on an ethical understanding of the nature and roles of the caring professions. Indeed, it has been the purpose of the discussion to explore issues in the content, focus, social relations and 'social mandate' of the caring professions in order to map out the way in which ethical questions are integral to these areas and not to seek specific 'answers'.

In the following five chapters the themes that have been introduced in this chapter are further extended in an exploration of recent advances in ethics. Each of Chapters 4 to 8 addresses a major contemporary approach to ethics in terms of their implications for the content, focus, social relations and 'social mandate' of the caring professions. In Chapters 1 and 2 the history and background of professional ethics were discussed and in this chapter current debates have been described. Having used the areas of the caring professions identified here to look at contemporary issues in ethics, the final chapters will explore the implications of these ideas for future developments in professional ethics.

CHAPTER 4

The Intelligence of Emotions and the Ethics of Compassion

Intelligence, emotion and compassion

Since the classical era, western moral philosophy has emphasised reason as the human faculty through which what is 'good' is known and from which 'right' actions follow. Reason thus became the foremost faculty to guide ethics, emphasising impartiality as a key value (Blum, 1994; Pizarro, 2000). The opposite of reason, in this view of human experience, is emotion. From the classical Greek philosophers, through medieval Europe, to the post-Enlightenment modernists, emotion has been widely regarded as insufficient to form any solid ground for a reliable ethics, whether as a philosophy or as a practice. Emotions, from this perspective, are unreliable and unruly, irrational precisely because they are subjective and particular.

Such an approach to ethics can seem dissatisfying for members of the caring professions (for example: Tuckett, 1998; Scott, 2000). Even when their focus is on physical or material needs, the caring professions work with those aspects of human life that are enmeshed with emotion. The objectives of their work concern those things that are important personally and socially precisely because they engage with people's emotional responses. Health, well-being, personal development, and so on, are not aspects of life about which our reactions can be confined to abstract reason. These are not only objects of the intellect, but of the variety of emotions that enrich our lives and from which we gain meaning. These are things about which we experience happiness or sadness, joy or anger, peace or suffering, and so on.

As Barbalet (2001) has noted, emotion has gradually emerged in western thought of the last two centuries as both an object of inquiry and as a factor in systematic explanations of the social world. A counter-trend to the dominant tradition of rationalism has run through western philosophy, from Hutcheson and Hume (Tronto, 1993), through Rousseau, Schopenhauer and Nietzsche, for example (de Botton, 2001). The idea of intuition and emotion as sources of moral judgement was developed further in the early twentieth century, for example by G. E. Moore and Ayer (MacIntyre, 1985; Murdoch, 1993). This shift in thought sought to take ethics further away from its foundation in rationalism, replacing rationality with emotion as the central human faculty in this respect.

In contrast, more recent attention to the relationship between emotion and ethics has sought to reconnect emotion and rationality. As we will see, this is not an attempt to justify emotion on purely rational grounds; nor is it a matter of adding an element of emotion to rationality. Instead, this developing set of views connects emotion and rationality as complementary forms of awareness of and response to the world that support ethical thought and action. To explore this development, I will examine two particular recent contributions, those of Nussbaum (1996, 2001) and Tallon (1997).

For Nussbaum, the importance of emotions in a consideration of ethics is that they are 'intelligent responses to the perception of value' (2001, p. 1). Emotions tell us what is important to us. In this, they constitute a part of our intelligence and they also make the connection between what we understand to be important and our own commitments or preferences. The emotions that Nussbaum identifies are 'grief, fear, love, joy, hope, anger, gratitude, hatred, envy, jealousy, pity, guilt' (p. 24). Each of these, she argues, are distinct from appetites, such as hunger and thirst, and they are distinctively unlike objectless moods. The elements of emotionality are cognitive and conscious (compare with Hinman's (2003) definition of ethics quoted in Chapter 1). Not only do the emotions have objects, but they are part of the process of making judgements about such objects, of valuing and responding. Thus, the emotions are, ultimately, an essential part of human 'flourishing' (Nussbaum, 2001, p. 31). In this idea, Nussbaum is drawing on the Greek concept of *eudaimonia*, which she takes to include all those things that not only make us 'happy' (in the utilitarian sense) but also contribute to every aspect of the wholeness of human life.

Tallon (1997) draws on twentieth century philosophers (notably in the traditions of existentialism and phenomenology) to argue that affection, or emotion, is such a powerful aspect of human consciousness that to ignore its impact on moral action is to have a deficient view of the basis of knowledge and action. Feeling, Tallon argues, is as much a ground for the will as is reason. The affective senses that Tallon is referring to include many of those that Nussbaum identifies (although his primary emphasis is on positive concepts, including joy, faith, hope and love). For Tallon (1997, p. 147) 'affectivity is the very essence of self'. This points to the same conclusion as that drawn by Nussbaum, that emotions are a clear guide to values. Moreover, they inform our actions, including and especially our ethical choices. Affectivity is as central to ethics as is reason. Human will, that finds expression in ethical choices and actions, responds to joy, faith, hope, and love, as much as these follow from experience of the world. The idea of 'love' is of particular importance here, as it frequently appears to *defy* reason, in the sense of a logical explanation of facts, but reveals the logic of values (Tallon, 1997, pp. 149–52). In this sense, the concept of love is not confined to erotic senses (as happens in much contemporary culture) but includes, perhaps even more powerfully, those affections that are expressed by the other ancient notion of *caritas*. This is a concept that became discredited in the nineteenth century through its reduction to an impersonal civic duty. More recently, in the caring professions there has been an increasing return to the idea that ethical practice cannot be understood impersonally and that the idea of emotional engagement implied by *caritas* is an important part of the professional relationship. It is in this sense, for instance, that Adams (2002) writes about the ethic and practice of love in medicine and health care (although his own practice of 'clown therapy' is a unique way of expressing it).

In order to examine the significance of emotion for professional ethics in more detail, I want to consider compassion. Let us consider the following situation.

Amina, a nurse with over 20 years in practice, is surprised to hear a newly qualified nurse, Angela, express anger at 'having to do so much for people who have just brought their illnesses on themselves'. Angela has recently nursed a young man who had tied to commit suicide and her patients now include several older men whose conditions are related to smoking tobacco and excessive consumption of alcohol. Angela thinks that it is wrong that some people have to wait for treatment because others have made what she regards as poor choices in their lives. Amina asks Angela to consider whether 'being to blame' should affect how nurses respond to their patients and whether blame is part of good nursing. Compassion, Amina argues, is the heart of ethical nursing.

In this scene, the older nurse is in agreement with Nussbaum, who describes compassion as that which has been 'most frequently taken to provide a good foundation for rational deliberation and appropriate action, in public as well as in private life' (2001, p. 299). This last point is crucial, that compassion is the emotion that bridges the public and the private, in much the same way as do the practices of the caring professions. The other emotions may be powerful aspects of the lives of both members of the caring professions and their clientele, in such a way as to shape personal motivations, actions and so on, but it is compassion that enables them to be brought into the public sphere and which enables personal emotions to enter the social realm.

Compassion can be defined in several ways. Nussbaum (2001, p. 301) says that it is 'a painful emotion occasioned by the awareness of another person's undeserved misfortune' (or plight, or predicament). She rejects any conflation with 'pity' or 'sympathy', seeing these concepts as laden with implications of condescension. 'Empathy' is seen as 'the imaginative reconstruction of another person's experience' (p. 302), but this, while necessary for compassion, is insufficient as it may or may not involve misfortune and does not require any particular evaluation. As Scarry (1999) argues, imagining another person's misfortune is difficult, even when the other person is a friend. When the other person is a stranger, this is even more the case. Furthermore, although the notion of empathy is more normally used to refer to beneficent reconstructions (for example, see Stephan & Finlay, 1999), it may be associated with 'indifference, malicious delight in [another's] suffering, or intense intellectual interest' rather than bringing to the appreciation of another's misfortune an 'active regard for his [or her] good' (Blum, 1994, p. 175). It is the sense of a particular evaluation in compassion that distinguishes it from empathy. Blum calls this evaluative aspect 'responsiveness' and, for him, this means that compassion is as robust a basis for beneficence as is duty or a rational application of principles, whereas empathy alone would be insufficient (p. 180).

Nussbaum is also strict about the element of 'non-desert' in compassion (2001, pp. 311–13). Not only does her approach to compassion require that the suffering has moral 'size' (it is serious, as opposed to trivial), but that the suffering was not caused by the bad choices and actions of the person. In contrast, Blum (1994, p. 178) argues that compassion is not incompatible with a rational observation that someone has caused their own plight. Likewise, Whitebrook criticises Nussbaum for insisting that 'non-desert' plays a role in compassion and argues that compassion is independent of attribution of blame; it is 'distinguished by its generosity' (2002, p. 535). This is the response of the older nurse, Amina, in the situation described above.

Whitebrook suggests that the notion of suffering should be replaced by that of 'vulnerability', the capacity to be harmed by actions or events (p. 537). This removes any sense of tragedy from the aspect of the seriousness of someone's plight and permits a more contemporary and democratic understanding. This idea of plight also includes the harm that may come from the way in which institutions and powerful individuals (which I take to include caring professionals) might humiliate or mistreat those who seek assistance. In addition, Whitebrook is insistent that compassion not only requires emotional engagement with someone who is vulnerable but also acting on that emotion; she reserves the concept of 'pity' for the emotional response that does not lead to action (p. 530).

The final element of compassion is the necessity of a belief that one's own life possibilities are similar to those of the person who is suffering (Nussbaum, 1996, p. 31; 2001, p. 315). Although this may be in the form of emotional awareness that arises from an actual experience of suffering (as we will see below), this is not an essential feature of compassion. Blum (1994, p. 177) puts this in terms of 'a sense of shared humanity, of regarding the other as a fellow human being'. In other words, it is not that to be compassionate a person must actually believe that the observed misfortune is a concrete prospect for her or him self, but that it is the type of event that could occur for anyone. Blum also notes (p. 178) that it is in this sense, too, that compassion is not condescending (see comments above about the distinction from 'pity'). On this point there is wide agreement (for example, see: Pizarro, 2000; Boleyn-Fitzgerald, 2003).

The question of desert or non-desert is the main point around which different conceptions of compassion part company (Nussbaum, 2001; Whitebrook, 2002). Questions of seriousness and of the possibility that all or many people might suffer a plight are more consistent. These distinctions are of significance for the caring professions. First, it matters whether the issue of desert or non-desert enters professional ethics. The stance that is taken will affect whether members of the caring professions are to be expected to make judgements of moral worth in clinical practice, or to implement policies that do so. Second, although the notion of seriousness of a plight appears quite robust, this can change over time, so that what is a predicament now was not seen as such in the recent past, or may not be seen as such in other cultural contexts. Thus, different professionals might reasonably have different views of what is serious. Third, the requirement that the caring professional should have a belief that their own possibilities are similar to the person with whose plight they are assisting might, I think, place a great number of service users outside the potential for compassion, depending on how it is understood. By definition, there are many situations in which caring professionals intervene that they are highly unlikely to have any possibility of facing (perhaps because they do not share the social characteristics or the preferences of a particular service user). Such a concept could restrict the idea of compassion as the basis for professional ethics to situations of accident or 'fate' and thus create categories of practice in which moral blame was the underlying value where particularities were not shared. However, if understood in the more general sense of shared human potential for responses to particular circumstances, then the perception of commonality may play a role and it is in this sense that Nussbaum (2001, p. 343) argues for the 'similarity of possibilities'. It is in this way that a positive empathy may be essential to compassion. For patients, these questions might have a practical consequence, if they were nursed by Angela as compared to Amina.

Nussbaum (2001) identifies emotions that are impediments to compassion, impeding its development and practice. These are shame, envy and disgust. We can speak also of resentment, fear and anger as emotions that act against compassion (Barbalet, 2001). Envy and resentment arise when someone cannot accept the realities of others, that other people might have something that they do not or that they might suffer a loss that others do not. The emotions lead to an inability to empathise or to form appropriate judgements of similar possibilities (Nussbaum, 2001, p. 345). Shame and disgust are similarly related, tying together the rejection of weakness, uncertainty, decay, death and so on. Nussbaum argues that shame and disgust are often associated with the human condition – of 'vulnerability and mortality – stickiness, stench, liquidity, ooze ... decay, foulness' (p. 347). Such emotions can be seen in the apparent durability of misogyny and homophobia in western societies (Stephan & Finlay, 1999). Lane (2001) also points to hostility to poorer sections of society, the labelling of them as 'welfare cheats' (or 'bludgers', or 'scroungers'), and resentment of ethnic minorities, immigrants and refugees, as entrenched in western societies.

Compassion and its impediments have implications for the caring professions, in terms of their practices, their goals and their social organisation. While it may be supposed that one of the reasons that people choose to train and work in caring professions is that they have a tendency to feel and act on those emotions, compared with the general population, this cannot be assumed to apply equally in all cases. For example, Lane (2001, p. 479) cites claims that nurses who demonstrate empathy avoid working with people who are terminally ill because they are unable to relieve pain or prevent death. Such an observation points to the question of 'compassion fatigue' (or 'burnout') that has been identified as a challenge to ethical practice in several professions (see, for example, Cherniss, 1995). Moreover, just as the general population displays a range of moral judgements about the relationship between desert and appropriate social responses to those deemed to be 'in need', so too it may be reasonable to suspect that there is a range of emotions felt by members of the caring professions and their ethical responses to the users of their services. It should not be surprising to find nurses who hold Angela's position, even though Amina's views correspond with formal nursing codes of ethics.

Emotions, especially those that support or impede compassion, raise many questions about ethics in the caring professions. How do ideas such as the recognition of and positive response to the plight of others (on the one hand) and shame, envy and disgust (on the other) inform our understanding of professional ethics? Nussbaum's analysis shows the way in which emotions are a core part of the logic in reaching moral judgements. As both Blum (1994) and Pizarro (2000) argue, moral judgements constitute the bridge between principles and specific situations. Therefore, in so far as the caring professions are concerned not only with material needs but also with emotional, psychological and social aspects of human lives, a consideration of professional ethics must include attention to emotions and interpersonal relationships, and their link to social values, as part of the conscious intelligent basis of ethics.

Emotional rationality and practice

The very existence of the caring professions can be said, in some sense, to be an expression of a compassionate response to tragedies, misfortunes and the challenges of life. Their objective is the good of those persons for whom professionals apply their disciplines. Knowledge and skills are not developed for their own sake, but for the purpose of promoting the good of service users. Sarason (1985) makes a particularly trenchant attack on those caring (his terms is 'clinical') professionals who 'dilute' compassion in a pursuit of 'science' that is reductionist and sometimes self-serving. For Sarason, ethical practice must be guided by a holistic interest in the person for whom knowledge and skills are being applied. Only in such circumstances, he argues, will compassion be possible. This is an important challenge to those caring professions that make explicit claims to an ethic of service based on compassion (see, for example, the review by Johnson *et al.* (1995) of codes of ethics from psychiatry, psychology, school counsellors and social workers, in which all make such a statement).

Service users certainly can be seen as facing tragedy, misfortune and challenge. Indeed, in some caring professions most or all of the work that is undertaken is with people whose situations can be described in these terms. Many of the discussions of compassion as the ethical heart of professional practice draw on situations of illness and disease, disability, the breakdown of relationships or material want. There are two dimensions to compassion in these situations. The first is in the emotional engagement of the practitioner in the interpersonal encounter with the service user, the second is in the overall orientation of the practitioner towards the need experienced by the service user.

For example, Fischer (2001) reviews how her own experience of a life-threatening condition (breast cancer) equipped her to be a more compassionate psychologist. Through the personal understanding that she gained from dealing with her own illness, she draws implications for responses to her patients that are grounded in positive empathy, so that Fischer's 'willingness to listen to the patient's account of her struggle allow[s] her to realize that her story is comprehensible and meaningful' (p. 108). Lynch (2002) describes how the capacity to engage emotionally with patients enabled a medical student to express her compassion towards those who were severely ill, which was, at times, the only response she could offer (that is, there were no technical medical procedures she could resort to in response to the patients' requests for assistance). From evidence about a range of caring professionals, Johnson *et al.* (1995) summarise service users' views of 'helpful' professionals as those who do not blame service users for their plight, and who do take time to listen, show courtesy, show they understand what the service user is going through and provide clear information. The professional responses that service users found helpful were those that the professions themselves have defined as 'good'. Each of these examples, in different ways, provide concrete instances of the elements of compassion discussed above. These are professionals who recognise the moral seriousness of service users' situations, who recognise common humanity with service users and who do not ascribe desert (that is, blame) for the misfortunes to which they are responding.

Not all of the work of the caring professions can be seen as a response to plight or misfortune. School teachers and ministers of religion may at times be faced with responding to such needs, but their professions are more directed to challenges that might be seen as positive aspects of human life, in the intellectual development of young people or spiritual growth of anyone who seeks it. Even in health situations, the caring professions may not be responding to illness or disablement, but to occurrences such as childbirth or more preventative matters, such as routine health checks, vaccinations and so on. But here, too, compassion expresses the intelligent emotional dimension of ethical practice. For example, the nurse at a clinic for babies who does not demonstrate compassion towards the normal uncertainties and anxieties of parents, especially those who are young, is unlikely to be experienced as helpful (Cherniss, 1995, p. 65). (That this is most likely to involve women professionals working with mothers does not of itself guarantee compassion. I note this point as an empirical observation and not as a normative judgement – the same point also would apply to male nurses and to fathers.)

Other examples from professional contexts that are not necessarily about plight or misfortune include those from education. For example, Brown (1999) proposes that good practice in teaching rests on an empathic response to the world-views of the learner, in which the teacher is able to grasp the significance of issues and ideas as these relate to the wider experiences of students and to understand the common humanity of each student. This applies to all aspects of the way in which each student approaches education, both those that show the student's positive engagement with learning and those that reveal resistance. Sumison (2000) gives an example of a student who repeatedly seeks extensions on submission dates for assignments and appears to change her explanation between different teachers. The ethical challenge for the teacher who sees this is to avoid the pitfall of acting in anger ('this is a "bad" student') while balancing compassion for the individual with the needs of other students and the educational reasons behind the limit on how many extensions can be given before students fail on grounds of non-completion of the task. It is only, Brown argues (1999, p. 73), through such a compassionate stance that the teacher will be able to respond helpfully to students' learning needs. It may be, but does not require, that the teacher has experienced the same things; however, compassion understood in this way would demand that the teacher recognise in her or him self the emotional responses that are generated by interactions with students. As we have already noted, empathy in itself does not guarantee compassion, but may also lead to anger, shame, envy or disgust. For compassion to become the ethical basis of teaching, and any other professional practice where the professional may act to exercise power over service users, it requires that professionals consciously address their own emotional responses to ensure that these are 'other directed' in the caring relationship.

Olsen (2001) calls this 'empathetic maturity'. He puts this in terms of a nurse seeking to have a 'positive regard for a patient with difficult behaviors' (p. 40) by seeing such behaviours as human. The problem in this sort of situation, is that it appears to invite an 'excusing' of the moral agency of service users, which is in itself dehumanising. Olsen's example (p. 41) is that of difficulties for nurses empathising with people who appear to have caused their own health problems, such as through drug mis-use. The same negative reaction may be experienced by some caring professionals who have to respond to someone who has tried to take their own life. Olsen's argument is that the empathetically mature professional is the one who is able to differentiate their assessment of culpability from their emotional responses. This is not the same as ignoring the reasons why the person may be requiring professional care, or their own part in that; nor does it demand that the professional abandon her or his own moral values. Rather, it involves shifting attention away from concern with 'blame' and towards understanding the person with needs in the complexity of their situation and the potential for any person to experience distress. In the earlier illustrative situation, Angela may reasonably feel affronted by others' apparently self-destructive actions, but 'good' practice informed by compassion would require her to act compassionately towards patients, regardless of 'desert', on the basis of shared humanity.

This notion is more widely recognised as 'emotional intelligence' (Mayer & Salovey, 1993) or 'moral perception' (Scott, 2000). However this is categorised, the central theme is that through conscious and considered attention to the emotional elements of work in the caring professions, it is possible to sustain practices that are service user centred (Stevenson, 2002). As the caring professions all, in some way, base their formal statements of ethical duties on notions such as respect for persons or service to humanity, such intelligence and perception are helpful in understanding how we might engage ethical principles in practice (Gallagher, 1999). Seen in this way, the intelligence of emotions constitutes a practical wisdom ('phronesis') that supports good practice.

Emotion in the focus of caring professions

In the previous chapter I noted that professional ethics not only concern the way in which caring professions undertake their work but also the goals and purposes towards which their work is focused. Von Dietze and Orb (2000) point to this when they note that '[c]ompassion is inextricably linked with action: listening, feeding, clothing, visiting, sheltering, educating, comforting, forgiving ...' (p. 171). These are the intended outcomes of intelligent emotion being put into practice. Through these quite specific goals, the wider objectives of health, well-being, intellectual accomplishment, spirituality and so on may be achieved. They give the example of the way in which a nurse might practise compassion through mobilisation of 'hope, confidence and trust' between her or him self and the patient, with the goal of achiev-ing healing (p. 172). Even palliative and terminal care contexts have this goal, as the notion of 'dying well' on which such work is based implies (see, for example, Tuckett, 1998, p. 225).

Let us consider the example of people who are admitted to a hospital. Whatever their age, it is probable that they will encounter several professions; it is also probable that both the individuals who are ill and their relatives (assuming that they have any in the locality) are likely to have many questions about what is happening to them. The reactions of medical, nursing and other health professionals to such questions can vary. Sometimes questions may be seen as an intrusion into the pro-fessional role. Indeed, where there are essential life supporting tasks to be performed, there may simply not be time to answer questions at that point. However, the compassionate professional will recognise such questions as expressions of the anxiety, even fear, that is a normal part of the human condition when facing ill-health and, as soon as possible, will seek to reassure the patient and family members with clearly understandable information. The idea of compassion may, in these circumstances, support the argument noted in the previous chapter, that 'too much information' *at a particular time* may be detri-mental to hope and confidence, but that this is a matter of timing and not a justification for being untruthful by omission (Veatch, 2002). Discovery of dishonesty not only destroys trust, but the act of being untruthful in itself could be seen, ultimately, as lacking in compassion because it fails to recognise the human dignity of the person asking the question. Indeed, at times the bland reassurance of 'everything's fine' can be both patronising and for the benefit of the person giving the reply, neither of which constitute compassion.

The purpose of the goals of hope, confidence and trust in the caring relationship, however, must be understood as going beyond the relationship in itself. In other words, compassion as the basis for professional ethics is not intended to produce a 'good' relationship for the sake of the relationship itself (although the relationship may be enjoyed by both parties because it is 'good'). The good relationship is a means to an end. Understood in this way, compassion, like any basis for ethics or any ethical principle, is an intermediary notion, which is why von Dietze and Orb (2000) argue that it is linked to action. I would go further than this, and suggest that compassion can only be expressed in action. Unless it forms a condition of practice, compassion would remain the internal and hence private experience of an individual. We would then be left with the question of whether it had any significance beyond that person's experience, a thought to which we will return below in relation to the phenomenon of 'burnout'.

One of the reasons why caring professionals in this situation might be evasive or cover up the truth with platitudes, apart from wishing to spare someone at a vulnerable moment from the impact of the full facts, might be a sense that it is not appropriate for the service user to ask questions, because this can seem to question the professional person's role. This is an emotional response that can be powerful, especially if the task being performed is complex, time is limited, or there are other pressures on the professional. While this is understandable (it is, after all, also part of the common human condition), it does raise the question of emotions such as anger, resentment and so on, which have been identified above as impediments to compassion. Momentary irritation is not, I think, an impediment of this kind, because it is much easier for the professional to be aware enough to amend her or his response – the emotions of anger and resentment go deeper and can be less open to self-awareness.

It has already been noted in this chapter that shame, envy and disgust also act as impediments to compassion. These are, perhaps, less obvious as emotional responses that might be expected in the caring professions, given the nature of the work that is undertaken. Yet they may be present. For example, Kushner and Thomasma (2001) cite many instances where medical students have to overcome innate shame or disgust at the things with which they have to deal and their own reactions to those things. All members of caring professions have to face these emotional responses in themselves in the process of becoming members of their professions. Such emotions can be expressed as rough humour, or in patronising or derogatory attitudes towards service users; at the extreme, these may be communicated directly to service users. Envy, disgust or anger, in the sense that Nussbaum (2001) intends, can emerge as a rejection of the ethical claims of the service user ('why do I have to help *this* person?', voiced by Angela in the earlier illustrative example), in the form of moralising or as inappropriately controlling action. However, whether or not directly expressed, these are all indications that compassion is absent. Respect for the human dignity of others is, therefore, closely linked to compassion, especially when the others are dependent in some way on an ethical response to achieve their own flourishing in the world.

Emotion and the social relations of caring professions

In practice, the relationships between service users and professionals are the major means through which the work of the caring professions is accomplished. Even where the nature of the identified need is physical, material, intellectual or spiritual, there will also be an emotional content and focus. In the previous chapter, it was noted that there had been a tendency of social relations in professional life to shift from those based on trust to those based on contract. That this may have occurred, at least partly, because of many instances of a lack of compassion, as well as integrity, by members of the caring professions, is not a reason to suppose that all members of these professions consider this an appropriate development. Those who argue for compassion as an ethical basis for practice are not only asserting an abstract ideal, but point to concrete examples in which compassion is evident.

For example, Lynch (2002), in a short descriptive account, illustrates his argument that compassion is more meaningful to many service users than technical skill (at least in terms of what is seen and remembered) with reference to a medical student in an oncology service who acted compassionately towards patients, such as by giving clear encouraging information, by using appropriate physical touch and by attending empathically to non-verbal communication. That such practice enabled the more technical aspects of treatment to be given effectively is not, in itself, the reason why Lynch affirms the ethics of this person's practice. At the same time, Lynch emphasises that compassion is no substitute for technical competence – the two are not separable.

Such examples are also given by, among others, in occupational therapy Barnitt (1993), in nursing Gaul (1995) and Tuckett (1998), in school teaching Brown (1999) and Sumison (2000), in psychology Fischer (2001) and in medicine Kushner and Thomasma (2001). Although these discussions provide different types of descriptions (some are research reports, some are self-reflections on practice) all of the descriptions of compassionate practice share the understanding that it is an action, not just an attitude. In each case it is the social relations between service users and professionals that reveal the ethics of compassion. Such accounts do what, to an extent, compassionate practice seeks to do, that is they rationalise the emotional dimensions of social relations. By this I mean that they make it possible to render an account of ethics in practice that is concrete, grounded in action, but which at the same time reveals ethical meaning that is applicable beyond the specifics of the individual situation (Gaul, 1995). The acts that constitute our measure of compassion are not simply to be seen as 'good' in the contexts in which they occurred, but can be recognised as instances of what might be enacted in other situations in order to act compassionately.

The type of situations that are described in terms of compassion not only include those in which the interests of the service user can be seen explicitly as matching the objectives of the professional but also those in which power is being exercised by the professional without an explicit agreement on the part of the service user. The former occur most obviously in health contexts where the patient understands the meaning of a procedure, even though it may be distressing, or in the relationship between a minister of religion and a member of the faith community. The latter occur more for social workers, medical practitioners and others dealing with situations such as child protection investigations, or at times for teachers responding to a child who does not wish to be in school. I want to be careful here to avoid misidentifying these latter sorts of situations with those of abuse and exploitation by professionals that were discussed in the previous chapter. Compassion clearly does not occur in those instances, which may be an indicator of a way in which they are 'unethical'. In contrast, where the caring professions are exercising authority legitimately there is still the possibility of compassion in the content and focus of their practices. In these situations, where power is more explicit, it is also the case that the impediments to compassion can be heightened. Particularly emotions such as anger, shame and disgust can challenge ethical practice in these circumstances. An example of this would be a social worker who is motivated by feelings of retribution; such a person is very likely find it difficult to practice ethically in child protection because they will lack the necessary positive empathy to be compassionate. For this reason, although compassion is evidenced by actions, the emotions behind it must be understood. Thus motivation is important even though it is not in itself a sufficient measure of compassion.

Good intent is also not a guarantee for compassion because it may be subject to corrosion by the realities of practice. Service users are not always grateful, colleagues are not always supportive and the task that the beginning practitioner sought to accomplish may have been too idealistic. The resulting loss of compassion has been identified as 'burnout' (Cherniss, 1995). Cherniss' longitudinal study is based on nurses, social workers, teachers, psychologists and 'poverty lawyers' working in the public human services. Burnout is defined in terms of responses to work stress that lead to caring professionals reducing their professional goals, losing commitment to their job and to the needs of service users and blaming others for this, having less empathy with service users, becoming self focused in their motivation and even leaving their profession. Not everyone left literally, as for some people there were opportunities to move out of clinical work into administration. Other people developed an emotional distance from service users, which undermined the empathy that is necessary to do a 'good' job, which can become a self-reinforcing process. Cherniss argues that when compassion depends on the extrinsic rewards of the responses from service users or colleagues, then it is too fragile to form an ethical basis for practice. However, this does not mean that professionals should gain no satisfaction in their work. Rather he suggests that intrinsic rewards provide a stronger foundation for maintaining an ethics of compassion in respect of the social relations of practice.

Emotion in the 'social mandate' of caring professions

The work of the caring professions, and the 'mandate' under which they have developed, can be seen as the 'social expression' of compassion. This not only applies to publicly funded services, but to all areas of professional work. That such occupations have developed and are accorded a positive value in the wider society comes partly from the tangible services that they are able to perform, but this is also buttressed by a belief that their existence reflects compassion at a social level. The caring professions are regarded positively because they embody the social emotion of responsiveness to those who face 'misfortune'. In this way, they are 'goods' both in the sense of being commodities and in terms of the way in which they exemplify a positive social ethic.

It is in this dimension of professional ethics, however, that the impediments to compassion (Nussbaum, 2001) and the difficulties in imagining the misfortune of others (Scarry, 1999) operate at a social level. For example, limits to the social expression of compassion through the emotions of shame and disgust can be seen in public responses to issues such as the abuse of children. Baartman (1998) reviews the way in which the fact of the occurrence of child sexual abuse has been repeatedly challenged over a long period of time, both scientifically and in the public arena, despite the strong evidence. As early as the late nineteenth century physicians and other professionals were subjected to such scepticism that to publicise the idea of child sexual abuse required a moral commitment to the truth of this concept, and its implications for victims, as well as a scientific commitment to the facts (Baartman, 1998, p. 192). In the face of scepticism, Baartman notes a predominant denial of the very idea, or else an interest in and compassion for perpetrators as opposed to victims (p. 193). His explanation is that child sexual abuse breaks such powerful taboos that shame and disgust, about both the sexual exploitation and the sexualisation of children, lead in many instances to the blaming, either totally or partially, of the victim. Caring professionals (he lists 'GPs, social workers, teachers, therapists and priests') may not be any better at responding to victims with compassion than is the society at large (p. 200), when their ethics might suggest that the professions should challenge the lack of compassion towards those who are abused.

Sznaider and Talmud (1998) see the problem with compassion at the social level stemming from the contradiction between compassion and instrumentality. That is, the actions of caring professionals to intervene in situations of child abuse are supported if they represent 'public compassion' acting to promote 'private goals ... namely the creation of better families', while at the same time they are criticised if they are seen to undermine the social order (p. 17). Parton (1985) argues that this is the foundation of an ethical double-bind for the caring professions, who are held culpable both if they fail to act and when they do act. The consequence, according to Sznaider and Talmud (1998) is that child abuse has been turned from a clinical and moral issue into a legal matter, especially in those countries where a statutory obligation to report instances of child abuse to designated authorities is placed on caring professions. The professional role is, thus, increasingly constructed around instrumental expertise to respond appropriately to a problem that has been publicly defined and in which '[u]niversal compassion for the helpless becomes institutionalized' (p. 24). As a result, the moral dimension of child abuse for members of the caring professions is dramatically reduced and replaced with formal rules of conduct.

Von Dietze and Orb (2000) perceive the impact of neo-liberalism on the 'social mandate' of the caring professions as being another impediment to the expression of compassion, whether publicly or in clinical practice. This is not because the economic restructuring of welfare states is, in itself, inimical to compassion. However, it has introduced two factors into the organisation of the caring professions. The first of these is competition. This can be seen between caring professionals in terms of competition for jobs and a consequent lack of compassion for each other as well as for service users (von Dietze & Orb, 2000, p. 172). It can also be seen in the competition between services (whether state, non-government not-for-profit, or private for profit) for contracts, in which notions of efficiency and effectiveness have displaced compassion for those who are in need. Here again, the prevailing political environment emphasises the instrumental expertise of the caring professions as against any claim to a role in the social expression of compassion.

A concrete example of this shift can be seen in the changing response to people who have chronic health problems that can be attributed to life-style, illustrated in the example of Amina and Angela. Formal professional ethics suggests that no-one should be refused treatment because of what amounts to a moral judgement about their life-style. However, in the context of health resources that are not increasing as rapidly as is demand, some choices must be made about who receives treatment and in what order. Historically, the practice of 'triage' developed to deal with this reality, in the use of clinical judgement to distinguish between those who would get well without treatment, those whose situation is not treatable and those who will get well but need treatment in order to do so. The underlying ethics of this practice is utilitarian, but it can be approached on the basis of the four central principles of autonomy, beneficence, non-maleficence and social justice (Beauchamp & Childress, 2001, p. 271). The competitive neo-liberal environment, however, has introduced the ethical impediments of envy and resentment into the dynamic of such decisions. The difficulty of imagining the other person (Scarry, 1999) appears to be connected to an increasing reluctance to fund social health and welfare programs in situations where the person in need can be held culpable for their own plight. The 'taxpayer', we are led to believe, does not wish to forgo wealth in order to assist fellow citizens whose plight is 'self inflicted' (Bauman, 2001b). In this sense, Nussbaum's (2001) notion of 'desert' has empirical validity, even if it sits awkwardly with her normative framework. So the person who smokes tobacco may be refused treatment because of that 'life-style choice'. Yet medical practitioners and nurses, in particular, have to reconcile these trends with their formal professional ethics. The involvement of health professionals in litigation against tobacco firms can be seen as one way in which compassion becomes redirected rather than blocked.

Nussbaum (1996) argues that there is a clear link between compassion and social justice. Without a normative framework such as that supplied by the ideal of justice, she suggests, compassion cannot be realised. As most of the caring professions subscribe to the notion of social justice in their codes of ethics, this seems to be a strong basis for connecting formal ethics with the practices of individual professionals. Indeed, for many caring professionals it is precisely in the detail of practice that principles such as social justice become enacted through a compassionate response to particular service users (Stevenson, 2002). With this comes the risk that, in the particular situation, the difficulty of imagining the plight of another person may become very complex. For example, empathy between people of different cultures in respect for privacy in a nursing examination of patients (Browne, 1995), or whose socio-economic class and sexuality may give them a different perspective on the meaning of the family (Wise, 1995) are certainly challenging. Yet, as Sen (2001) argues, it is precisely in the use of principles to understand the ethical demands of the particular that the necessary imaginative capacities can be developed. Compassion, as an intelligent emotion, may not in itself be robust enough to provide the foundation for professional ethics. But when understood in connection with a normative framework, and the necessary debates between positions which that will entail, compassion can be seen as necessary for the enactment of ethical principles in the clinical context.

Conclusion

This chapter has examined recent developments in thinking about compassion as an intelligent emotion. Blum (1994) and Nussbaum (1996, 2001) argue for the central place of emotion in ethics as a balance to the reliance on abstract reason as the basis for ethical thought. Blum, Nussbaum and others see compassion as the emotion that achieves this objective. In the caring professions, too, there has been a growing interest in both the general approach to acknowledge the role of emotion and specifically in the place that compassion plays in balancing the more abstract principles of autonomy, beneficence, non-maleficence and justice (Gallagher, 1999). However, as Nussbaum's (2001) analysis shows, there are also emotional impediments to compassion, including shame, disgust and envy, and these also can operate in the caring professions and the social contexts that surround them.

By examining the practices and the goals of the caring professions, as well as the social relations and the 'social mandate' under which they operate, the complexity of compassion as a basis for professional ethics is revealed. Professional ethics may (perhaps even must) attend to compassion because it involves the recognition of the person, or situation, in a way that demands a moral response. Yet, at the same time, the emotional impediments to compassion are powerful factors that cannot be ignored. Not only do they appear in various ways in the policies that shape the work of the caring professions, but professionals themselves also feel such emotions in different ways. This ambiguity suggests that compassion ultimately cannot do all that is required to sustain a robust professional ethics. What is needed is a normative framework within which compassion may be able to play a key role in guiding clinical practice, the development of knowledge and skills (for example through research), the management of services and wider policy formation (compare with Gallagher, 1999). Thus, compassion is necessary but it is not sufficient on its own to provide a distinct and self-sustaining approach to professional ethics.

CHAPTER 5

Feminism and the Ethics of Care

Gender and care

Arguments for an 'ethics of care' have grown from a debate in moral psychology, in particular that between Kohlberg (1981, 1984) and Gilligan (1982). Kohlberg's extensive, transcultural research on moral development argues for a hierarchy in which the most basic level is one at which moral behaviour follows from learned obedience and avoidance of punishment, while at the highest level a person is capable of identifying complex moral issues and applying universal and abstract principles. Gilligan challenges this model on the grounds that the research sample was entirely male. When Gilligan conducted a different experiment with young women she observed that values of caring for others and maintaining social relationships were predominant. These are the middle stages of Kohlberg's hierarchy, which he termed 'conventional morality'. Rather than accepting the conclusion that young women are morally less developed than young men, Gilligan argues that Kohlberg's model is flawed because it assumed *a priori* a view of morality in which particular notions of the moral person are embedded, such as objectivity, rationality and so on. Gilligan argues that by not including women in his research, Kohlberg had obscured the possibility of seeing a focus on 'caring' as a higher order stage of moral development. This has the effect of consigning (most) women to a 'lower level' of moral capacity and over-emphasising the proportion of men who attain a 'higher level'.

Against this view Gilligan (1982) argues for a view of ethics in which women's voices should be heard as clearly as men's voices, resonating with the differences between women's and men's moral perceptions. For Gilligan, morality must be understood in terms of relationships and not of personal autonomy, of 'human connection rather than through systems of rules' (1982, p. 29). This is not just a matter of including a 'feminine' perspective in otherwise 'masculine' moral frameworks, but of asserting a *feminist* view of ethics, in which women's perspectives must be valued in their own right and in ways that enable women to be understood as moral agents (Gilligan, 1995). This means that although a women's voice will emphasise relationships and caring in morality the more 'traditional feminine virtues' of subservience and self-sacrifice are criticised as ways of confining women within patriarchy.

The importance of this view for the caring professions can be seen in Johnstone's (1994) critique of arguments that ethics education for nurses should focus on 'the middle stages' of moral development and not to be concerned with 'the higher stages', as it was argued by some educators that nurses (almost all of whom are women) would be unlikely to be able to develop the capacity for 'Kantian morality'. Johnstone, herself a nurse, responds with an extensive review of the criticisms of Kohlberg's *a priori* reliance on quite restricted and specific notions of justice (1994, pp. 113–14). This point will be developed further below.

To illustrate how the notion of care is encountered in practice I want to consider the following instance.

Sara, a social worker, is discussing a forthcoming court appearance with Michelle, a teenager who has been charged with several offences of shoplifting. Sara has to present a report to the court on Michelle's social circumstances and Michelle asks Sara to miss out facts about her poor record of school attendance. Sara explains to Michelle that although she will ask the court to consider other facts about Michelle's life (her father does not live with the family and does not support them financially and her mother does not have a job, for example) Sara is not willing to deceive the court by missing out relevant information. In response to Michelle's tears and angry words, Sara patiently explains again how she intends her report to help Michelle and that it is unhelpful for her to collude with Michelle about her school record.

From the perspective of care that Gilligan (1982) outlines, Sara is attending and responding to Michelle's anxieties about the court appearance, but this does not mean that she simply takes Michelle's demand at face value. Nor does Sara resolve the matter by reference to duty, although this might be plausible. Rather, she sees Michelle as someone with whom she has a relationship of responsibility and for whom she must engage with the difficult task of helping Michelle also to recognise her own responsibilities.

Noddings (1984) argues that caring, like compassion, is connected to the emotion of empathy. However, caring is not compassion, as the latter is understood in terms of the ideas that were explored in the previous chapter. For Noddings, care is relational, in so far as the 'one-caring' is receptive to the 'cared-for', attending to and taking responsibility for responding to the other person, rather than projecting her or his understanding into the other person's situation (1984, p. 30). The 'cared-for' person, in turn, is called to respond ethically to the 'one-caring'. The ethical person, in this view, is the person who feels and acts in caring for others rather than someone who follows abstract principles, even when those principles may point to that which is right. However, the ethics of care is not dependent on just how an individual might be feeling at any given time. As Noddings puts it, 'ethical caring requires an effort that is not needed in natural caring' (p. 80). While love or respect may provide the foundations for caring, an ethics of care demands a thoughtful and considered nurturing of capacities to tease out ways in which the 'one-caring' may be receptive, attentive and responsible to the person who is 'cared-for'. Unlike rationalist ethics, this is an approach that 'is conditioned not by a host of narrow and rigidly defined principles but by a broad and loosely defined ethic that moulds itself in situations and has a proper regard for human affections, weaknesses, and anxieties' (Noddings, 1984, p. 25). It is for this reason that an ethics of care emphasises that Sara's actions are responsive both to Michelle's immediate needs and to her moral development.

The way in which Noddings understands caring is derived from the distinction between 'caring about' and 'caring for' that was encountered in Chapter 3 (1984, pp. 18, 112–13). For her the difference between the two notions is the degree of receptivity and attention. 'Caring about' can lead to limited action (such as a casual donation to a hunger relief agency) or to an intellectual response which remains within the confines of the thoughts of the person who is claiming to care. 'Caring for' is seen as the stronger foundation for ethics because it is expressed in the concrete relations between the person caring and the person who is cared for. In this approach, acts are good or bad because of the bearing that they have on relationships, not simply because they do or do not conform to an abstract principle. Ethics is the means by which we discern how we might be moral; morality is sought in order that we might maintain relationships. Thus, duties, principles and virtues may be plausible ways of explaining what is good or right, but what makes them so is the context of caring in which they have meaning.

Like Gilligan, Noddings argues that the distinction between the ethics of care and the dominant traditions of philosophy is to be understood in terms of the differences between feminine and masculine, or patriarchal, approaches to morality. Noddings sees a very clear connection between women's relationships, in families and in communities, and the ethics of being receptive, attentive and responsible to those who are cared-for. Her model of caring is that of motherhood. By extension, she also refers to education as a professional field in which the operation of the ethics of care can be seen. It is not that all women are inherently ethical and all men innately not so; rather, Noddings suggests that the biological and psychological differences between the sexes are such that, under patriarchal social relations, men have not developed a masculine caring, but have instead sought abstract and decontextualised principles that place ethics outside relationships (Noddings, 1984, pp. 128–30).

Tronto (1993) and Sevenhuijsen (1998), among others, have argued that it is important for a feminist ethic of care to avoid any essentialism, either in the form of the exclusion of men from caring or in the appearance of trapping women in relationships that can be exploitative and oppressive. Tronto (1993) argues for an open view of caring as a basis for ethics, seeing the strengths of this perspective in the potential to focus on practice and the context of action. Sevenhuijsen agrees, and in addition argues that both Gilligan and Noddings create a binary system of thought, in which sex (male and female) replaces the more subtle notion of gender (feminine and masculine) (1998, p. 82). Rather, what is needed is a broad way of conceptualising care as action – 'what care is and where it takes place' (p. 83). This leads Sevenhuijsen (following Tronto) to question the binary divide between care and justice as primary values, but in doing so to ask how justice may be rethought in order for it to be held in a more dynamic relationship with care. Similarly, Held (1995, p. 130) suggests, tentatively, that care may be seen as the 'wider moral framework into which justice can be fitted'. Care is the more basic moral value because relationships are foundational to human life. At the same time justice is necessary for a more complete human flourishing, in the sense that justice is the outcome of trust enacted between individuals and groups. Deveaux (1995), likewise, argues that the ethics of care is compatible with, even essential to, ethics grounded in principles such as justice. The point is that the ethics of care is not a 'grand moral theory', but rather a framework for understanding moral context and relationships in concrete experience (p. 117).

Like compassion, an ethics of care can only be achieved through action (van Hooft, 1995). Active caring is expressive of commitments that have human well-being as their goal. Similarly, Blum (1994) states that 'responsiveness' as the expression of care for another has to be enacted – it is 'a kind of initiative and is not merely a passive response' (p. 198). There is an important connection between emotion, thought and action. This leads, for Blum, to a particularistic view of ethics, in which what is 'right' is to be judged in context and in relation to a given person. In the framework of an ethics of care, the capacity to discern issues and to respond appropriately cannot be left to the workings of abstract principles but has to be teased out in the context of specific relationships, for example between *this* nurse and *this* patient, or between *that* teacher and *that* student.

The question of particularity raises the most pertinent challenge to the ethics of care, namely the question of partiality. To deal with this, Gilligan argues that a contextual way of looking at morality is not simply relativism by another name, but is necessary to be able to deal with the complexity of the relationships within which ethical choices are made (1982, pp. 111–12). Noddings similarly demonstrates the way in which the particularity of a concrete situation has its own dynamic with examples of relational teasing out of ethical choices (1984, pp. 93, 109–11). It is not that the ethics of care supports partiality in the sense that anything will do providing it enables a person to maintain relationships, or that it promotes nepotism. Indeed, the justification of choices from the ethics of care may appear to be very like those made from abstract principles – the point is that the basis on which they are made is very different and the way in which those choices are arrived at makes them more sustaining of human relationships. Does this, then, make the ethics of care a type of 'universal principle'? Blum argues that the ethics of care proposes 'a morality for all': it is not relativistic 'in the sense of applying to some but not to others or of being confined to one particular group' (1994, p. 233). However, he asserts that this is very different from being a 'universal principle' in the sense that the term is used in either deontology or utilitarianism, precisely because the ethics of care cannot be separated from the relationships, choices and actions in which it is enacted.

As the ethics of care has, in many ways, been developed from two of the professions with which we are concerned, psychology and education, it might be assumed that this approach would have special implications for these and the other occupations that have been defined as 'caring'. So, for the remainder of this chapter we will examine the issues raised by this approach for these professions.

Care in professional practice

As the ethics of care is described by Gilligan (1982) or Noddings (1984) it can only be understood in terms of individual actions in specific contexts. Particularity and the emphasis on relationships make it difficult to consider the ethics of care in any other way. As Davies (1995) has put it, the issue is how we consider the moral aspects of professional care-giving. Ethics and practices should not be separated; ethics, in this sense, concerns the integration of the moral and technical aspects of 'how' good professional practice is to be achieved.

The ethics of care has been widely addressed in nursing (Allmark, 1995, 1996; Davies, 1995; Gaul, 1995; Bradshaw, 1996; Tadd, 1998). In each of these discussions there is an emphasis on the concrete practices of nursing as the embodiment of caring in sets of particular tasks. For example, the nurse who is performing specific tasks for a patient, such as changing dressings, giving injections, monitoring intravenous rehydration, and so on, may do so in a way that is attentive and responsive to the patient as well as seeking to be technically competent. At times a patient may find procedures distressing or uncomfortable, and in the context of ill-health find it difficult to co-operate with the nursing process. According to the ethics of care, good practice leads the nurse to respond to the patient's distress or discomfort through reassurance, explanation, and encouragement. The maintenance of antisepsis and other matters of technique are important, as they may have a critical effect on the health of the patient, but responsiveness to the person should be considered as significant. Responses that reflect a view of patients as 'difficult', 'demanding', 'wanting to know more than they need to' and so on, fail to take responsibility for caring for the whole person.

In education the role of the teacher, while not concerned with the physical needs of students in the way a nurse's concerns include such needs, can also be seen as 'caring-for' as well as 'caring-about'. Such practice may take the form of being attentive and responsive to the importance of the student understanding that which is being studied, rather than simply learning information (Friedman, 2002). In a different context, it may take the form of challenging a student who does not address her own responsibilities in the process of learning (Sumison, 2000). As was evident also in the illustrative example of the social worker, Sara, there are strong parallels here with Noddings' discussion of a parent who talks through a moral issue with a child, caring for the child in her moral development (1984, pp. 90–4). (This point will be developed below.) Both Friedman and Sumison are aware that a teacher is rarely relating just to one student at a time, but is having to juggle responsiveness to many individuals in the context of a class or group (Noddings too is aware of this). As with nurses, who will usually have several patients to care for at one time, ethical practice requires a fine judgement about attentiveness. This is also seen in Acker's description of teachers as 'a kind of reflective practitioner mother' (1995, p. 23), using the metaphor of attending to the plural needs of a family. Also making the comparison with women's domestic roles, Acker's study found that teachers' 'work is never done', that they 'are accountable to practically everyone' and, in order that their students are not disadvantaged, routinely spend 'vast amounts of time' in additional preparation and marking (p. 24).

Not only do nurses and teachers care for their patients or students in terms of promoting their health and learning, but they (and other professions, such as psychology, religious ministry and social work) may also 'care for' in the sense of nurturing the identities of those for whom they care. Mujawamariya (2001) identifies the way in which teachers' responses to students from ethnic minority backgrounds may have a negative influence on the care for their identities that such students receive, and as a consequence a detrimental impact on their learning. Parsons (2001), in contrast, provides a case study of a teacher who found ways to value students from a variety of ethnic backgrounds and to challenge white male privilege in a non-confrontational way. The specific practices observed in this case study include positive confirmation in verbal exchanges, emphasis on the responsibilities of students in their behaviour towards each other and explicit appeals to values such as fairness, not being rude and so on, in feedback on unacceptable actions. The teacher in this example is not only caring for the students who otherwise experience marginalisation (the girls, the black students) but is also caring for those whose actions marginalise others (the white boys), in that she is modelling ways in which the students may learn to care for each other.

There is relatively little attention to the ethics of care in relation to the details of practice in other caring professions. Taylor's (1995) discussion of occupational therapy and MacLeod's (2001) discussion of palliative medicine are notable exceptions to this. MacLeod identifies the care of people who are dying as an important aspect of medical practice, in which a focus on care rather than cure leads to the possibility of a different ethical approach to that which often prevails in medicine. The way in which medical practitioners in palliative care encountered patients appears to be the major reason why an ethics of care makes most sense in this context (compared, say, to surgery). Medical practitioners, among all the caring professions, are most likely to be trained to regard distance from patients as the correct ethical response, so situations in which care can only be accomplished through intimacy can be surprising and confront expectations of how the practitioner is to act ethically (MacLeod, 2001, p. 1723). Of course, it may be precisely because the palliative care context is, by definition, an area of medicine in which there are no other responses available that the ethical challenge of caring appears in ways that it does not in other medical fields.

Gilligan cites an example of a 'woman physician who, seeing the loneliness of an old woman in the hospital, "would go out and buy her a root beer float and sit at her bedside just so there would be somebody there for her" ' (1982, p. 62). Kushner and Thomasma cite a similar observation of rural physicians caring for patients by emptying bed-pans (2001, p. 13). However, while demonstrating ways in which medical practitioners can 'care for' patients in that sense, these acts were being performed not *as* medicine but because there were insufficient nurses or others to do these tasks. Such acts, while ethical in themselves, therefore can be seen as exceptional rather than normative. (Indeed, it may be imagined that some medical practitioners might wish for time to 'care for' within the immense pressures on their time.) Nonetheless, MacLeod (2001, p. 1720) points to the way in which general medical practitioners also often demonstrate positive regard for caring in their routine practice. The actual practices that he observed, while drawing on medical knowledge, were primarily like those of other professions, with listening to patients being the most important. Ethically, these were situations that called for attentiveness, responsiveness and responsibility to people who were dying. Similarly, an illustration of how an ethic of care might appear more routinely in other types of medical practice would be in the instance of a surgeon who, having just performed an emergency operation on a child, before leaving the hospital stops to talk with the child's parents in order to provide them with an explanation and reassurance about what has happened.

The ethics of care is not necessarily seen uniformly in a positive way in every aspect of the caring professions. Acker (1995) refers to the way in which the 'feminine' role of caring can be a source of exploitation of teachers, who can feel responsibility towards their students that intrudes into their responsibilities for caring in other relationships. Similarly, in nursing there is a concern that just as the nature of the tasks that embody 'caring-for' are feminised, or seen as 'women's work', so the ethical demands placed on nurses will draw on ideas about the 'good woman' from domestic roles that emphasise subservience and subordination, whether explicitly or implicitly, to the cost of nurses (for example, see Johnstone, 1994, pp. 106–7). However, Sevenhuijsen argues, it is important to see the ethics of care in its proper perspective and not allow notions of duties or rules to slip in by the perceptual back door (1998, pp. 56–7). In its positive mode, the ethics of care asks questions such as 'how might my attentiveness and responsiveness to another person best be expressed?' and 'in what ways is it justified for me to be held responsible in this situation?'. Ethical practice, seen as that which is attentive, responsive and responsible can only be worked out in the detail of concrete situations.

The caring focus of 'caring' professions

To discuss 'care' in the practices of the caring professions may appear to be a tautology. The goals of the caring professions are *to care for* service users, in the sense of promoting their health, well-being, intellectual development, spirituality and so on. So for that reason it is plausible to approach the idea of care as commitment to the good of the service user in terms of the provision of care as a concrete set of tasks. Yet, as Jecker and Self (1991) point out, the connection between these two cannot be assumed. They question an assumption that they see in the relationship between 'caring-about' and 'caring-for'. Jecker and Self (1991, pp. 296 ff., 301) provide a four-fold model of the permutations in the link of 'caring about' and 'caring for':

- caring for and caring about, in which the professional undertakes the tasks of providing assistance and has a commitment to the well-being of the person who is cared for that is expressed in the way care is provided;
- caring for but not caring about, in which the tasks of providing assistance are accomplished competently, but without any commitment

to the well-being of the person who is receiving the service (perhaps disliking or morally judging the person);

- caring about but not caring for, in which the professional has a commitment to the well-being of the person but does not undertake the tasks of caring (the person in need declines assistance, or there is another professional who is more appropriate to address the specific needs, for example);
- caring neither for nor about, in which the professional avoids responsibility for the tasks of providing care because of a lack of commitment to the well-being of the person in need.

Jecker and Self argue that each of these potential responses is empirically verifiable, but that the distribution between them is not determined either by gender or profession. Specifically they challenge the tendency that they see in the application of these ideas to medicine (cares about but not for) and nursing (cares both about and for). In this model, the position that most clearly meets the ideal of care ethics is the first, in which 'caring about' and 'caring for' are brought together, which, they argue, applies to actions not to specific occupations. Thus Jecker and Self are sceptical about the implicit conclusion in the attention to writing about the ethics of care that nursing (and, by extension, allied health professions, social work and teaching) are *more* ethical than those professions which rely to a greater extent on technical skill and the direction of other professionals' actions to accomplish their objectives.

A different challenge to assumptions about the ethical relationship between caring about and caring for is made by Graham (2001), who states that it is necessary to avoid implicitly privileging the idea that in order to be ethical care must be provided directly, to an individual and over a period of time. There are, says Graham, other ways in which a professional may care. These include ensuring that one's skills are up to date, being attentive and responsive in a brief contact, ensuring that a good alternative is available if one is not able to undertake direct tasks, and so on. This conception, Graham argues, can be applied to allied health professions, medicine, nursing, religious ministry, social work and teaching (2001, pp. 50, 53). In other words, Graham is claiming that either 'caring about' or 'caring for', not only the combination of the two, may suffice for care to be seen as 'good'. However, although this view does permit brief responses and 'indirect' forms of practice to be understood as 'good practice', it also seems to stretch the meaning of care much further than can be sustained by the ethics of care. If professional ethics is to be founded on attentiveness, responsiveness and responsibility, this has to mean more than 'being careful' or 'maintaining competence' in the everyday sense of these phrases.

Allmark (1995) is also critical of the ethics of care on the grounds that it fails to provide a specific enough concept of how practices relate to the goals of caring professions. The approach, he states, 'lacks both normative and descriptive content', it conflates 'care-for' with 'good' and it uses the presence or absence of specific acts to infer feelings and judgements (rather than focusing on the acts themselves). In summary, Allmark's critique amounts to a charge of inconsistency, arbitrariness and a failure to recognise that a practical ethics must include a way of judging actions in relation to goals. In other words, caring involves a commitment to the 'right' objectives as well as acting in the 'right' way, 'with sensitivity and skill' (Allmark, 1995, p. 23). Bradshaw (1996) responds to Allmark by arguing that the ethics of care is relevant for nursing, but in doing so she effectively upholds the point that it requires normative content (also see Allmark, 1996). Bradshaw argues that the most pertinent issue for the professions in considering the ethics of care is that it is modelled on personal relationships, whereas professional work is almost always about 'the care of the stranger' (Bradshaw, 1996, p. 10). Moreover, the inconsistency of the ethics of care is not that it lacks normative assumptions, but that these assumptions are avoided. For Bradshaw, the plausibility of the ethics of care for the caring professions is that its normative base can be found in the objectives of the professions themselves, in their commitment to serve others in the promotion of health, well-being, intellectual development, spirituality and so on. As has already been noted above, concepts such as justice cannot be separated from caring in such objectives.

The need to find a normative ethical basis for care as the focus of the caring professions can be seen in the illustrative example of Sara and Michelle that was given above. Noddings' (1984) own discussion of education refers repeatedly to the ethics of a teacher responding to a student who is cheating. Here, as with the social worker, the professional objective from the perspective of the ethics of care is not the enforcement of rules, but rather it is to face the student with the consequence of their actions in their own care of themselves and of others, such as fellow students and, indeed, the teacher. Physicians and nurses might face a comparable situation in the patient who is dependent on controlled drugs and who seeks illegal access, such as by means of an illicit prescription. Again, from a perspective of caring, the ethical importance of refusing such a request lies not in whether it breaks with abstract duties (in this case to the law), but in that such an act would not be consistent with the relationship of healing.

Values, such as honesty that is contained in these illustrations, can thus be seen to provide a normative content to the ethics of care. Yet seen in this way they appear to have their origin outside such ethics. This would suggest that ethics of care is a means by which we might act rightly rather than a framework for considering what is right. The arguments of Tronto (1993), Held (1993, 1995) and Sevenhuijsen (1998) that a more discursive way of thinking about how values such as justice, honesty and so on can be balanced with that of care provides one way out of this circularity. It suggests that each should be judged against the others, so that, for example, the meaning of care may be found in the promotion of justice, while the meaning of justice may be found in the promotion of care. This would not challenge the primary values of the caring professions (Bradshaw, 1996) but it would raise new questions about how they are interpreted and put into practice.

The social relations of professional caring

That 'caring' is women's work has been widely and regularly observed, whether in relation to care by family members (Finch, 1989) or to care by professionals (Witz, 1992). The connection between the two domains can be seen in the nature of the work that is performed in 'caring for', including the personal and intimate tasks of daily living, both physical and emotional. Therefore the boundaries of this type of professional work can easily become blurred if professionals or service users allow themselves to look for intimacy in such caring relationships. As Bradshaw (1996, p. 11) observes, the meeting between a caring professional and a service user is not that of friends or lovers, no matter how deeply commitment is felt (compare with van Hooft, 1995) nor how intimate is the contact between the two. Both Tronto (1993) and Sevenhuijsen (1998) point to the parallel but opposite dynamic that is operating, in that caring for family members follows from the relationship (compare with Finch, 1989), while in caring for clients it is the relationship that follows from the caring practice. In other words, unlike the mother caring for the child, or the daughter caring for her infirm parent, the professional meets the service user as a stranger and the social distance between them remains, at least to a degree. For the relationship to have integrity its bounded nature must be explicitly acknowledged and respected. Caring may not be bounded for the mother (or the father) but it is for the caring professional (Taylor, 1995). Perhaps only for the minister of religion do such boundaries not appear to be quite the same, but even in this profession there are ethical limits arising from the need to balance the demands of many parishioners and to maintain trust with each (Goldner *et al.*, 1973; Koehn, 1994).

The point is that the relationships of professional caring combine intimacy with a degree of social distance (Davies, 1995). This not only permits the work of caring to be accomplished, as Sevenhuijsen notes (1998, p. 83), without the necessity of affection between the one who is caring and the person who is cared for, but it also enables the professional carer to respond to others who are cared for, to the network of other professionals with whom the one who is caring may have to relate (both immediate colleagues and a professional association) and in many instances to an employing agency. This can be seen in the limits to confidentiality that apply in all these professions. While all professionals expect to maintain confidentiality in the sense that they do not share information about service users with those for whom the person concerned has not given explicit permission, confidentiality is not absolute (Sim, 1996). Although it may be surprising to many service users, even medical practitioners and ministers of religion may be required by a court of law to reveal information (Bersoff, 1995). From the perspective of the ethics of care, the professional who is caring would not deceive the service user, but would find ways of enabling that person to make informed choices about what to reveal about her or him self. Of course, the professional may choose to defy a court, but in doing so must accept the likely consequences of punishment by the court. The service user has no right of expectation, in such circumstances, that a professional should choose such an option, as the ethics of care suggest that the one who is cared for exercises reciprocal attentiveness, responsiveness and responsibility. Confidentiality is better understood as careful attention to privacy than as an absolute maintenance of secrecy (Collingridge *et al.*, 2001).

It is in relation to the implications in the ethical 'ideal' of caring that Noddings has been most strongly criticised from feminist perspectives (Tronto, 1993; Held, 1993, 1995; Sevenhuijsen, 1998). Because this ideal is based on the ethics of mothering, extrapolated to teaching, it is grounded in the notion of the 'self-giving' of caring, in which the person who cares is primarily other-directed. As we have already noted, this is practically unrealistic in a professional context, as many other people, both service users and others, have a reasonable call on the attentiveness, responsiveness and responsibility of any one caring professional (Kuhse, 1997). Whereas it could be argued that many mothers also may have to find ways of balancing the demands of several children, the total number is unlikely to be the size of a normal school class or clinical workload; nor, indeed, will the children in a family be considered as a 'workload'. As Carr points out (2000, p. 164), the question for any profession in which a degree of personal involvement is necessary (which particularly includes the caring professions) is that of whether differentiation between individual service users follows from an appropriate recognition of their differences or is due to favouritism.

More than this, an ethic that is grounded in this way in the domestic relationships that pertain mostly to women appears to bring with it the risk of a sense of 'self-sacrifice'. Indeed, this potential is criticised from within the professions (see, for example: Barnitt & Partridge, 1997; Coulehan & Williams, 2001; Fry & Johnstone, 2002). The underlying pattern to this concern is the proportion of women in the different professions, and the degree to which the formation of their formal ethics, their practices and their organisation reflect the institutionalisation of 'women's work'. Just as 'women's work is never done' in the family, the same may be observed in many areas of professional life (Acker, 1995). To raise this culturally embedded notion to the level of an ethical expectation would be to the detriment of both professionals and service users, resulting in the 'burnout' (or 'compassion fatigue') that was discussed in the previous chapter (see Cherniss, 1995). The ethics of care, if understood in this way, could well become a trap for the caring professions, both in terms of the demands on the time of individual practitioners (and hence their responsibilities elsewhere) as well as in taking on responsibilities that cold be said to lie with the wider society.

What, then, of the idea that in caring for others one must also care for oneself? This is of particular importance for professions that not only serve direct clients but also provide services to and on behalf of other professions. Here again the issue of gender is important, as it is the professions in which women historically are in the majority that are most concerned with the balance of care for service users with the care of their own professional selves (for example: Corbett, 1993; Tadd, 1998). Such concern with self-care is understood as important both in order to ensure that care continues to be provided to service users and because there is a reciprocity to caring: quite simply, those who are caring for others themselves have needs that may be considered as quite legitimate. Even so, the more that the relationships between the caring professional and those who are cared for is extensive and lasts over time, particularly as in school teaching, but also in many other areas, there is a tendency for practitioners to find it necessary to justify an attention to the care of the self (Acker, 1995; Tadd, 1998). A comparison with physicians in palliative care who engaged with holistic caring (MacLeod, 2001) suggests that this is not as much of an issue for medical practitioners because they feel more in control of their context than do other professions. Indeed, the power of medicine over other professions in the health field is often discussed as a factor in the ethical tensions of caring, as prescriptions or instructions may be experienced as requiring action that is contrary to the other profession's ethics, or more dominant professionals may simply disregard the opinion of colleagues whom they perceive to be 'junior' (Taylor, 1995; Barnitt & Partridge, 1997; Fry & Johnstone, 2002).

Care and the idea of a 'social mandate'

At a surface level it might appear that the social mandate of the caring profession is to do just that: to care. However, as with compassion, the question of how recent shifts in public policy that emphasise economic issues in relation to wider notions of fairness have affected the possibility of an ethics of care. Moreover, what implications does a feminist approach to ethics as embodied in the debates about the ethics of care have for the policies that affect the particular practices of caring professions? In order to answer these questions, three aspects of contemporary practice will be discussed: the social authority exercised by the caring professions; the increasing value that is placed on esoteric knowledge and skills in the neo-liberal political economy; and the connections between the ethics of care and a feminist critique of patriarchal social relations.

First, there are aspects of the caring professions that are concerned with some form of social authority, rather than with relationships of direct accountability to the immediate service user. How does the objective of 'caring for' provide an ethical basis for practice in such circumstances? Many caring professions exercise socially sanctioned power to act 'for the good' of the individual, where this is defined by powerful social institutions. Courts of law, delegated authority derived from statute and government policy may all place responsibilities on the caring professions to act in ways that require the exercise of power and authority over individual service users.

Examples of this include measures to compel someone to be placed in a psychiatric hospital or similar facility. Many countries have such laws, which tend to be based on the notion of protection of the person from the risk that they might harm themselves or of other people from the risk of harm by the person with the mental health problem. Such laws tend to emphasise the use of the least restrictive options and are subject to legal review. While formal codes of professional ethics support such uses of authority, based on principles such as beneficence, there are some critics who argue that such actions breach ethics of respect for autonomy and integrity (Szasz, 1991). However, the ethics of care appears to support the idea of questioning whether someone is 'fit to plead' in a court of law, for example, which is relevant to the many situations in which people might be compulsorily admitted to a hospital as a consequence of having committed a criminal act because of a mental health problem.

Applying the ethics of care to situations of power and authority draws on two particular models, that of the adult–child relationships in the family or the school (Noddings, 1984) or the provision of care for adults (such as in aged care, disability services or mental health services) (Sevenhuijsen, 1998). While the former places quite clear expectations on professionals, in that an adult who is caring for a child will listen carefully to the child, the latter is more complex. Practice based on the ethics of care in such circumstances, especially when the immediate service user may have their consent over-ridden, would still be attentive and responsive and in taking responsibility would still seek to maximise accountability to the individual person, for example by explaining their actions clearly and carefully and ensuring that they used as little compulsion as was possible. However, there is a risk of 'parentalism' (that is, treating an adult as if they were a child) that is clearly counter-productive to an ethical relationship of care.

Second, the increasing value that is placed on esoteric knowledge and skills in the neo-liberal political economy is not conducive to the ethics of care. This approach to ethics assumes a high level of individuality and attention to the particular aspects of the feelings, thoughts and social circumstances of the person who is cared for. However, in the neo-liberal political economy there may be pressure on the caring professions to ration services according to whether the service user can pay or there are other (non-government) sources of funds. Under these conditions an ethics of care, embodying values of attentiveness, responsiveness and responsibility, although possible, may be more difficult to achieve (Kuhse, 1997). The neo-liberal environment also places importance on other forms of accountability, seen in the privileged status given to certain sorts of professional knowledge, especially those that can be demonstrated through numerically measurable outcomes (Held, 1993; Taylor, 1995). While the value of competence is embodied in the ethics of care, this is not understood in terms of instrumental practices. Rather, it assumes broader ways of knowing about human need and practices that are based on a more holistic view of people in their social contexts (Yerxa, 1991; Wise, 1995). To be capable of being attentive, responsive and responsible, caring professionals require the development of knowledge and skills that are grounded in listening to service users and their views of the world.

Third, this point about forms of knowledge leads towards a consideration of the connections between the ethics of care and a feminist critique of patriarchal social relations. Both the insistence on privileging numerically based knowledge and ways of organising health, education, social welfare and religious institutions have been critiqued as patriarchal by feminist scholars (Held, 1993; Stanley & Wise, 1993). Not only does this apply to the relationships between the professions (as discussed above) but also to the way in which bureaucratic and managerial systems are inimical to caring as the ethics of practice. As Bradshaw puts it, the ethics of these systems is 'detached and dutiful, correct and philanthropic, meeting needs of patients but without "heart" ' (1996, p. 11). Although as Tadd (1998, p. 31) is correct to point out, not every patient wants an intense closeness with a nurse (or, we could add, with any other professional), and that all service users do expect technical competence in the care they receive, she does conclude that this must be provided 'with care'. Her counter-suggestion, that of respecting privacy and safeguarding dignity, is congruent with the ethics of care. Indeed, getting the right balance between individuals requires precisely the attentiveness and responsiveness that lies at the core of this approach.

As has been noted above, caution is expressed in several profession specific discussions of the ethics of care about its potential to appear to reinforce the status of many areas of the caring professions as 'women's work' (Acker, 1995; Taylor, 1995; Banks, 2001; Fry & Johnstone, 2002). Taylor's observations (1995, p. 170) that this is reflected in the disproportionately high number of men in management positions, in generally low salaries, in the relationships of power between professions and in expectations of 'non-assertive "feminine" behaviour in general' apply to teaching, nursing and to social work as well as to allied health therapies. This is not caused by a commitment to the ethics of care, or simply to 'caring for', but is a consequence of patriarchal social structures that distribute power and prestige differently relative to gender. At the same time the ethics of care stands as a critique of approaches that see ethics in terms only of rational calculation and abstract duties and principles. Such a position is challenged by a feminist view of the ethics of care, that is one which explicitly seeks to assert women's voices, not as a chorus or commentary to 'dominant' ethical approaches, but in its own terms. As Taylor (1995) notes, the difficulties of asserting a feminist position in professional life can be considerable (also see Wise, 1988), but it is congruent both with the commitments of these occupations to promote change and in caring for one's self through valuing one's own profession including its values and its moral perspective.

Conclusion

One of the major opportunities offered by the ethics of care for the caring professions, is that the approach is grounded in the professions themselves. It is drawn from the very issues that face members of these professions and so contains the possibility of ethics that relates directly to experience. It takes a critical stance on the implications of liberal ethics for the caring professions, seeing the different liberal approaches as depersonalising, cold, distant, and mechanical. In contrast, the ethics of care seeks to create an approach that responds to other aspects of the human condition, including interpersonal relationships, affection and so on. There are many similarities between the ethics of care and the ethics of compassion (discussed in Chapter 4). However, the former is grounded in social relationships as a primary value, while the latter emphasises the emotional responses of the individual.

The ethics of care assumes that 'care' is its own normative base (that is, the primary value from which all others are derived). Although some advocates of the ethics of care assert that a concept of justice can, even must, be integrated with the value of care, the complex relationship between the two prioritises care as basic. In the context of the neo-liberal political economy this may not be sufficient to construct a strong ethics, in a context not only of accountability to measurable outcomes but also where impartiality is codified in organisational procedures and 'public standards' (Banks, 2001, p. 50). Some proponents of the ethics of care may find the debate about its connection with the ethic of justice to be tiresome (Deveaux, 1995) but this is vital for those who seek both to care and to be accountable in professional life. It is also important that appeals to care as a primary value do not reinforce gender oppression (although this is a feature of prevailing patriarchal social relations and is not inherent in the ethics of care). Kuhse (1997) argues that care is necessary but not in itself sufficient for an adequate professional ethics. If it is to be a more central element in thinking about professional ethics, the debate about the relationship between care and justice (and, indeed, other values) must continue.

CHAPTER 6

Ecology and the Ethics of Life

Ecology and sustainability as ethics

In this chapter, I want to examine the influence of ecological thinking and the perspective that may be defined as 'ecologism' (Smith, 1998, p. 1). Although it has made a mark in political and social life, and may have been embraced by individual professionals, ecologism has not been widely considered from the perspective of professional ethics. In some ways, this could be seen as surprising, as the concepts on which ecological debates are based are also found in professional ethics, such as 'care', 'justice', 'need' and 'responsibility' (Park, 1996; Cairns, 1998). As we will see, ecology not only connects with issues of virtues and care, but also raises questions about the ways in which the dominant ethical approaches (deontology and utilitarianism) can be addressed in pluralistic principles.

Julius and Amanda are medical students on internship in geriatric medicine in a western country. They both think that the resources available are insufficient because each day they have to make decisions in which their clinical judgement is not about whether patients have a need but whose need is greater. They both think that care is denied to people who have clinical needs. Julius argues that this reflects the social devaluing of old age, and wants to see health budgets increase. Amanda disagrees with him and suggests that unless resources are rationed then other parts of the world and future generations will not have a chance of basic opportunities in life. For her this may even require considering the suggestion of non-voluntary euthanasia in cases of irreversible loss of capacity to function as in cases of advanced Alzheimer's Disease.

These different responses to the rationing of health care reflect social and political values; they also have practical implications for professionals and others in resource allocation. This chapter examines the way in which attention to ecology as the basis of ethics would assist Julius and Amanda in considering their ethical disagreement in more depth.

Through the second half of the twentieth century some ethicists have begun to take a view of humanity that does not (necessarily) place humans at the centre of the universe (for example: Singer, 1975, 1993a; Regan, 1984; Mies & Shiva, 1993; Cairns, 1998; Midgely, 2001). Singer's work represents a major strand in the development of an ethics of ecology; it is extensive and has been very influential (Smith, 1998; Preece, 2002). Singer bases his arguments on a preference utilitarian view of ethics, that what matters are the consequences of action and the preferences that choices express (Singer, 1993a, pp. 12–14). His position that humanity is not privileged is derived from the older utilitarian view that what matters in considering ethical responsibilities owed to living creatures is whether they can suffer (as opposed to whether they can reason, or talk) (Singer, 1975, pp. 8–9). Singer's unique contribution is to extend the original point to argue that sentient animals other than humans should be considered as having interests, or 'preferences', in the utilitarian calculus of 'good' and 'bad', solely on the ground that such creatures are sentient. Within this perspective, the use of sentient creatures in ways that would cause them to suffer is 'bad', because it increases pain to satisfy the preferences of others. From this argument, Singer coined the term 'animal liberation' as the practical expression of ethical ecology, and advocates strongly against the use of animals in experimentation, against factory farming and in favour of vegetarianism.

From a different ethical framework, namely deontology, Regan (1984) argues that utilitarianism does not go far enough, as it still permits a calculus in which the balance of well-being over pain could ultimately be achieved at the expense of non-human animals. For Regan, the only way for non-human animals to be accorded equality with humanity is for them to be recognised as ethical 'ends-in-themselves' and thus as having rights. This permits Regan to go further than Singer (for example, see Regan, 1984, pp. 206 ff.) and to suggest that, in addition to the benefits of better use of resources and the subsequent implications of global equity, an ethic in which respect for all animal life was central would be one that would have a positive influence on the human treatment of other humans (p. 179). But this is a by-product, not a justification, as for Regan there is not only a negative responsibility not to harm non-human animals, but a positive duty to promote the well-being of all sentient life simply because it is life. Ecological ethics thus demands, for example, attention to habitats so that species may be preserved as of value in themselves and not simply in terms of future human utility. The debates around the ethics of ecology have tended to follow these two main threads and so to address either the utilitarianism of Singer or the deontology of Regan and to examine the logical and practical strength of their arguments (Smith, 1998; Preece, 2002). Some practical implications of these approaches will be explored below, before which it is necessary to make some further brief remarks about the differences between the two positions.

First, Singer's utilitarianism allows for such possibilities as the relative value between sentient creatures (1986, pp. 216–17). However, Singer goes on to note that just as the idea of equality between human persons is not a description, but rather a value statement providing a moral prescription that can be built on utilitarian principles, the notion of relative value does not implicitly favour human life (p. 220). In contrast, Regan asserts that everything that has inherent value has it equally, which is the basis of all rights to respect (1984, pp. 240–1). His definition of living beings has similarities with that of Singer, as it includes characteristics of a displayed capacity for desire, a sense of memory and anticipation, intention, emotion, awareness and so on (Regan, 1984, pp. 73–8). This way of seeing the complexity of non-human animal life is supported from starting points in different ethical theories (Hare, 1991; Nussbaum, 2001; Gaita, 2002). For Regan there is no relativity of value; moreover, where particular creatures lack the capacities generally exhibited by their kind, they are to be accorded value as members of the overall category of animals to which they belong in kind (a pertinent example of which is that of a person with Alzheimer's Disease). In turn, Singer and other utilitarians (such as Hare, 1991) would claim that this is a type of consequential rather than duty-based argument. At the same time, Hare (1991, p. 13) concedes that the value base of the utilitarian position is identical to Kant's categorical imperative (or the 'Golden Rule') and that for both utilitarians and deontologists the universality of the intention behind an action should include its impact on all sentient animals, not just human animals. So, although there are differences between Singer and Regan in their philosophical paths, there are some commonalities in the destination they are seeking. (We will return to this point below.)

Second, the implications of the two approaches outlined here can be seen most clearly as diametrically opposed when consideration is given to humans who do not fit the criterion of 'sentience'. This not only applies to foetuses, but also to (all) infants and to older children and adults with mental disabilities. For Singer (1975, 1993a), human beings who lack the capacity to experience suffering, because they are without awareness, memory or anticipation, do not have the same ethical standing as do mature non-human animals who have such capacities. In contrast, Regan (1984) widens rather than narrowing the net, because his underlying principle is that of duty to inherent value rather than that of utility. Infants, or people with profound mental disabilities, are of a kind of animal that normally has the features of sentience and so they are included as of inherent value.

Singer is (in)famous for his logical conclusions that it might be 'right' to experiment on very young infants where there were no sentient others with preferences for the life of the child, or to actively kill very young infants with disabilities (or even, simply, where the utility of the life was 'negative' in the context of the preferences of sentient others) (Preece, 2002). It can be argued that qualifying statements of the kind 'if X then Y' in passages comparing research on non-human animals and research on infants suggest hyperbole to make the underlying point about ethical responsibilities to non-human animals (Singer, 1986, p. 24). However, a critical reading of Singer's logical conclusions, in his apparently more literal discussions of infanticide in the case of disabled infants and non-voluntary euthanasia of older people who have lost their mental capacities, shows that his arguments do in fact lead to principles that support experimentation on infants (for example, see Singer, 1993a, pp. 179–93). Regan, in contrast, argues that all individuals, whether 'moral agents' (having the capacity to understand and engage in ethical reflection) or 'moral patients' (not having such a capacity) have the same moral *rights*. It is moral *duties* that are held by 'moral agents' alone (1984, pp. 279–80). On this point the formal ethical statements of the caring professions tend to emphasise the importance of integrating abstract arguments with basic principles. The involvement of caring professionals in Nazi atrocities (see Johnstone, 1994, pp. 19 ff.) remains a powerful reminder of the logical conclusion of Singer's position, despite Singer's protests to the contrary (1993b).

As noted above, both Singer and Regan are concerned with sentient creatures. The arguments of ethical ecology can be taken further than this, to consider ecosystems and the whole of the planetary ecosystem (Kinnevy, 1999). Seen in this way, the issue goes further than defining duties or utilitarian obligations, but embraces 'human responsibilities towards other animals, other forms of life and the conditions which make life possible' (Smith, 1998, p. 44). Smith's argument draws on

Beck's (1992) 'risk theory', which states that ecosystems are complex, uncertain and interconnected. Extending the debate between utilitarian and deontological consideration of non-human animals, Smith argues that the 'moral boundary between present and future generations' is arbitrary (1998, p. 97). From the utilitarian approach he draws the notion that any claims of the interests of present generations must be balanced against the anticipated claims of future generations, using as a gauge the question of whether our actions would harm our own children. As Gower (1992, p. 11) puts it, we are not obliged to sacrifice everything for the sake of posterity, but we are required to accept limits on our own well-being. If our actions or preferences leave future generations worse off than they would otherwise have been, except where we can be sure this was the only possible course of action, then we will have acted in ways that do not promote the maximum of well-being over harm. Although this is a utilitarian argument, for Smith it also means that we should give moral value to the whole of the ecosystem, including that which is inanimate as well as animate. Only by doing so can we grasp the inherent importance of the whole system for the well-being of all its interconnected parts. Smith argues that such a position means that we should be inherently sceptical of technological developments, placing a prospective burden of proof on new ideas, rather than the retrospective burden of proof that currently rests on those who have been harmed (Smith, 1998, p. 96).

Of interest, also, must be the arguments of ecofeminism, that the treatment of the natural world, including non-human animals, simply to meet the needs of humans is an expression of patriarchy. In a manner similar to the feminist 'ethics of care' (Sevenhuijsen, 1998), ecofeminism suggests that the environment is not something to be managed but to be cared for in a relationship (Mies & Siva, 1993). The subject of care is valued for its place in the relationship and for itself, not only in terms of what it can contribute to human flourishing (Plumwood, 1993, 2002). Mies and Shiva (1993, pp. 16 ff.) point to the actions of women in various parts of the world in defence of the environment as parallels to the ways in which women have had to resist being used as means to an end by health and welfare businesses (such as women in third world countries being the unwitting subjects in pharmaceutical experiments) (pp. 190–1). Ecofeminism thus suggests that the oppression of women and the exploitation of the environment have a common origin in patriarchy and so all three must be challenged (Plumwood, 2002). As sympathetic critics of ecofeminism have noted, this must necessarily seek to embrace men as well as women, although in different ways and from different starting points (Smith, 1998, p. 86).

The implications of the different approaches to the ethics of ecology go beyond the realm of technology. While it is easiest to see the relationship between these ideas and mining or agriculture, for example, the whole of advanced society is based on the relationship between humanity and the natural world that is critiqued by ecologism (Kinnevy, 1999). Not only the economy and technology, but all other aspects of advanced societies are bound up in the uses made of non-human animals and the inanimate world. Health and social welfare systems are no less a part of this than any other part of the complex set of institutions that comprise such societies. If this point is accepted, then the ethics of ecology has implications for the form and extent of health and social welfare services, as well as for the professional practices engaged in within these institutions. Such an ethics raises questions about the sustainability of both systems and practices.

Ecological practice in caring professions?

As we have seen in previous chapters, the practice content of caring professions has been based on the prevailing scientific world-view of the modern era. This is evident in the skills and the knowledge of the caring professions, as well as their values and ethics. The problems and issues to which caring professions attend, as well as the practices used to respond to these problems and issues, have been developed in an intellectual tradition that separates human consciousness from the surrounding world. From the perspective of ecologism, therefore, the caring professions no less than any other human activity approach the non-human world as an external 'other', different and separate from humanity. The ecological critique of modernism, that it fails to understand the interdependence of human and non-human life in the ecosystem, thus applies to the caring professions as much as to manufacturing industry, financial services, the military or any other major social institution. In so far as the forms of knowledge, and hence the skills, of the caring professions are grounded in the modernist world-view they are 'reductionist' – that is, they break problems down and address them through dealing with their separate constituent parts. This is the opposite of the 'holism' that is inherent in the systems perspective of ecology.

Park (1996) offers four examples of ecological social work practice, which include concerns with air and water quality, a campaign against toxic sites used for public housing, youth work based on gardening, and therapies that use experience of wilderness to encourage personal growth. These are quite standard types of practice, but are oriented to the environment both as means and end. Ethically, an ecologically informed critique approaches the knowledge and skills of the caring professions from the same range of positions as do other perspectives. Questions of respect, beneficence, non-maleficence and justice are as relevant in this context as in others. However, from the viewpoint of ecologism the meaning and significance of these principles is different from that which is normally understood. To illustrate this point, I want to consider an aspect of the development of knowledge and skills in caring professions in the use of the non-human world to produce knowledge and test its application.

A considerable amount of knowledge in the health and human sciences has been gained from the use of non-human life, especially in the form of experimentation. Especially in biomedical and psychological fields a great deal of knowledge has been gained from the use of non-human animals, which are routinely used in experiments that are designed principally to benefit humans. Discussions of the ethics of this use of non-human animals tend to concentrate on the minimisation of suffering (Beauchamp & Childress, 2001; Campbell *et al.*, 2001). However, there is always some suffering involved if an animal is to be used in experiments that are physically invasive or induce stress. From an 'orthodox' position, this matter is usually resolved by reference to the question of whether the probable outcome in the further development of knowledge makes such suffering justifiable. Not only should the knowledge that may be gained from such experiments benefit people, but the research process should be rigorous enough to produce usable findings. (The same standards, of course, are applied to the use of human subjects in research.) This is a straightforward utilitarian argument, clearly anticipating that the balance of well-being (human) over pain (non-human) is positive. It is in questioning this point of view that the ethics of ecology is united, whether from a utilitarian basis (Singer, 1975, 1993a), deontology (Regan, 1984) or feminism (Mies & Shiva, 1993; Plumwood, 1993, 2002).

Although caring professionals do not seem to take Singer's (1984, 1993a) suggestions about experimentation on human infants seriously, as noted in previous chapters however, some medical researchers have made use of foetal tissue for research purposes (Redfern, 2001) and there are wide ranging debates continuing about the use of stem-cells taken from foetal tissue (Morgan, 2002). While many of the ethical problems with the former example arise from the lack of openness and the failure to obtain consent from the parents, the debates about stem-cell research focus on ethical disagreements about the status of a foetus as 'having life', or 'being human'. Such debates go outside the professions themselves and involve political and wider social deliberations about these ethical issues. Disagreements exist not only between different ethical approaches (utilitarian versus deontological versus pluralist) but also within each of these positions. It appears that on this issue the premises from which any consideration begins are as important as the logical path taken in an argument. So the question of whether a virus or bacterium should be regarded as living in these terms is not frivolous, but has serious ethical implications if the capacity to kill viruses and bacteria is a major aspect of health care for humans and many other sentient non-human animals. However, the practical response of ecological ethics is to draw this line between such forms of life and *sentient* life.

The primary issue in the ethics of ecology can be seen as the underlying problems with experimentation on living entities as the basis for assisting *other* entities. However, there is also the larger question raised by ecologists who point to the systemic nature of life. Systems theory suggests that if an action takes place in one part of the system it may have consequences several stages away in the chain of systemic relationships. Such consequences are very hard to predict, leading to the identification of 'chaos theory' to describe the unpredictability of the resulting patterns of effect. Beck's (1992) concept of 'risk' describes the social implications of this theory. He argues that advanced society is now based on technological capacities that produce many benefits but of which there may be many unintended and harmful consequences, 'risks' with which the world then has to cope. Ethically, therefore, anyone who seeks to develop such capacities (knowledge and skill) has a responsibility to think as carefully and plan as much as possible. However, as risk is ultimately not open to such a fine degree of calculation, there is a corollary in the obligation to exercise caution and not to be guided by too simple a view that benefits outweigh risks, or to be driven by potential 'vices' (such as fame or fortune as ends in themselves).

Applications of the concept of risk to the work of the caring professions are not confined to the more obvious areas of health sciences, but are spread across all types of practice. The use of theories such as 'recovered memory' in cases of alleged child abuse have had serious consequences for those involved in disputed situations (Cossins, 1999). Forcible removal of Aboriginal children from their mothers in Australia in the twentieth century was based on 'scientific' ideas (as they were seen at the time) (Kidd, 2000), as was the export of children from poorer families in England to Australia, Canada and New Zealand (Humphrey, 1996). Educational practices have shifted according to developments in learning theories, with implications for each new generation. And so on. These few examples embrace almost all of the caring professions at some time and in some way. Not only do they demonstrate the 'risk' inherent in all such theories, but they point to the issue of *social* ecology that follows from the recognition of ecological ethics. In a social as well as in a material sense the knowledge and skills of the caring professions are indeterminate, in the sense of requiring situational judgement, and the ethics of ecology faces professional ethics with a challenge to take responsibility for consequences that cannot be fully anticipated.

'Social' ecology, in this sense, refers to the inter-relationship between individuals and groups. It is not just a euphemism for 'society', but encourages a view of social relations and structures as systematically inter-connected and also as dynamic over time. Just as chaos theory applied to the natural world may describe the link between industrial pollution in Europe and weather patterns in Asia (Beck, 1992), the idea of social ecology raises question about the use of knowledge and skills by caring professions in terms of their unintended as well as intended impacts, not only in the present but also in the future. The ethical consequences of the actions of caring professions are, thus, both considerable and enduring.

An ecological focus in caring professions?

Professional goals and objectives are also challenged by the ethics of ecology. Otherwise diverse ecological perspectives all voice a criticism of other ethical positions as being 'anthropocentric'. Yet there are two challenges to the application of ecological ethics in the caring professions. Not only must judgements about the interests or preferences of non-human animals or future generations of all life be made from the perspective of present human preferences and choices, but the subjects that concern the caring professions are humans. To respond to the challenge of the ethics of ecology, therefore, a consideration of the goals and purposes of the caring professions would not only be in terms of what immediate impact they would have (for example in terms of resource use, the exploitation of non-human animals and so on) but also on their future impact on non-human as well as human life and on the ecosystem, as far as these can be presently known and understood. So, for example, if our increasingly high expectations of health and well-being can only be sustained through ever more rapid depletion of material resources to the possible detriment of future generations of all life then the policies and practices that delivered them would not be 'good' or 'right' unless necessary to defend present interests, notably survival (Smith, 1998, p. 31).

To examine how this might appear in concrete terms, let us return to the two medical students with whom this chapter began, Julius and Amanda, and look at issues raised by ageing populations. The rapid ageing of the demographics of most national societies can be considered as one of the success stories, in human terms, of health and social welfare technologies (McCallum & Geiselhart, 1996). There are many factors that have produced this phenomenon, among which cleanliness in childbirth, clean water and closed sewerage, improvements in nutrition, and the development of antibiotics, vaccines and anaesthetics, have all been major contributors (Hugman, 1994). Relatively recent high-technology medical procedures, in this sense, represent the culmination of such changes rather than being a major cause. The consequence is that in the more developed countries most infants can now look forward to growing old as mean average life expectancy continues to approach figures that throughout human history have been achieved by relatively few (McCallum & Geiselhart, 1996).

An unanticipated consequence of this success, however, has been in the demands placed on health and social welfare systems. Although debates continue to run concerning the exact economics (for example, whether the costs associated with end of life health needs are simply put back further in the life-span or are spread out over a longer period of people's lives) there is agreement that costs must be considered (McCallum & Geiselhart, 1996). The underlying question is whether such costs are 'sustainable', not only in the economic sense, but also in the sense of the demands placed on the ecosystem both now and in the future by the economic growth that would be necessary to support ageing populations around the world at the level of the material expectations currently enjoyed by older people in the most developed countries. These issues concern justice and equity both between nations and cultures and between generations (Daniels, 1988; Callahan, 1990). In short, does the provision for older people made today conflict with the interests of a future generation in that it uses resources in ways that are not sustainable? In terms of professional practices this question suggests a corollary, which is whether an assessment might be influenced by how much of a given resource an older person would use in receipt of care.

The answer must be that, to some extent, this already happens: part of Amanda's utilitarian argument tends to prevail over Julius' deontological position. Some older people are offered forms of care based not solely on an objective assessment of their needs, but also taking into account measures of 'quality of life', cost-value calculations or public preferences (Beauchamp & Childress, 2001, pp. 256 ff.). Age is used in many developed countries for rationing health care, using arguments about 'prudence' (maximising each person's chances of achieving a normal life span) and 'equity' (older people have already had their go at life). Callahan (1990) qualifies this perspective with the view that moderation of suffering should replace life-extension as the goal once a person has reached mean average life expectancy. This accords with Singer's (1993a) basic position, in which he argues that active euthanasia may be as ethical as the passive euthanasia that is currently practised through withholding of treatment (for example, 'not for resuscitation') or the use of very large doses of pain-relieving drugs (also see Rachels, 1986). Singer's advocacy of 'non-voluntary' euthanasia as an option for older people who have lost their capacity to reason (and hence to have preferences) is a practical extension of this argument (Singer, 1993a, pp. 191–2). In this concept, he advocates that when a person had lost the capacity to be said to have preferences then others could be empowered to make a decision to end the person's life. Quality of life and costs may play a legitimate role in the factors weighed in reaching a decision.

Such an example is relevant to caring professions involved in aged care. But would most of the caring professions involved in this type of activity accept the move from a limited 'passive' sense of allowing life to end and the 'active' steps of deliberately ending a life that in other circumstances would not end? This is a different argument to that which supports 'assisted suicide' in the face of irremediable pain (Tschudin, 1998). On this point rule utilitarianism, deontology and the ethics of care would not support non-voluntary euthanasia. The moral rights of the infirm older person not to be killed remain, for these approaches. Moreover, as I have summarised elsewhere

(Hugman, 1994, p. 156) the use of age as a factor in utilitarian calculations has been extensively criticised as oppressive discrimination ('ageism'). From a rights perspective the choice to apply particular values to some but not all members of a species is unjust (Regan, 1984). On those grounds it is contrary to many codes of ethics of the various caring professions to discriminate on grounds of age.

It can be observed that the notion of the sanctity of life that is inherent in a reluctance to contemplate active non-voluntary euthanasia is historical and cultural (Silverman & Maxwell, 1982, pp. 66–7). Thus, the objection to euthanasia could be seen as a particular rather than a universal value. However, the evidence suggests that such customs tend(ed) to exist in nomadic or semi-nomadic hunter societies rather than those that are settled and based on agriculture or industry (Hugman, 1994, pp. 75–6). In the few recorded cases of systematic non-voluntary euthanasia of older people, widespread poverty was a significant factor. In other words, the values that they express are those of necessity, and in all cases non-voluntary euthanasia was (or is) embedded in the cultural honouring of very old people. None of these factors apply in advanced industrial societies. So while globalised professional ethics may reflect the particularities of Judaeo-Christian culture, these values can also be seen as grounded in the necessities faced in advanced industrial societies, which are matters of degree rather than those of absolute survival. To this extent, neither of the views of our medical interns can apply intact. Amanda's argument for limiting the care of older people in favour of future generations is moderated by Julius' claims for the valuing of older people in and of themselves, as human lives.

The utilitarian calculation about the use of resources is not a new issue for any caring profession (Fry & Johnstone, 2002). The practice of 'triage' in nursing, that is of allocating priority to patients based on assessment of need and risk, is well established. All caring professionals will routinely make decisions about prioritising between service users (whether they are individuals or groups), whether this is in making appointments for direct interventions such as interviews or meetings, whom to respond to in a group situation, or allocating time for indirect interventions such as advocacy with third parties. All of these practices tend to be pragmatic, in that they are based on a calculation of the 'most effective' use of scarce resources to respond to problems faced by service users. Some decisions in specific cases may be based on principles such as 'social justice' or 'equity' and thus draw on utilitarian arguments in weighing fairness in the distribution of social 'goods' that include time and skills as well as material resources (Barnitt *et al.*, 1998, p. 53; Clark, 2000, pp. 74–7). More often, principles are applied at the level of policies within which practitioners make decisions on a case-by-case basis.

However, the point remains that such practices as triage apply to that over which the caring professional has tangible control (their time and other specific resources). To make such calculations based on wider costs, especially if these are imprecise future ecological costs, would lie outside the scope of professional codes of ethics or standards of conduct. While rationing, in this sense, takes place at the level of individuals, the basis on which individual decisions are made does not originate in the individual situation. Caring professionals apply rationing as a utilitarian framework that is provided by the context of their practice, including policies, organisational procedures and wider social values. In this sense resource limitations constitute a 'condition of necessity' which is implied by utilitarianism (Mill, [1861] 1910). Yet, in making such calculations they will also be guided by more absolute values, such that at the point of making specific decisions all people under consideration will be viewed in terms of the same principles. As Pellegrino and Thomasma note (1993, p. 103), in facing escalating health costs it is the responsibility of everyone in a society to consider who should have a right to 'medical technology' or 'health care' and who might be excluded from such rights. In arguing that age should be a factor in rationing health and social care, Daniels (1988, p. 141) acknowledges this and argues that such judgements should be made at the social level. To leave it to individual professional practitioners would be untenable, as they could not have a sufficiently broad view at the point at which they would have to make decisions.

At such points utilitarianism and deontology effectively have the same practical impact as both are universal in their implications (Hare, 1991, p. 13). It is, therefore, significant to note that when faced with his own mother's impairment by Alzheimer's Disease Singer felt unable to act on his own philosophy and made the decision to purchase expensive care for her, contrary to the preference-utilitarian or ecological aspects of his formal ethics (Preece, 2002, pp. 29–30). It may be a reasonable hypothesis, therefore, that at the level of individual practice, as opposed to that of policy, caring professionals also would give some priority to the person they were actually facing, in a manner suggested by the ethics of care, as against a more abstract sense of 'countless others' for whom the resources could theoretically be redistributed. In wider discussion about goals and purposes, however, a utilitarian approach to the ethics of ecology might serve to assist the caring professions to examine matters of principle about 'equity' and 'justice'.

Ecology and the social relations of caring professions

The human service systems within which caring professionals act (education, health, social welfare and so on) operate at several levels. These can be seen as local, national and global, and of these increasingly the most powerful is the global (Bauman, 1998; Singer, 2002). Globalisation as a process implies not only the integration of national economies into a less differentiated global economy (although it does mean this) but also the homogenisation (at least to a degree) of various aspects of culture and of civil society. So, as part of this process, the professional service systems of the advanced industrial countries have become a model for developing nations, while at the same time, where necessary, they have been subject to massive reconstruction to fit with the demands of the global economy (Leonard, 1997). Issues of child-welfare, education, health, and aged care, for example, are ever more clearly defined as a personal responsibility, even in countries where these had come to be seen as social issues in the latter half of the twentieth century. In practice, such matters are defined as 'risks' against which the prudent citizen should insure privately so that constraints are not placed on others.

It is not without irony that in a globalised economy 'sustainability' is seen not in ecological terms, of the careful nurturing of the natural world, but as the capacity for continual growth of profits through consumption – the very antithesis of ecologism. A major critique of the social relations of the caring professions under these conditions is that they become defined in terms of consumerism, with service users being defined as 'customers' (Hugman, 1998). In terms of formal codes of ethics of the caring professions, consumerist social relations need not necessarily be problematic. For example, the same duties of fidelity, veracity, truth, confidentiality and so on operate in the private market as well as in public services or hybrid 'mixed markets'. For Koehn (1994), however, it was noted that the contractarian basis of private market relations in professional work limits ethical obligations and takes away part of the claim to professionalism. One of the solutions to this, which at times draws explicitly on ecological ideas in terms of ethics as well as organisationally, is to locate the work of caring professions in community-based non-government agencies (Ife, 1995, p. 87). The maxim of 'think globally, act locally' applies here as a principle to think about how caring professions might relate to service users. Park's (1996) examples of ecological social work practice that were discussed above also are all community-based.

Ife (1995, p. 89) takes a community development approach to professional practice in advanced industrial societies and argues that a preference for local solutions to problems is in itself an ecological way to construct practice. Not only does such an approach tend to minimise the use of resources, through the likely impact on the use of fuel for transport and so on, but is *socially* ecological in that it is consistent with an empowerment model of practice. That is, by seeking to work with local resources, caring professionals are required to recognise and respond to the strengths in communities and to seek to work with them. This has long been understood in community development as the most effective approach and it has been used in community education, community health, community medicine, community nursing and community social work.

For caring professions using a community approach the same ethical challenges that are faced in more individualised forms of practice also remain, especially in how to balance attention to questions of fairness with responsibilities to individual people. Communities are not monolithic, but contain great diversities of interests and values. Indeed, it could be argued that social diversity is as much an ecological issue as is bio-diversity. However, local values can be discriminatory and oppressive as much as can professional practices or government policies. Feminist critiques of community-based approaches have highlighted that there is a risk that this can become a covert (albeit often unintended) vehicle for the further oppression of women (Ungerson, 1987). For example, if 'locally based' services that seek to support family and community relationships simply take for granted a particular view of women's roles within households, the outcome may be to reduce rather than to enhance options. Similarly, for Aboriginal or ethnic minority communities options may not actually be available at all (Anderson & Brady, 1999). Good community practice in such contexts may require that the professional role is focused on working with a community to identify the resources it needs to achieve empowerment and then seeking to obtain those resources. The point is that community-focused professional practice does not operate with a 'one size fits all' model, but begins from a position of respect for the community, with all the complexity and potential for contradictions that this implies. Again, the ethical tension between ensuring the best possible outcome for the largest number of people and respect for each individual person has to be addressed in the particular context of practice. As such, the ethics of ecology helps to identify clearly the issues that are to be faced but does not remove the responsibility that rests with each practitioner.

Ecology and the 'social mandate' of caring professions

Although the implications of the ethics of ecology have been discussed in relation to the practices of the caring professions, many aspects of the issues that have been considered go beyond the responsibilities of individual practitioners. Questions of the use of non-human animals in research, rationing in aged care, or adopting community-based approaches, have to be dealt with at the individual level but they reflect wider policies and social values. The ethics of ecology confronts prevailing policies and social values as much as it challenges individual choices.

At the level of policies and social values, the use of non-human animals in experiments is institutionalised as a preferable option to experimentation on humans on the grounds of an anthropocentric utilitarianism. There is a widely held belief that the possible suffering of such animals is preferable to the risks faced by human research subjects. The alternative, however, would not necessarily be the use of human subjects, but might be a massive reduction in the scale of experiments and therefore of developments in health, especially in pharmaceuticals. Yet although decisions to act in different ways can be made by individual professionals, such as choice by clinicians not to be personally involved in experiments (Kushner & Thomasma, 2001), any larger scale change would require a more major shift in views of non-human life that have an extensive history across many cultures.

Arguments for inter-generational equity in aged care do not specifically consider the impact on the environment of ever growing demands for care, but there is an implicit assumption that current usage of natural resources would at least not be increased. Nor, for that matter, do such arguments consider that notions of inter-generational 'unfairness' are framed in the context of the rapid growth in levels of overall material affluence in the last fifty years, or that there are other types of 'unfairness' that could be addressed (such as those arising from factors of social class, 'race', disability, gender and so on). If these factors are taken into account, then it could be argued that expectations of the quality of care in late life need to be *reduced* so that the natural resources of the environment are preserved as much as possible for the next generation. The debate between the two medical interns, Julius and Amanda, could be resolved by older people agreeing themselves to ask less of the health care system on such grounds, as an act of asserting their moral agency. This, however, is an extension of arguments for everyone in advanced industrial societies to rethink their expectations of continual growth in material standards of living (Singer, 1993b). In other words, the level of quality of care in late life should not be seen separately from the general standard of living for everyone in a society and not just for those of a particular age. At this point, the broad implications of utilitarian and deontological approaches to ecological ethics again appear to be similar.

The question of 'fairness' between generations has implications for a view of the work of the caring professions that seeks to balance the interests of different groups of people on a straightforwardly utilitarian basis (Smith, 1998). It suggests that ethical preferences are more complex than simply asking what the best course of action might be in a given instance, but should be framed in terms of the balance of consequences both now and in the future arising from present choices. While individual practitioners may anticipate the future, they do so in modest ways (such as 'this treatment should reduce the symptoms') and, as the discussion of 'risk' above indicated, larger attempts to control future events are less certain. This ethical risk must be shared; it is political as well as professional.

In relation to practitioners 'acting locally', practice outside the state or the market faces precisely the same ethical issues as does practice in state institutions or private market relationships. Practice in non-government not-for-profit settings do not occupy a ground in which ethics can be taken as given, and it is certainly not 'high ground' simply because it is outside the state or the market. These aspects of the caring professions have as much an obligation as any other to be ethically equipped and accountable. They may become advocates for the communities they serve, but the arguments about what it is 'good' and 'right' to pursue with those communities will remain contested.

There are also issues to be faced in the logical implication that local practice would suggest that practitioners become closely connected with the community that they are serving. Singer (2002) observes that we may give preference to meeting the needs of those to whom we feel great attachment, on the basis of family relationships or national identity, but that this is not the best possible choice when it is given considered thought. From this view of impartiality, it can be argued that the wealth of many sections of western societies should be compared with the level of need in other countries not only with the poorer sections of their own society. If more than ten million children die each year from lack of clean water and from preventable diseases (as happens), while expectations about well-being and health continue to grow rapidly in developed countries, the outcome could be seen as 'unjust' (Singer, 2002, p. 167; also see Bauman, 1998, pp. 70–1). Given that these situations are outcomes of choices, such injustice effectively means that developed societies choose ever-finer degrees of comfort over the basic subsistence of others. It appears that the policy implications of the utilitarian argument about comparative justice between countries are no more acceptable politically than are similar arguments about redistributive policies within countries, even though there is much to commend them (Singer, 2002, pp. 197 ff.). In neither case are those with wealth (at least in general) apparently willing to forgo the benefits that they could obtain in order to ensure that others might achieve minimum benefits. Acting locally will not, of itself, address such injustices. Caring professionals who take seriously the ethics of ecology may, therefore, seek to contribute to the democratic processes in their societies, to act as 'ecological citizens' (Smith, 1998, p. 98), but citizens who are informed by both expertise and an ethical awareness.

Conclusion

The examples that have been discussed in this chapter show that the application of ecological ethics to the caring professions is not necessarily straightforward. In none of these instances is there a sense that these concepts enable us to identify a specific 'correct' practice. However, there are also many points on which thinking about ethical practice is enhanced by attending to the implications of the ethics of ecology. Although an ecological perspective does not provide easy solutions to the challenges of research, resource issues in aged care or competing perspectives within local communities, it does assist in thinking more clearly about ethics in practice. In this chapter the ethics of ecology has been identified as an aspect of ethical thought that has not been widely attended to in the caring professions. The central feature of ecology is that the well-being of humanity is not the only ethical concern, but rather the well-being of all sentient life should be considered. This then leads, for some ecological thinkers, to the argument that in order for this to be achieved the well-being of the inanimate world must also be an ethical consideration. Thus, guided chiefly by the principle of justice, but also the principles of respect, beneficence and non-maleficence, an appropriate balance must be found between the interests and preferences of all sentient life, including humans, not only in the present but also for future generations. Thinking only one generation into the future provides a reasonable basis for applying this notion, because it balances a concern for the future with the difficulties of making accurate judgements about the consequences of actions.

Recognising the issues of material and social sustainability that ecology raises for the caring professions particularly directs ethical concerns to a re-examination of justice. The complexities of achieving fairness in the distribution of material and social resources in finite conditions mean that justice must in practice be a relative concept, achieved through balances between interests and preferences and not in their absolute fulfilment. So, this challenges the caring professions to face the consequences of policies and practices for diversity, for the way in which choices not only 'use' people as 'means to an end' (such as in taxation for the benefit of others) but may 'use' other sentient life either directly or indirectly and may use resources that have implications for the interests and preferences of future sentient life. Therefore, the caring professions are faced with the need to examine policies and practices from the perspective of sustainability and to consider this not only as a practical issue but also as a matter of professional ethics. Just as in ecological ethics there remain debates between perspectives, so too in professional ethics such a dialogue is to be seen positively.

CHAPTER 7

Postmodernity and Ethics Beyond Liberalism

Postmodern ethics

As we saw in Chapter 1, the historical development of ethical thought in western society can be seen in terms of successive eras that are characterised by different world-views. Contemporary approaches to ethics are grounded in the liberal individualism that has distinguished the 'modernist' period of industrial society that followed the European 'Enlightenment'. Both deontology and utilitarianism embody this world-view, which privileges rationalism and positivist science against tradition, religion and other ways of seeing the world that increasingly were regarded as 'irrational'. Principlism is derived from an interplay between the two. However, in the late twentieth century critiques of the dominant modernist position began to influence social and moral thought in a wide-ranging movement of thinking that has come to be known as 'postmodernism'.

Jill (an occupational therapist), Anne (a nurse) and Rob (a social worker) are discussing a seminar on ethics they have just attended. Jill is critical of the presentation because it did not provide conclusive arguments for an overall theory to explain the issues they face in practice. Anne and Rob disagree, as both think that ethics is a matter of one's own values. Rob states that it all just depends on who you are and what your background is, including which profession you belong to. Anne argues that it is more than that – there is a basis for agreeing how to define a 'good nurse' or a 'good social worker' but it would still be up to each individual to make the best attempt they can to be such a person.

This hypothetical scene illustrates the conditions of postmodernity. In this chapter arguments about the limits of 'overall theories' and the return to the ethics of virtue will be explored to examine the issues raised in such a conversation.

The main theme that links the disparate contributions to the development of postmodernism is that the 'meta-narratives' of modernism have lost their credibility (Lyon, 1999). A 'meta-narrative' is a theory or set of theories that seeks to provide a universal explanation of the world, particularly including social phenomena, such as a notion of 'human nature' that applies to all people. Against the modernist approach, postmodernism asserts the flexible, floating, plural, contingent and uncertain nature of social life (Irving, 1999). Postmodernism is concerned with attention to language and the way in which knowledge and understanding are produced through language. From this point of view society is best understood as a network of meaning that is constructed through the use of language, so that society is to be 'read' like a written text, art, or a dramatic performance. As with a text or art, meaning is not fixed but changes according to the differences between readers or viewers. Likewise, any particular 'reader', or analyst, of society may return to phenomena and see different insights. In this way any analysis is never final in its judgements, but is tentative, with finality of meaning always 'deferred' to the possibility of some future new insight (Sim, 1999, pp. 30–8).

Seen in this way, in contrast to the emphasis in modernism on objectivity of method (roughly equivalent to the everyday view of 'science'), postmodernism proposes a subjectivity of method where any claims to truth can only be understood as reflecting the particular stance or position of the person who is asserting that truth. Postmodernism, in this sense, is a loose grouping of concepts, rather than representing a single coherent body of ideas. Many postmodernists trace ideas to earlier writers, such as Nietzsche, who in the nineteenth century challenged the core ideas of modernist philosophy and science (for a summary, see Robinson, 1999, pp. 47 ff.). The ideas on which postmodernism draws also range across the different eras that were defined in Chapter 1, including classical and medieval thought. To some extent this eclecticism is part of the defining features of a postmodern approach (Lyon, 1999). Yet there are sufficient common themes in the postmodern approaches to ethics for them to be regarded as a distinctive set of ideas that present particular challenges to thinking about professional ethics.

This shift in the way in which the world, both physical and social, may be analysed has profound implications for the caring professions. All, to varying degrees, derive their knowledge and skills, as well as their values and ethics, from modernist views of 'science', 'truth' and so on. This is so not only for those that are concerned more with the physical aspects of human needs, but also those that are concerned with social needs. In ways that differ only by degrees, all the caring professions tend to embody a view of being human that emphasises similarities between people, each focusing on problems in terms of the core knowledge and skills of their specific profession. In this way each individual service user is seen in relation to the common objective features of the problem for which they are seeking help. Ethics, too, from the modernist perspective, emphasises the common, universal and objective aspects of the relationship between caring professionals and service users. Formal codes of ethics that can be treated as 'duties' or 'laws' clearly operate in this way. However, although many postmodern approaches to philosophy and social theory address matters that concern ethics, and can be said to have ethical consequences, most postmodern writing does not consider 'ethics' in explicit terms. So, for the purposes of this discussion I want to focus particularly on three theorists who have explicitly articulated issues of 'ethics' in relation to postmodernity: MacIntyre, Foucault and Bauman.

MacIntyre: ethics after virtue

Although not often cited among 'postmodernists', MacIntyre's position is clearly within the broad critique of the limits of modernity, as the tradition of virtues is to be regarded as the antithesis of modernity (MacIntyre, 1985, pp. 254–5). His starting point is that 'the language of morality is in the same state of grave disorder as the language of natural science', so that what we now have 'are the fragments of a conceptual scheme', and although 'we continue to use many of the key expressions' we have 'lost our comprehension, both theoretical and practical, of morality' (p. 2). Instead of the liberal vision of rational universal values, duties or calculations that lay behind the Enlightenment, the world is now to be seen as uncertain. Where the Enlightenment thinkers had emphasised the foundation of ethics in abstract rationality, MacIntyre suggests that 'the good' is to be understood as rooted in human character. MacIntyre therefore looks again at the idea of ethics grounded in 'virtue', returning to the insights of Aristotle (1985, pp. 109 ff.). For Aristotle, the virtues describe the character of a 'good' person and are evident in thoughts and actions. The virtues are that to which a good person is inclined, they are not simply a duty (deontology); and they are important because of what they embody about a person's character, not just because of what they produce (utilitarianism).

It should be noticed that 'the good' is not defined by virtue, but virtue (as an ethics of excellence) is productive of 'the good'. The virtues are those qualities of character that will enable a person to flourish (MacIntyre, 1985, p. 148). In this interpretation, MacIntyre is following Aristotle and not Nietzsche. For Nietzsche, there are no rational defences of morality, so his answer to the question 'what sort of person am I to become?' led to the solipsistic idea of the 'great' (not 'good') person who asserts his or her own morality (MacIntyre, 1985, pp. 117–18, 258–9). This is liberalism without rationality. Against this, MacIntyre returns to Aristotle, whose concept of virtue is social. Thus, if the idea of 'good [is grounded in] such notions as those of a practice, of the narrative unity of a human life and of a moral tradition, then goods ... can only be discovered by entering into those relationships which constitute communities [with] a shared vision of and under-standing of goods' (1985, p. 258). In other words, to be a virtue a char-acteristic must be related to specific practices, the whole of a human life and a moral tradition or community (p. 275).

The virtues that were identified by Aristotle included 'friendship, courage, self-restraint, wisdom, justice' as well as others (MacIntyre, 1985, p. 134). MacIntyre is not suggesting that these are the only way of understanding what is virtuous (he goes on to note that specific concepts have changed through the centuries). His argument is that we should look within our present communities of relationships (which would include professions) to discern what is virtuous, other-wise the definitions of 'good' and 'virtue' become circular in a closed self-referencing system. Thus, in considering virtues in the caring professions it will be necessary to consider them in the contemporary context. However, the underlying notions of 'good' and 'virtue' are sufficiently general for them to be considered comparatively between contexts.

Foucault: ethics and subjectivity

Foucault is very widely regarded as 'a postmodernist' (for example, see Robinson, 1999, pp. 47–8), although his own attention to 'postmoder-nity' was both ambivalent and brief. His work reveals a much greater interest in using a wide range of intellectual methods (sociology, anthropology, history, psychology, philosophy) to examine the development and the inter-relationship of ideas, values and actions (see, for example, Foucault, 1997, pp. 309–10). This approach he called 'genealogy', a term that conveys the sense of tracing the antecedents of ideas, values and actions. Using this historiographical method, Foucault (1973) looked at the emergence of professions (disciplines) that seek to manage (to discipline) human life and conduct. These are the occupations that have been defined here as the caring professions, and include medicine (especially psychiatry), psychology, social work and teaching. By inference, others such as allied health professions and nursing are part of the broad social trend that Foucault identified in the inextricable connection of 'care' and 'control' in the practices of these professions (Foucault, 1980).

Foucault's major ethical concern was to understand 'the ethics of the self [and] technologies of the self' (1997, p. 255). By this, he meant the question of how we decide what sort of person we should be and how we seek to become that person. Such a notion is based, quite explicitly, on Socrates' concern for the 'care of the self' and Aristotle's idea of 'habits of the soul'. Socrates, Foucault observed, 'would greet people ... with the question "are you caring for yourself?" ... He is the man who cares about the care of others' (1997, p. 287). This idea is very different from the approach to ethics of universal principles, rules or laws of 'right conduct'. In Foucault's terms, ethics is (only) possible to the extent that a person can be responsible for and responsive to her or his own self and from that to her or his encounters with the world. So the ethical self is not grounded in knowledge of principles, rules, laws, duties or consequences, but in the practice of self-scrutiny. Foucault's ethics can, like that of MacIntyre, be seen as a return to virtue as a core value.

In professional life, Foucault's approach would imply that ethics is to 'know one's professional self' and 'take care of one's professional self'. This would mean that the ethical professional would not only seek to use self-knowing to be the 'best possible' practitioner of their profession, but also to be rid of self-deception. Such deception would include belief in the neutrality of practices because, using the same processes of inquiry and analysis, it would be seen that practices are based on the 'discourse', that is the combination of knowledge and power, of the profession. In other words, the ethical member of the caring professions would be aware that their knowledge, skills and values are the product of a particular way of seeing the world at a particular time and so avoid the degree of certainty that can become the domination of others. At the same time, they would seek to be as knowledgeable and as skillful as possible, constantly reviewing and developing these aspects of the professional self.

Bauman: ethics after certainty

For Bauman (1993), as for MacIntyre and Foucault, 'postmodernity' is a condition of 'uncertainty' in knowledge and values. More than this, all efforts to delineate social laws are suspect because every attempt at objectivist grand planning has led to totalitarian outcomes, such as the horrors of the gulag or the gas chamber (Bauman, 1989). If this is the case, Bauman then asks, how are we to know how we should live? The answer is that we should cease to look for universal rules (what Bauman terms 'ethics') and should seek to understand the ways in which we relate to each other (which he calls 'morality') (1993, pp. 16 ff.). (It should be observed that his usage here is exactly contrary to the tradition that was noted in Chapter 1.)

To accomplish this task, Bauman draws on the notion of morality that was set out by the philosopher Lèvinas (1981, 1985, 1987) as the impulse to respond to 'the Other'. This concept refers to the necessity for each moral agent to live with the all-embracing responsibility of relationships that are each unique and that do not depend on any type of qualification, such as the expectation of reciprocity. The moral response to 'the Other' cannot be limited, reduced to contract, treated as a commodity or ever be seen to be finished; nor does it depend on who 'the Other' is or what 'the Other' does (compare with Gaita, 1991, pp. 6–7). This relationship of self-and-other Bauman describes as a 'moral party of two' (Bauman, 1993, pp. 82 ff.). Yet the human world does not consist of dyadic relationships, but of many varied relationships that at times present conflicting moral demands; society makes demands 'beyond the moral party' (1993, pp. 112 ff.). It is in society and not in relationships that ethical rules are necessary, but for Bauman such rules take away the discretion that is the core of moral relationships.

Seen in this way, morality is ambivalent and full of conflict and contradiction (Bauman calls this state 'aporetic'). If this view of morality is accepted, then it means that we must constantly struggle with the moral demands of relationships in the context of society. This struggle is revealed in Bauman's own apparent self-contradiction between the argument that 'care' is a deceptive value because it so easily turns into power (1993, pp. 91–2), and his later assertion that the caring professional may (indeed, must) 'speak-for' or 'act-for' 'the Other' when the other cannot speak or act, such that a refusal to do so would be morally irresponsible (2001a, pp. 80–2). In this sense, therefore, caring must be 'for' an other and not simply done in terms that have meaning for the carer.

Bauman also applies a critical sociology to contexts that are significant for the caring professions, in his analysis of the morality of modernist organisational structures, namely bureaucracy and business. The late twentieth century saw a shift from the former to the latter in many industrial countries as the politically preferred way of delivering education, health and well-being. However, argues Bauman, neither mode of organisation deals with the morality of these human endeavours. 'Bureaucracy strangles or criminalises moral impulses, while business merely pushes them aside' (1994, p. 13). Ethics in both is reduced to rules of conduct – in bureaucracy these are procedural, in business they are contractual. Both make strangers out of people who should be able to see themselves as being in a relationship where discretion and moral responsibility go hand in hand. The *moral* person is, thus, the one who can speak out against the tide of public (or collegial) opinion when this is the only way to be responsible (p. 14). More recently, Bauman (2001a) has reasserted the possibility of such 'speaking out' coming from shared values, such as those of a professional community.

Postmodernity, virtue, the self and responsibility

Between these three approaches to ethics in conditions of postmodernity there are several common features. First, each, in some way, deals with the idea of 'virtue', whether this is explicit (MacIntyre, Foucault) or implicit (Bauman). All three approaches are concerned with the aspects of human character that enable people to know what is 'good' or 'right' and to act on that understanding. Second, all three conclude that ethics (or morality in Bauman's terms) is a matter for each human self, because it is a facet of the self. The self in postmodern conditions exercises intuition in the face of demands from all that is around her or him, being capable of separating her or him self off from the context in which she or he is situated, of being able to stand back from (or stand above) the tide of social expectations. The postmodern virtuous self is, therefore, someone who is able to take responsibility because they can be accountable, in the sense of giving an account for the stance that is taken on matters of what is 'good' or 'right', even when this is contrary to the prevailing social orthodoxies. For the three colleagues who were described at the beginning of this chapter, such a position would be inadequate for Jill (who seeks universal principles), while it would be congruent with Rob's ideas; for Anne, however, although this position is necessary it is not sufficient.

The remaining problem is that of how we are to know what is 'good' and what is 'right'. A central problem for the postmodern condition is whether subjectivity must be reduced to solipsism, in which all values are personal and arbitrary. As Pellegrino and Thomasma note (1993, p. 19), there is a risk that in seeking to overcome the limitations of formal rules and principles caring professions will find themselves confronted by a degree of subjectivity that isolates individuals from each other. The three approaches that have been considered here share the answer, more or less tentatively, that the way forward is not in seeking to develop a new objectivity, in the sense of fixed external standards, but in the efforts of 'inter-subjectivity', in which each individual seeks moral responsibility in themselves and looks for it in others. This is an understanding of ethics that cannot be confined by codes or rules but must be encountered in practice.

Postmodernity and virtuous practice

In their discussion of the virtues in practice, Pellegrino & Thomasma (1993) identify eight virtues of the medical profession. These are: fidelity; compassion; phronesis; justice; fortitude; temperance; integrity; self-effacement. This is a somewhat augmented version of the Aristotelian virtues of friendship, courage, self-restraint, wisdom and justice that were noted above. As we shall see, the additional elements and nuances come more from the contemporary situation than from a basic disagreement with the classical Greek view of human flourishing. In the following discussion I want to consider these ideas more widely, both in applying these virtues to all the caring professions and also in exploring the extent to which this specific list is sufficient to describe virtuous practice.

In order to examine the virtues and the ethical self in relation to the content of practice, the ideas of phronesis, fortitude (or courage) and temperance will be explored. The first of these, phronesis, is a term from classical Greek that refers to the notion of 'practical wisdom' originally stated by Aristotle (Pellegrino & Thomasma, 1993, p. 84). This is the virtue of being able to know and do what is right in a specific situation. This can be seen as equivalent to the medieval notion of 'prudence' (developed by Aquinas), in which practical wisdom is joined by other virtues (Pellegrino & Thomasma, 1993, p. 85). More than that, it is the virtue that enables the other virtues to be placed in their appropriate context. However, these are not notions that guarantee a particular idea of what is 'good' or 'right', or that people will always agree on those qualities. In that sense, Bauman's assertion that we are all 'alone' in the face of moral responsibility (Bauman, 1994, p. 14) is consistent with the idea of practical wisdom. This means that colleagues who are equally prudent will disagree, at least from time to time.

Prudential action is that in which moral complexity is not ignored simply to achieve technically 'correct' outcomes. For example, the beliefs of a service user may conflict with what the professional 'knows' is the correct course of action. Many medical and health ethicists give the example of people whose religious convictions preclude the use of antibiotics or of blood transfusions even in life-threatening situations (Pellegrino & Thomasma, 1993, p. 88; Beauchamp & Childress, 2001, p. 60). Similarly, other factors, such as pain, fear or previous bad experiences of treatment or intervention, may influence a person in need to withhold their permission or co-operation with an action that, from a technical point of view, the professional knows to be the most effective. In human service practices there are equivalents, such as the concerns of Aboriginal Australians or members of ethnic minorities in dealing with many aspects of the child and family health and welfare and the education systems (Carrese & Rhodes, 1995; Anderson & Bardy, 1999). Prudence, in all such contexts, is the capacity to bring together respect for the autonomy of the individual, including cultural aspects of people's lives, with beneficence and non-maleficence, sometimes to do so very quickly, and to be able to give a plausible account if called on to do so. It can also mean the wisdom to refrain from acting, even when colleagues or service users are assertively asking for something to be done.

The idea of 'fortitude' or 'courage' may sound almost quaint to the contemporary ear, especially when applied to professional practices. Yet this virtue is concerned with the capacity to act well (that is, to do what is 'good' or 'right') over a sustained period and in the face of potential disagreement or opposition. Examples of courage in practice would include choosing to work with people who have highly communicable and life-threatening conditions, such as HIV, Hepatitis C, or (at the time of writing) SARS. Less dramatic, but no less virtuous, are those members of the caring professions who demonstrate fortitude by choosing to work with groups of people whose needs are great, in situations where resources are limited, where professional status (and rewards) are low, and where service users may not even recognise that the provision of the service requires such an individual commitment. Of course, to make such a choice in order to get acknowledgement, even the verbal thanks of service users, would remove the virtuous nature of the choice. (There are parallels here with a Kantian notion of duty.)

The caring professional who decides to make a public stand about something that is wrong about the service in which they work, or in the practice of a colleague, could be said to be acting courageously. Such an act, usually referred to as 'whistle-blowing', may not seem to be an obvious example, as to some people it can appear to be confrontational, and therefore aggressive, lacking in the virtue of loyalty, or even self-serving (because it is seen as 'holier-than-thou'). Yet for the professional who is convinced that some serious harm has been or is being done to others, especially to vulnerable service users, taking this type of action can be the only way to challenge what is seen to be 'bad' or 'wrong'. 'Whistle-blowing' takes fortitude and courage, because it is likely to produce resistance from colleagues and others, including those who are concerned about what is 'good' and 'right', as well as potentially being very costly in personal and career terms. For example, when Graham Pink, a nurse in the UK, challenged dangerously low staffing levels in the aged-care wards of the hospital where he worked in a senior position, he was sacked and ostracised (Pink, 1994). Making such a choice must, therefore, not be seen frivolously. Bauman's injunction to stand out against the unanimous opinion of all those around (see above) is credible largely because of his own actions in the face of what was 'bad' and 'wrong', that led to losing his job, his reputation and then having to accept exile from his country of birth (Smith, 1999).

Temperance also now has connotations as a concept that links it to censorious or moralising attitudes. In this context, however, temperance refers to the virtue of balance, self-control or self-restraint. Foucault's (1997) notion of the self-disciplining person who takes care of her or his own self is based on his reading of Plato and other classical Greek philosophers on this concept. Having self-control or balance of judgement enables the professional to avoid excesses in thoughts and actions, some of which may be vices not in themselves, but because they are excesses of virtues. An example of this would be the practitioner who excuses unjust or criminal actions by a colleague on grounds of 'loyalty'. Similarly, as Banks observes (2001, pp. 141–2), the caring professional who, having only partially understood Aristotle and Bauman, befriends a service user to the point where appropriate role distinctions are lost, and who then favours the one person over and above other service users, could be said to lack balance. The 'ethics of proximity' ('being for the Other') is a starting point, from which the temperate (and prudent) practitioner struggles with the limitations set by material circumstances, law and policy and so on, but does not try to act as if such constraints were not there.

Another example of a lack of self-restraint or of balance would be that of the practitioner who appears not to be able to live by the advice that she or he would give to a service user. The obese dietician, the physician who smokes, and the teacher who derides the value of applying oneself to learning would all be examples of a lack of temperance. In this sense, the caring professional who takes care of the self would display respect for the objectives of their own profession's practices in a balanced approach to their role, their colleagues and service users.

There are also implications for the caring professions in the pluralistic idea of knowledge that lies behind the return to virtue ethics. The postmodern 'condition of uncertainty' not only covers ethics, but stretches across all conceptions of 'truth'. What, then, of the postmodern idea that 'truth' is always provisional? This leads both to the claim that 'good' and 'right' are not fixed and it also challenges the scientific basis of practices in the caring professions. In a discussion of social work, Howe (1994) argues that under postmodern conditions the idea of expertise, seen as that of grasping fixed truths about the world and skill in applying those truths, gives way to 'performance' of a role, in which the practitioner continually reworks their grasp on truth in demonstrations of 'competence' (also see jagodinski (2002) on a similar point in relation to teaching). It is not necessary to embrace the more extreme version of this aspect of postmodernism (that there is no such things as 'truth') to see that an appropriate degree of humility about knowledge and skills may be an ethical virtue that brings together practical wisdom and self-restraint. This point may be most pertinent to those practices that lack the material science of surgery, for example; by this I mean counselling and other types of intra- and inter-personal therapies (Flaskas, 1997). However, Pellegrino and Thomasma (1993, pp. 120–2) also point to the risk in medicine of 'playing God', by withholding interventions or forcing them onto patients (which can be extrapolated to other caring professions). Their point is that there is a balance to be found in careful and competent consideration of issues to ensure that the service users' needs are served rather than the self-opinion of the professional. Yet they also note that in the current social and economic climate, caring professionals may be caught between the demands of service users and those of managers and policy makers. In such circumstances, courage is required along with phronesis and fortitude.

A postmodern focus for caring professions

Any consideration of professional ethics must be grounded in the objectives or focus of the caring professions. As has been discussed in previous chapters, the common thread between the caring professions is that of service to the 'good' of the service user, through the application of knowledge and skill (Koehn, 1994). The 'good' of the service user, as I have noted above, is not just to be understood in the technical sense but also as a moral matter. However, as with the 'knowledge' and 'skill' in the content of the caring professions, the notion of postmodernity can be seen as creating problems with the idea of 'a focus'. If 'truth' is flexible, floating, plural, contingent and uncertain, then what of the goals of 'health' or 'well-being' or 'education'? Are these all simply subjective and to be understood only in terms of individual preferences, based on the differences between individuals?

If we look at the actions or commitments of the theorists of postmodernity, we can see that in practice they do not appear to have had difficulty in identifying what was 'good' and what was not. Foucault, for example, was active in prisoners' rights and gay and lesbian rights campaigning (Foucault, 1980, 1997), while other theorists such as Lyotard have been committed to environmental and other issues in a way that presupposes a judgement about what is 'right' (Sim, 1999, pp. 25, 27). Bauman has used his work to make very clear attacks against the ethos of neo-liberal individualism as the basis for privatising health, welfare and education (Bauman, 1993, 1994, 1997, 2001a). Each of these responses to the social world, from theorists who focus on the self, are explicit in their commitments to social, and not to individualistic, views of responsibility for health, well-being, education and so on. A postmodern perspective does not, it seems, preclude a clear view of what is 'good' and what is 'right', although this appears to undermine the more relativistic interpretations of postmodernism.

Criticisms of postmodernist perspectives applied to questions of health, well-being and education have tended to concentrate on this very issue of purpose. For example, Leonard (1997), in a discussion of social welfare in conditions of postmodernity, makes it clear that his intention is to defend core values such as universal 'human rights', 'empowerment' (of people to exercise power in their own lives) and 'social justice', all of which are modernist in that they assume an objective view about social reality. Leonard's purpose is *ethical* as much as it reflects any other motivation. Recognising the ethical consequences of a completely relativist view of values, he seeks to renew the argument for some core universal values to be defended. Flaskas (1997) makes a similar point about family therapy, noting that while truths may be conditional, partial and open to various interpretations, they are connected to concrete empirical experiences of reality. The good therapist assists the client to pursue the truth of his or her situation.

Postmodern ideas point to the difficulty of reaching fixed and final positions about specific practices out of context. Yet, at the same time, the critics of postmodernism (or at least of its most relativistic interpretations) challenge the view that 'anything goes' (Cheek & Porter, 1997). Such an interpretation of postmodernity cannot be sustained in a meaningful way if notions such as health, well-being and education are to continue to be taken seriously as professional values. This can be illustrated by reference to the issues of inter-personal violence, including domestic violence and child abuse, for example. Proponents of postmodern ideas about difference and diversity do not seriously challenge the argument that violence and abuse should be opposed. There is an ethical 'truth' about domestic violence and child abuse that continues to have universal validity among the caring professions. Indeed, it would be hard to imagine an example of an ethical defence for either.

Postmodern social relations in the caring professions

From this brief discussion of 'focus', it becomes clearer that the implication of postmodern ethics for the caring professions is an increasing individualisation of the relations between professionals and service users. Of course, at the level of everyday practice relationships are between individuals; the point is that within other ethical frameworks (deontology, utilitarianism, principlism and so on) professionals and service users encounter each other in terms of their membership of more general and universal categories of social roles. The emphasis on subjectivity in postmodern ethics changes this view, suggesting that ethical practice is something to be worked out in each situation. In Bauman's (1993) terms, it is only in the 'moral impulse' of the caring professional and not in formal codes that an ethics of practice can be found. So, if this is the case, to what should the 'morally active practitioner' (Husband, 1995) turn as the basis for knowing what is 'good' and what is 'right' in practice?

To answer this question, it is helpful to look again at the notion of the virtues. In their discussion of virtues in medical practice, Pellegrino and Thomasma (1993) identify three key examples that relate to the immediate relationships between practitioners and patients. These are fidelity, integrity and self-effacement. Each of these reflects an attitude that the professional's role exists, first and foremost, to meet the purposes of the service user and not for the ends of the professional. Fidelity and integrity concern the basic characteristics of honesty and openness that are most aptly expressed in the notion of 'truth-telling' (Higgs, 1998). This particular expression of virtuous action is widely discussed among health professions (for example: Brockett, 1996; Tadd, 1998; Francis, 1999). The importance of truth-telling is found in the combination of fidelity and integrity. These virtues can be seen as being respectful of the other (the service user) and being respectful of one's self (the professional). It is not just a matter of duty or the particular consequences, but of choosing the type of professional self that one will be.

The example that is widely discussed in relation to truth-telling is that of breaking bad news, such as a poor prognosis. While there are some recent defences of 'therapeutic privilege' (that is, the claimed right to deceive a patient 'for their own good') (such as Jackson, 2002), in most discussions this is now seen as a form of self-deception by clinicians about how they are perceived by the rest of society. As Campbell *et al.* (2001, p. 31) put it, the prevailing view is now turning to the idea that deception, even if it is in the form of concealment of certain facts or obfuscation with jargon, is not 'kind' to patients and damages the integrity of caring professions. Only in rare circumstances (they cite the immediate aftermath of serious accidents) might the whole truth be temporarily withheld from someone, but such instances should be resolved by eventual disclosure and always seen clearly as exceptions. Social workers in child protection, similarly, have recognised that although the truth can be difficult to deal with, the alternative is to undermine the very integrity of the profession (Wise, 1995; Banks, 2001, pp. 176–7). In Australia, at the time of writing, the Christian churches are also facing the implications of truth-telling in relation to child abuse, or rather the legacy of concealing truth. This can seem most scandalous because it involves ministers of religion, but scandal accompanies all the caring professions when they are perceived to have been parsimonious with the truth. The alternative to fidelity and integrity would be that the caring professions are prepared to be the type of people who use deception as stock-in-trade; this clearly goes against the self-image that lies at the heart of professionalism, in which trustworthiness, honesty and reliability are as crucial as technical competence (Koehn, 1994).

Another aspect of individual action that has been extensively discussed in the caring professions is that of 'paternalism'. This refers to an attitude in which it is assumed that the professional knows better than the service users what are the latter's interests (because professionals have access to knowledge and skills that others do not have). This assumption is regarded by those who hold such a view as benign – indeed, this attitude holds, it is precisely because professional knowledge gives a clear view of the service user's best interests that the professional ought to act as he or she sees fit irrespective of the service user's views. Pellegrino and Thomasma (1993, pp. 57–8) suggest that some paternalism may take the form of the professional believing that they have a 'prerogative as the privileged proprietor' of professional knowledge and skills. However, they and others (for example: Fry & Johnstone, 2002) argue strongly that paternalism is not beneficence, but is often its opposite as it violates the service user's autonomy and, as such, should be seen as maleficent. Clark (2000, pp. 175–84) notes that the classic liberal notion of freedom operates in situations where someone may have a differing idea of their interests from those held by professionals. Laws are framed to give caring professions the right to exercise power over others only when the person may be a demonstrable threat to themselves or someone else. In all other circumstances consent is assumed. Examples include situations where a service user has severe mental ill-health or mental disability, including that arising from organic conditions in late life (such as Alzheimer's Disease). Where paternalist actions are undertaken within the framework of law they are subject to review and accountability. Where they are not, the professional who is determined to be paternalistic must be reliant on subterfuge or deceit and, as discussed above, is not enacting the virtues of fidelity and integrity.

These issues relate to the question of participation, which is identified by Howe (1994) as an aspect of postmodern practice. This not only includes the notion that professionals should listen carefully to service users' views of the world, but also the expectation that professionals should act in such a way as to promote the capacity of service users to participate, for example by sharing knowledge. This takes time and commitment, especially where the situation is highly complex and the service user does not have the prior educational background to grasp facts and ideas quickly. As such, participation is derived from the virtue of self-effacement, which is the virtue that is opposed to self-interest – in other words, it is to act on the interests of the other in such a way as to seek to find out what those interests are.

However, Pellegrino and Thomasma (1993, pp. 148–50) note that the virtues of fidelity, integrity and self-effacement are not necessarily shared, even within the caring professions. For example, they say, we can see the rejection of these virtues in members of these professions who own hospitals, nursing homes, retirement villages, child care facilities, pathology services and the like, to which they then refer service users who have consulted them for a diagnosis or advice. Self-interest is, perhaps, most startling in the multi-million dollar religious ministries based in electronic media. At the same time, it must also be recognised the wider society has encouraged the caring professions to become entrepreneurial and competitive in a free market (Pellegrino & Thomasma, 1993, p. 154). Thus, the postmodern world, while appearing to give greatest ethical plausibility to virtues has, at the same time, created conditions that promote self-interest as legitimate and given moral approval to the pursuit of profit as a measure of success in areas of life where the previous ethical gauge has been that of service to humanity. Nonetheless, consideration of postmodern ethics suggests that the caring professions can find 'good' and 'right' in reflection on practice. If attention to subjectivity and virtues is to contribute to a new way of thinking about and engaging with professional ethics, then this could only happen in the context of the professions as moral communities. These communities are as pluralistic as any other, despite formal codes of ethics. Therefore, the impact of postmodern ethics in practice would be likely to take many forms.

Postmodernity and the idea of a 'social mandate'

In discussions of nursing and social work, Cheek and Rudge (1994) and Parton (1994), respectively, have argued that in the absence of a moral consensus on the social basis of health, well-being, education and so on, the primary social mandate for the caring professions is to manage various forms of social risk. Child protection is an example of such an area of practice. Whereas the previous social focus on the needs of children permitted each profession to concentrate on its own contribution to the well-being and development of children (compare with Koehn, 1994), the increased emphasis on child protection as a paramount concern subjects each profession to processes of monitoring, reviews, evaluation and so on. A mandatory requirement to report suspicions of child abuse now exists in many western countries as a means of ensuring that if professionals do not do the 'right' thing, then they can be held accountable legally as well as morally (Breckenridge, 1999).

It is not just that the professions are being called to greater accountability. Rather, such a change reveals a weakening of the social mandate for caring professions to establish their own content and focus. It is no longer acceptable that a professional should exercise judgement about whether a suspicion of child abuse could be dealt with in other ways (although it is still a judgement call as to whether an event constitutes suspicion). Where previously the way in which professionals acted was taken to be 'right' precisely because it was based on professional judgement, now what is 'right' is defined and applied to the professions through the management of their actions.

In the context of professional ethics, such an analysis suggests that what is 'right' is now more clearly to be found in following correct procedures. Moreover, there are also implications of greater social controls on the caring professions embedded in the market model of service provision that is now so influential, even in the state and not-for-profit sectors. The professions are expected to have formal codes of ethics, perhaps more explicitly than ever, but these are intended to provide the basis for the quasi-contractual consumer relationships rather than to form the basis of an encounter between moral selves (to use Bauman's terms). Indeed, Bauman's distinction between bureaucracy and business that was discussed above may even be transcended, in that the form of governmentality expressed in mandatory reporting of child abuse can 'criminalise the moral impulse' of professionals judging how to act while at the same time step round moral processes by taking judgement out of the situation.

In this way of understanding contemporary society it would appear that the virtues, along with care of the self and the response to 'the Other' become privatised. Of course, MacIntyre, Foucault and Bauman are all in agreement that ethics is actually a matter for each autonomous individual. This is part of the post-liberal individualism to which each points. However, there is one virtue that goes beyond individuals and which has to be grounded in a moral community, namely justice. This virtue can be seen at the level of individual action, in the sense of rendering to others what is their due. Pellegrino and Thomasma (1993, p. 94) equate this with the balancing of the demands of the other virtues, along with the needs and interests of the individual service user and others who have a claim on the professional. The clinician has to exercise justice, with wisdom, in responding to an individual and in choosing between individuals, such as in rationing time or other scare resources.

However, justice also refers to a concern with those whose needs are particularly acute, whose rights have been breached, who are less able to speak for themselves and so on. This social interpretation of justice has a long pedigree, having been of interest to the classical Greek and medieval philosophers as well as in the present day. It is in this respect that postmodern society confronts professional ethics, because the social mandate of the neo-liberal market does not include the legitimacy of advocacy concerning social injustice (against unjust policies, for example). It is not that all such action is prevented, but that in pluralist conditions the caring professions may be seen as simply one more interest group. Bauman (2001a) argues strongly for the legitimacy of the voice of such informed interests, precisely because they are expressions of wider interests and not the self-interests of the group that is speaking. Examples of this debate in Australia include the hostile response from government and other powerful groups to caring professions' public statements about Aboriginal rights or about the treatment of asylum seekers in mandatory detention, challenging the legitimacy of such statements.

To return to the three colleagues with whom this chapter began, clearly postmodern approaches to ethics do not provide a clear signpost to particular definitions of what is 'good' and 'right'. However, nor do such approaches lead necessarily to totally subjective and particularistic conclusions. At least in the guises offered by MacIntyre, Foucault and Bauman it is possible to find a way of exploring inter-subjective agreement, especially through renewed attention to virtues as the basis for ethics. Such postmodern ethics, while not providing explicit answers, creates another dimension to such a conversation, with its emphasis on subjectivity, diversity and the inexhaustible demands of the ethical life.

Conclusion

In examining particular approaches to ethics in postmodernity, this chapter has identified subjectivity as a central theme. This understanding of social reality leads our attention away from abstract rules, formulae and principles and towards ethics based on the self and context. Virtue ethics have been explored as the common thread between different approaches to postmodern ethics, extended by a consideration of ethics as the impulse to respond to others as moral selves who each have a unique value. The same social change, it has been noted, also creates circumstances in which the legitimacy of the moral dimensions of the caring professions' roles is limited to individual actions and encounters with other individuals. Thus, to paraphrase Bauman (1994), each caring professional finds her or him self 'alone again' after moral certainty has been declared to be at an end. In these terms, codes of ethics can be seen as rules that constrain the moral impulse of autonomous (professional) selves and are no guarantee of the pursuit of 'good' character or 'right' action (Lichtenberg, 1996).

One of the few attempts to consider how this analysis might apply to everyday practice is the notion of the 'morally active practitioner' proposed by Husband (1995). This is the caring professional who recognises that codes, and the duties, formulae and principles they embody, are 'a reasoned and legitimated set of externally prescriptive guidelines' and that, although 'implementation of professional ethical guidelines [i]s desirable', at the same time they are 'permanently irreducible to routine' (p. 87). The outcome is that the ethical acts of different individuals may well look different but be equally ethical. The point is whether it is thought through, connected to the values of the profession and can be accountable (in the moral sense). For this to happen, members of the caring professions must engage with ethics as part of the core of what it is to be professional. This requires what Sellman (1996) has called 'moral fluency', which is the capacity to consider the relationship between means, ends and values, to grasp options and to be able to base practice on the morally conscious exercise of choices. This can only be achieved as part of a profession as a moral community. Thus, the 'care of the professional self' includes the engagement of the self and others in ethical discourse as part of the professional life.

CHAPTER 8

Discourse Ethics: Constructionism or Critical Realism?

Discourse ethics and the caring professions

In the previous four chapters we have examined major developments in ethics that in the latter part of the twentieth century began to present challenges to the dominant ways of looking at ethics in the caring professions. As Tronto puts it, '… the hegemony of Neo-Kantian ethics has been challenged by moral theories that rely upon compassion, care, the emotions, and to some extent, communication', drawing on a variety of perspectives that share roots in the ideas originally set out by Aristotle (Tronto, 1993, p. 149). So far the discussion has focused on compassion seen as an intelligent emotion, the ethics of care, the ethics of ecology and of postmodernity; it has emphasised questions of emotion, perception, context, character and virtue, subjectivity and inter-subjectivity. In this chapter the other element that is identified by Tronto as part of changing approaches to ethics will be considered, namely that of communication.

Gadamer's (1979) discussion of the Aristotelian view of the relationship between ethics and knowledge is significant for members of the caring professions, drawing attention to the way in which knowledge is an important part of being ethical. Unless a person knows things about the world and forms an understanding of them, it is not possible to speak about conscious action or values. However, this is not the same as the technical knowledge and skill that form part of the basis of the very idea of a profession (and which, for Gadamer, includes theoretical knowledge). It is the sort of practical knowledge, or wisdom, that Aristotle called 'phronesis'. Such knowledge cannot be developed simply through objective study of an object, but must be gained also by practice and by reflection. This distinction can also be seen as that between 'knowing about' and 'understanding' an object, a person, or a situation. For example, the clinician may 'know about' the biological, psychological or social elements of a problem faced by a service user, but unless the clinician also 'understands' the context in which the service user is acting and the values that the service user brings to the encounter, as well as her or his own self as a clinician interacting with the service user, then technical knowledge and skill will not be sufficient to grasp all aspects of the problems faced by the service user. It is in this sense that we may think about a 'wise practitioner' or an 'insightful clinician'.

In order to see the implications of this view in practice, let us return briefly to the hypothetical situation that was presented in Chapter 1. This concerned a girl, aged 15, disclosing to a teacher her use of illegal drugs and active sexual relationship with an older man, from whom the girl thinks she may have contracted a sexually transmitted disease, and where the girl asks for assistance in getting medical attention without her parents knowing. Seen within an objective, universalist framework, the practitioner would be required to consider duties and principles in the abstract and then apply them to the specific situation. In this case the responsibilities of men who have sexual relationships with girls who are under the age of consent, and the rights of parents to know what is happening to their children compared to children's rights (which, as legal minors may be more limited), would be matters that would be of ethical importance. In contrast, an inter-subjective approach moves the practitioner towards a more relational position, in which the person to whom the practitioner is responding, the practitioner her or him self, and various facets of the situation (including laws, rules and other external forces) are all considered together. Where the former approach is often understood in terms of knowledge and skill in applying principles, the latter embodies the idea of practical wisdom in terms of 'making moral sense in action'. *This* girl, *this* man and *these* parents in the particularities of *this* situation (which also includes *this* teacher, *this* nurse and so on) all become ethically crucial to a response grounded in compassion, caring, or even 'being-for-Other'.

Banks (2001, pp. 141–2) argues that these inter-subjective approaches are not strong enough on which to build a professional community in which there is consistency, accountability, or which addresses the very specific yet potentially limitless demands that may be placed on professionals by the roles that they perform *as* professionals. Banks gives the example of a social worker who, while out shopping, gives money to someone begging on the street and asks, if we affirm this as an ethical act on grounds of compassion, caring or postmodern 'being-for-Other', whether this enjoins the social worker to give money from her or his own pocket to someone who is a client. Banks concludes that this would be both impractical and would undermine other aspects of the client–professional relationship. Indeed; but agreement with this point does not of itself suggest that ideas of compassion, caring, sustainability or 'being-for-Other' have nothing to say in considering and acting on professional values. Rather, Banks' argument can be seen as indicative of the way in which practical ethics are particular and contextual. Although Banks does not make this point as such, she also criticises the opposite perspective, that universal and impartial ethics may be held to require professionals to completely separate personal moral values, emotions and so on from their responses to service users (2001, pp. 142–4).

What Banks' discussion illustrates is that, despite the philosophical differences between objective and inter-subjective approaches to ethics, there remains a possibility for debate and dialogue. Underlying the distinction between acts performed in the context of personal life and those performed in a professional role are the elements of 'agency' and 'structure' (Giddens, 1991). This distinction points to questions about the extent to which human action is free or is constrained, or to use other terms is 'voluntary' or 'determined' (a debate that is as old as philosophy). From Socrates and Aristotle we inherit the view that only in conditions where rational choice may be exercised can people be held accountable for their actions. So, where social structures are seen to determine actions moral responsibility is limited, but where human agency is sufficiently free to operate people may be regarded as morally responsible. Giddens' (1991) conclusion is that the social world is formed in the interplay between these two opposites: human agency is neither totally constrained nor totally free. The caring professional has choices about how she or he responds to the service user, or acts in relation to colleagues, in doing research or developing policies, but such choices are formed within the limitations of circumstances that include resources, the actions of others, law, agency procedures and so on.

Human agency is not only affected by issues of social structure and the material conditions of the world but also by cognition and emotion. The relationship of what we know and how we know it, as indicated by Gadamer (1979), therefore lies at the heart of any attempt to relate moral values to ethical practice. Apel (1984) argues for a view of knowledge in which ideas about what is true are achieved through an open consensus. This differs both from the strict empirical methods of positivism (only formally tested objective knowledge is acceptable) and from relativism (all knowledge is seen as valid in its own terms). Apel's model has been summarised by Delanty (1997, p. 89) as consisting of three elements: (1) knowledge is built on consensus; (2) consensus is achieved through communication; (3) communication is possible only if there is a commitment to a public understanding of knowledge. What this means is that the validity of knowledge comes from the open debate about the meaning of evidence, in which all parties are accountable to each other for permitting each other to speak, be heard and to take account of all views. This model can be said to describe an ideal form of a profession, as a community in which consensus is reached through open communication about knowledge and skills and in which all members can share their ideas and learn from each other. As we will discuss below, this has implications for the formation of knowledge and skills, in research and in education, as well as requiring an ethics of openness, in which reaching agreement is the aim, rather than winning the debate.

These ideas have been extended by Habermas (1990) in his concept of 'communicative action'. Habermas notes that there are different types of validity, each of which has its own logic that is expressed in language as the distinctions between 'truth', 'rightness' and 'truthfulness' (1990, p. 58). The first refers to what is propositionally true in the sense of being an objective fact. The second refers to what is normatively right in the sense of being legitimate in the inter-personal relationships within a society. The third refers to what each person may hold in her or his own subjective experience. For example, the statement that 'nurses must act as advocates for their patients' cannot be said to be objectively true (or false), but in so far as such a statement appears in a nursing code of ethics then it can be said to be normatively right; whether it is subjectively truthful depends on the individual situation of specific nurses. Of course, the statement that 'nursing codes of ethics require nurses to act as advocates for their patients' may be objectively true, in that such a statement can be examined by looking at such codes of ethics.

Habermas' model of discourse ethics then proceeds to set out the social basis by which normative rightness can be developed in such a way that it is not forced to fit into either notions of objective facts or of subjective experience. For Habermas, the importance of such an exercise is that although the validity of ethics cannot be reached by the methods of positivistic science (that is, they cannot be tested empirically on the basis of evidence), the alternative of ethics simply being a matter of subjective experience leads to the Nietzscheian conclusion that there is no such thing as truth. Although it may be argued that what Nietzsche was actually proposing is that the 'correspondence' view of truth (the world actually corresponds exactly to what we experience directly through senses and reason) is incorrect, this view has been used to argue that all ideas about what is true are equally valid (Robinson, 1999). Habermas is concerned that such a view undermines the very possibility of a democratic society, if taken to its logical conclusion. Thus it becomes clear that the sort of consensus that Habermas envisages is not simply one in which a closed group of people decide something among themselves. For example, medical practitioners and nurses contributed to the mid-twentieth century horrors of the Holocaust, especially in research on unwilling human victims (Johnstone, 1994, pp. 19–23). Yet, although these practices were deemed to be ethical by the professionals who were involved, in that they regarded these acts as normatively right among themselves, they were regarded as wrong by other contemporary groups in medicine and nursing, including others in Germany.

Habermas' (1990) concept of democracy is important here. He characterises a democratic society as one in which all people are able, as far as they have the capacity, to exchange ideas about truth, rightness and truthfulness. Seeking to preserve the idea of universal moral values, but recognising that the difference between truth and rightness means that this is not simply a matter of empirical observation to see who is factually correct, Habermas proposes a view of ethics derived from the 'practical discourse' of a society. By practical discourse he means the way in which people talk about things, in this case about ethics. He sums up in a 'principle of discourse ethics' that 'only those norms can claim to be valid that meet (or could meet) with the approval of all affected in their capacity as participants in a practical discourse' (Habermas, 1990, p. 93). The ethics of Nazi medical research clearly fail to meet such a principle, not least because the victims were denied the opportunity to withhold approval, but also because to the extent that they attempted to be included in the practical discourse they were not listened to. Similarly, from the perspective of ethics in practical discourse, it applies in any context that if any ideas or statements the agreement to which of anyone who is affected is either not obtained or could not be reached through appropriate processes, such ideas become sectional preferences. In that sense their enactment becomes a matter of power or force. Put simply, if service users could not agree with a profession's code of ethics, such a code does not meet the principles of discourse ethics. Habermas' argument (p. 122) is that, because his principle is a method and not a substantive statement of ethics as such, different formulations of ethics may be possible each of which meets the primary value of democratic communication.

Objectivity, subjectivity and relativism in professional ethics

An example of how this might appear in the practical discourse of caring professions is provided in Carr's (2000) discussion of different religious beliefs in the construction of the teaching profession. He observes that in the UK schools based on particular faith communities have expanded considerably in recent decades. (The same point can be made about Australia, Canada, New Zealand and the USA.) However, Carr argues (p. 136), debates about the ethical purposes and conduct of teaching should permit a discourse of teaching in which it does not matter if the participants are Buddhist, Christian, Jewish, Muslim or Secular Humanist. From this point, Carr extends his argument by linking the actions of individual practitioners with the larger purposes of the teaching profession, for example in the congruence of promoting the physical, psychological and spiritual well-being of children along with their intellectual development. Thus the actions of any teacher, no matter in which cultural setting they were practising, could be evaluated using moral norms that were accepted by the teaching profession as a whole and which would be supported by parents and pupils from diverse cultural backgrounds. At least with regard to matters of great seriousness, such as sexual exploitation of pupils by a teacher, the possibility of such a consensus seems likely.

Carr's argument is directly contrary to that of Azmi (1997), which has already been introduced in Chapter 2, concerning the legitimacy of social work in the traditional Muslim community of Toronto. For Azmi, it is not possible for all those who are affected by health and social welfare professions to agree with their norms. Precisely because of the difference of cultural world-views, in particular concerning the family, personal relationships, the authority of spiritual leaders in resolving community problems, and so on, Azmi's argument is that a moral consensus is not possible. So on this basis, because there is no practical discourse, the interventions of social workers in the traditional Muslim community are illegitimate. This is particularly the case for social work, because of the considerable extent to which it is based on a normative understanding about well-being, irrespective of the extent to which social workers have a developed body of empirically derived knowledge and skills. By implication, other health interventions would not necessarily be illegitimate in this way, in so far as they remained focused on physical treatments. However, they would need to be practised in a way which was culturally appropriate. Thus, aspects of occupational therapy, psychiatry and psychology clearly would not meet this requirement at all and as with social work the imposition of these professional practices, for example through state health and welfare services, could be regarded as unacceptable from this perspective (Azmi, 1997). (Tjelveit (2001) raises similar objections to the idea of universal norms from a Christian perspective.)

The question remains as to whether a universal approach to values can be contested simply by a refusal to participate in a practical discourse, or if the apparent disagreement stems more from a confusion between levels of generality and specificity. For example, almost all the major faith communities have norms such as that which is sometimes called the 'Golden Rule', which can have the negative form of 'do not do to others that which you would not wish them to do to you', or in its positive form 'do to others that which you would wish them to do to you' (Fasching & deChant, 2001). The Kantian categorical imperative forms the basis of a secular humanist version of this. Despite the language of preferences, this principle can be seen very broadly as an ethic of consistency. In simple terms, it is a proscription of hypocrisy and a prescription of congruence and integrity. It is consistent with the ethics of duty and of consequences, as well as with inter-subjective approaches such as ethics based on compassion, the ethics of care and ecological ethics. In postmodern ethics, too, there is scope for this notion, but it is in postmodern approaches that relativism enters the frame. Yet each of these approaches assumes that values and the reasons for holding some values and rejecting others can be subject to communication in the form of explanation and justification. Where appeals to universalism break down is when a position is asserted in which all members of a society are forcibly included, but not everyone can accept the basis of the moral values in question. An example of this might be the statement that 'abortion is wrong under all circumstances, because it is contrary to the will of God'. Such a statement not only asserts the position of the speaker, but makes a claim on the listener as well, irrespective of the listener's own moral values (or belief in God). Where it is possible for the listener then to speak and to reject the claim, the conditions of discourse ethics are achieved. Where this cannot happen is when a party to the discourse cannot accept the right of others to reject such a moral claim, but who regard it as their moral duty to enforce particular values on all members of a society. Abortion, euthanasia, physical punishment of children and the nature of the family are all examples of areas in which consensus does not exist in the contemporary world, precisely because of the assertion of a variety of normative positions, all of which have implications for the caring professions.

As Johnstone (1994, p. 175) states, simply because there are situations in which radical moral disagreement cannot be resolved does not of itself mean that the professions should not seek to establish the basis for ethical dialogue. Indeed, the debates between deontology, utilitarianism and principlism have not prevented a moral discourse leading to the formation of professional ethics and the production of codes that combine elements of each of these ways of considering ethics. In formal terms the professions claim to be open democratic discourses, with a sufficient degree of normative consensus to produce codes of ethics. However, while this idea draws on Habermas' notion of discourse ethics, that conception is, quite explicitly, a method of thinking about ethics at a high level of generality. The caring professions require a way of thinking about ethical and moral diversity that enables more specific communication to take place. The argument for discourse ethics is that, if they are not simply to impose the values of dominant groups, the professions need to be communities of ethical communication. While this is possible, it is highly contested, as revealed in Azmi's (1997) discussion of traditional Islamic communities in western countries, or the debate between Tjelveit (1999, 2001) and Hathaway (2001a, 2001b) from different positions within the Christian faith community (respectively arguing for relativist and universalist views of Christian moral norms).

Constructionism and critical realism in ethics

To help us to look further into this debate about universal and particular ethics, I want to turn to another aspect of social theory in which a similar set of issues is discussed. Delanty (1997) identifies the central concerns of early twenty-first century social theory in terms of the different contributions of constructionism (also called constructivism) and critical realism. The notion of 'construction' comes from the sociology of Berger and Luckmann (1966), who argued that knowledge and values are created, or constructed, through social process (that is, by human action in specific contexts). Thus, what is known and valued comes from our subjectivity, but it becomes objective in being shared and experienced as external to any one individual. On these grounds natural science is as much a product of particular societies at particular points in history as is social science, philosophy or theology. In contrast, critical realism argues that although knowledge and values are developed through communication they reflect an objective reality, however imperfectly (Bhaskar, 1986). According to Delanty (1997, pp. 129–30), critical realism rejects traditional positivism (only that which can be measured can be known) but at the same time still seeks a sufficient rigour for the critique of social actions and social institutions. Put simply, this is achieved by recognising that all knowledge and values are created in social contexts, but that they are capable of being tested and falsified (shown not to be true, right or truthful) by empirical evidence, by theoretical analysis, or a combination of the two.

The significance of this debate for professional ethics lies in the extent to which it is possible to make claims for moral values that apply to groups of people, as members of professions, who as individuals may hold very different views of the world. To explore this point, I want to look at one of the principles with which many members of caring professions engage in practice, that of 'human rights'. As we have already noted in previous chapters, all the professions draw on ideas of 'justice' or 'social justice' in some way, many of these in formal codes of ethics. These notions may be expressed tangibly in ideas about fairness, for example in the distribution of resources relative to 'need', or they may be seen in the operation of broader concerns with 'rights'. In the instance of rights, there are different ways in which these principles may be articulated. At the individual level, which is where many caring professionals work, there is the idea of 'patients' rights', 'clients' rights' or 'citizens' rights', which can be understood in various ways, such as the right to participate in decision making, or the right to explanations in plain language (Rhodes, 1986; Francis, 1999). As Johnstone points out (1994, p. 278) these more specific formulations of the idea of rights are all part of the larger notion of human rights and therefore have the same ethical and practical significance. As Habermas has argued (1990, p. 105), it is this idea that has given strength and stability to the claim that ethics can be universal at the level of principle.

Yet, as Leonard (1997) suggests, without an agreement about principles and the way in which they are to be interpreted, notions such as human rights can appear to be elusive. Concepts such as 'emancipation', 'equity' and 'justice' have derived their meaning, from before Kant, from the sense that they apply to all members of a society. If the claims of inter-subjective ethics are to be heard, however, questions must be raised about whether the universality of this principle is plausible. To examine this in more detail, we may consider the issue of domestic violence from the perspective of human rights. Domestic violence takes many forms, including acts of violence between adult partners, between parents and children, or between carers and other adults for whom they care. Sometime such acts may be understood clinically as 'abuse', but they are all types of acts that in many countries are also defined as crimes (Breckenridge, 1999). Such acts lead to problems that are responded to in different ways by all of the caring professions. They lead to physical injuries and they lead also to psycho-social harm. If a human rights perspective is taken, then the person against whom domestic violence is perpetrated has rights to safety, so that professionals have a corresponding duty to intervene. However, if a relativist position is adopted, then rights and duties have to be seen in the context of beliefs about appropriate relationships and actions that are held by the individuals who are involved and the community of which they are a part.

This can be seen in the following hypothetical example.

Mary, a woman aged in her late twenties, has been admitted to the emergency department of her local hospital. She has cuts and bruises on her face, neck, upper torso, arms and hands. After initially refusing to say how she was injured, she eventually tells the nurse who is treating her that her husband has assaulted her. She also adds that he has done this previously, but without harming her to the extent that she needed to seek treatment. Mary then tells the nurse that her husband has started to 'bash' their two children, who are aged 3 and 6. She has concealed the injury he caused to the older child, by keeping her away from school, but is now concerned that as his violence is getting worse the children are increasingly at risk.

Such a situation, while clearly severe, is encountered by caring professionals in many situations. From the perspective of codes of ethics, it would be both right and good for professional intervention to be initiated in response to this event. Indeed, as with the young woman in a sexual relationship with an older man, there are also legal implications in many countries that would, at least, require caring professionals to take action with regard to the safety of the children.

What may be at issue in this sort of situation is not whether caring professionals should be prepared to respond, but the basis on which they might do so. From a human rights position, Mary has a right to personal security and safety, as do her children. Her husband does not have the right to harm or threaten them, irrespective of any reason that he may claim for doing so. Such a position can be supported from a Kantian argument about autonomy of the individual or from a utilitarian approach in which the benefit of all involved is weighed. It can also be supported from an appeal to intelligent emotion (the flourishing of all members of the family is impaired), the ethics of care (members of the family and their relationships are harmed by violence), ethics of ecology (the right of all life to develop), and postmodern perspectives (being for the Other of the person who asks for help). Indeed, it seems totally implausible that any of these approaches, whether objective and universal, or intersubjective and particular, would support the idea that violence towards one's spouse and children is acceptable on grounds of normative rightness.

So, where does the sense that the ethics of human rights may be 'just one position among many' come from? To answer this we need to look again at the arguments about cultural specificity. First, we must be clear that arguments such as that of Azmi (1997) quite clearly are *not* defending domestic violence, child abuse or other challenges to human rights. There are many issues about how practices in the caring professions might respond appropriately to cultural differences (Whiteford & St Clair, 2002). But arguments about whether western professions are a cultural colonisation of non-western communities in general are more about questions of *who* will intervene and *how* they will do this. For Azmi, it is not that domestic violence, child abuse or other serious problems in family life are acceptable, but that for the traditional Muslim the right person to intervene is an Imam, or some other person whose moral authority is grounded in that community. Similarly, for Aboriginal Australians there are issues from the past concerning the forcible removal of children for eugenic reasons (often now referred to as 'cultural genocide') which make it very difficult for many Aboriginal people to accept the plausibility of health and social welfare interventions (Kidd, 2000).

One way out of the apparent circle into which such observations appear to lead is provided by the debate between Honneth (1995, 2001) and Fraser (2001) about the 'recognition' that is due to each person (including their values and beliefs) in an open and democratic society. Recognition here means the way in which the rights and values of each person or group are sustained in social life. The core of the matter is whether recognition (and its opposite, 'misrecognition') is a matter of rights or of identity. For Fraser, misrecognition is 'a serious violation of justice' (2001, p. 26), in which more powerful social groups force their values on other less powerful groups, and recognition is the positive response to people's right to their place in the society. For Honneth (2001), recognition concerns equity of esteem in which all members of a society are able to participate in fair or just social relations and so achieve self-realisation; misrecognition is the exclusion of people from society, which Honneth calls a 'moral injury' (p. 48).

Using the counterpoint between constructionism and critical realism, we can see that while ideas about values and identity are socially produced and sustained, there are also issues of material resources that are integral to social relationships (within families and communities as well as in the professions). Both social and material aspects of the world simultaneously have objective and subjective dimensions. So, while it is possible to agree with Honneth's view that recognition concerns values, Fraser's argument that recognition is about material differences and not just social attitudes must also be taken into account. This means that inequalities in access to material goods cannot be ignored: recognition concerns material and structural inequality *as well as* values (also see Plumwood, 2002, p. 94).

So, to return to the example of Mary in the hospital emergency department, we can begin to think about the differences that her identity, in terms of her ethnicity or 'race', her socio-economic class, her age and so on, may present to the caring professionals who are responding to her situation. This does not mean that the values of human rights can only be applied to Mary, or her children, if she is recognised as having a particular identity. Rather, it means that the tasks of the caring professionals who would be involved include finding ways to promote Mary's participation in defining what is good and what is right in this situation, such as in working out what outcomes she wants and what she thinks is possible (Wise, 1995; Des Jardin, 2001a). Fraser's (2001) point is that it would also require ensuring that Mary can access the resources necessary for her to pursue a good resolution for her situation. Her husband's participation would also be required, in so far as his actions did not deny Mary her right to participation, as he too would be owed recognition even though his specific actions (and, perhaps, values) would be challenged in this process. As Whiteford and St Clair (2002) observe, cultural competence is a means to engaging with the ethics of practice, not simply a technique, and in this context 'culture' not only concerns ethnicity, but includes all issues of social values and relationships.

Towards discursive ethics

Habermas' (1990) concept of discourse ethics, which was outlined above, is based on the idea that agreement between all participants in a practical discourse is achievable at a fairly high level of generality. This might mean that a great deal of detail is left to be worked out in specific situations, in which problems of communication and recognition remain as matters of individual competence and performance. Of course, all ways of looking at professional ethics require individual practitioners to engage with the application of principles to concrete instances in the everyday world. However, while some approaches provide quite specific principles, discourse ethics outlines a process. In so far as it has a moral content, it is the principle (or value) of practical discourse in social democracy. As we saw in Chapter 5, a similar point has been made about the ethics of care (Allmark, 1995, 1996; Bradshaw, 1996) in the question concerning how we might know what values are congruent with care, which is also itself a value as well as a practice (Tronto, 1993). In this respect, discourse ethics can be seen as another 'new approach' to ethics in the same way as those that have been discussed in previous chapters.

However, it is also the case that discourse ethics as such cannot be 'applied' to the questions about practice that face the caring professions in the same way as ideas such as emotional intelligence and compassion, care, life and sustainability, virtue and so on. Yet, as a process the underlying notion of 'discursive' social relations, those that are based on the practical principle of open discourse, can be used to consider the ways in which professional ethics are developed and form the basis for practice. By this I mean that because all approaches to ethics have to be articulated in some way with the experienced realities of practice, a discursive process has the potential to enable all those who are participants in practice to speak and be heard. Discursive ethics is, therefore, the conduct of dialogue about that which is good (values) and that which is right (actions) in professional practice, in which all those who are affected can participate, including all members of the caring professions, service users, and other members of the societies in which these practices take place.

Discursive ethics not only concerns values at high levels of generality, but also the minutiae of the day-to-day provision of professional caring services. It is seen in examples that have been used in previous chapters, including the negotiation of the meaning of respect in an encounter between a European Canadian nurse and Inuit patients (Browne, 1995) and the reactions of palliative care physicians to relationships with dying patients (MacLeod, 2001). It is also seen in the debates within and between professions, and between professionals, managers and policy makers about the purposes of the work of the caring professions and how these may be achieved. Discursive ethics is a way of 'doing' ethics, in that it provides a methodology for the construction and reconstruction of values and actions, but it also embodies the specific values of participation, inclusion and recognition. In that respect it can provide a means by which competing theories and concepts in professional ethics can be considered and debated.

The main weakness of a discursive approach, as has been discussed above, is that it does assume open, consensus-building communication, in which the value of communication as a process itself is paramount over any particular outcome including that of an actual consensus. As Warnke (1995, p. 259) notes, in practical discourse the possibility of difference and disagreement remains, even where people share strong common values. Using the example of debates between feminist perspectives on surrogate motherhood, Warnke points out that 'agreeing to disagree' may be unavoidable. But this also requires that absolute points of view, which would exclude the right of others to be considered, are not allowable. Being accorded the right to participate requires a response that accepts Apel's (1984) third criterion, namely the commitment to participate and to give recognition to other perspectives and value claims. Where this cannot be achieved a discursive approach to ethics can only make an appeal to the possibility of communication. Between the person who seeks an open and participative discourse and the person who wants to 'win the argument' by asserting a position that has already been decided there can be little common ground. Nonetheless, where people are committed to open communication, discursive ethics is more likely to achieve this, and to assist caring professionals to negotiate the intricacies of ethical issues in practice, than is either an appeal to an absolute position or accepting that diversity means that only relativism can be plausible.

Conclusion

In this chapter the idea of communication as the basis of ethics has been examined and related to debates about objectivity and subjectivity in knowledge, values and action. Habermas' (1990) 'discourse ethics' provides a way of developing a shared ethical dialogue in which agreement is a primary value, as compared to the assertion of any single over-arching principle. In the realm of social theory, constructionism and critical realism provide models of how objectivity and subjectivity may be brought together in understanding how knowledge and values are developed through social action. The principle of human rights and its application in practice shows how a broad common ground of values can be achieved. However, some limitations of cultural relativity remain, especially when individuals or groups are not committed to seeking agreement. The debate between objectivity and subjectivity also shows that the possibility of achieving common values cannot be assumed. It is also important to consider material and structural limitations to participation, so that a discursive approach does not form an 'oppressive unity' that is superimposed on the values that different perspectives bring to ethical debates (Plumwood, 2002, pp. 91–2).

Discursive ethics, produced from extensive dialogue that involves all those who have an interest in the outcome, at least potentially, can be a process that enables each individual and group to be heard, to listen and to be accorded recognition. In the next two chapters this concept will be examined in more detail. First, in Chapter 9, the implications of new approaches to ethics for future possibilities concerning codes of ethics are examined. Then, in the final chapter, the implications of a discursive approach to the continuing development of professional ethics will be explored.

CHAPTER 9

Re-evaluating Professional Ethics

Challenges for ethics in the caring professions

In the previous chapter the idea of discursive ethics was discussed as a basis for a practical response to ethical pluralism. This chapter looks at the challenge that a discursive approach creates for the re-evaluation of professional ethics, examining in particular the implications of contemporary ideas for codes of ethics.

Four substantive approaches to ethics have been considered in detail in Chapters 4 to 7: the ethics of compassion as an intelligent emotion; the ethics of care; the ethics of ecology; and postmodern ethics. Each chapter examined a substantive approach in relation to key aspects of the caring professions that were outlined in Chapter 3, that is the content (practices), the focus (objectives), the social relations and the social mandate of these professions. However, these four developments in ethical thought have so far been discussed separately and in this chapter we turn to the task of examining commonalities and differences. In doing so we will also return to the questions that were outlined in Chapter 2, that is whether professional ethics is universal or particular, whether it is binding or guiding on practice, whether it is explicit or implicit and whether it should be understood as properties of individuals or of society.

Contemporary approaches to ethics each offer a challenge to the more traditional, liberal ethics. However, because in different ways and to different degrees they are relational, situational and contain elements of subjectivity, the incorporation of such approaches in *professional* ethics may appear to be problematic. A strength of the more traditional liberal ethics is that general statements can be made about professional practice, precisely because such ethical approaches are based on formal reason. A profession is a collective entity that is made up of people who, it is reasonable to assume, will not share all their values. So some means must be found to create a general set of principles for definition of good practice that can be taken to apply to all members of the group if we are to be able to speak of professional ethics at all and not simply of the ethics of professionals. As we have already noted in Chapters 1 and 3, codes of ethics have the function both of providing a moral framework for thought and action and of constituting 'laws' governing right action by individual members of any particular profession. The advantage of an ethics based on reason is that it permits the development of rules (which in the case of deontology are inherent). Such rules are easily communicated and can be applied generally across a professional group.

The issue of how relational ethics might be applied in practice is illustrated by Sumison's (2000) discussion of a student who seeks exemptions from assignment deadlines but gives self-contradicting explanations to different teachers and who resists taking responsibility for her own work (see Chapter 5 above). This has echoes in other professions, in which practitioners may also encounter patients or clients who similarly deny or resist their own responsibilities in achieving health and well-being. The challenge for the caring professions in such circumstances is to avoid the extremes of being drawn into collusion on the one hand or of anger in rejecting the person as a defence against the assumption about one's own integrity that the demand of the other appears to create. As Sumison (2000) notes, these extremes can only be avoided through conscious ethical awareness and emotional resilience (also see Stevens, 2000). The ethics of compassion, ethics of care, ethics of ecology and postmodern ethics each offer a different route to resolving this example of integrity. Yet their conclusions may appear to be very similar, in that all approaches are likely to agree that collusion or rejection fail to meet their core values: neither of these responses demonstrates compassion, embodies care, engages with the person in their environment, reveals the virtuous self of the professional or is 'for' the 'other'. Deontology, utilitarian and principlist arguments are also likely to support the same outcome.

However, as Tännsjö (2002, p. 136) points out, we cannot simply accept all approaches as equally valid, because they incorporate different assumptions. Although agreement on many matters may be possible there is also the question of our own intellectual and emotional integrity. In Sumison's (2000) example, the teacher may be expected on a variety of ethical grounds to insist on the requirements of the course being met but each of these grounds will be based on core values that affect both how and why a particular way of dealing with the matter is pursued. Thus, in a context in which competing value positions are brought to the task of what determines right action and good objectives, the means and ends that can be agreed by people holding different value positions will be the ones that command legitimate authority in formal ethical codes. In this case, we may agree that the teacher acts rightly by taking the student's circumstances *and* the rights of all students into account, while also upholding the importance of integrity in the process.

The way in which the professions have dealt with ethical diversity has tended to be through the formulation of codes of ethics that are held to apply to all members of a given profession. While there is wide variation in the specific approaches that are taken, there is a tendency to gloss over the possibility of contradictions and to combine elements from deontology, utilitarianism and principlism in the way such codes are constructed (Rhodes, 1986). Where elements of codes taken from different approaches produce an equivalent outcome in action this may not be of practical concern. Sumison's example of the teacher was intended to illustrate the ethics of care, but it also shows how other approaches can be brought together in a practical way. However, in seeking to combine insights from different approaches there are inherent risks that professionals may find themselves in a double-bind, for example in trying to operationalise a deontological notion of respect for persons and a utilitarian idea of justice in rationing scarce resources (see, for example, the debate about rationing health resources on grounds of age that is summarised in Chapter 6).

If contemporary developments in ethics are to have any impact in professional ethics (being less amenable to the formulation of rules than the more traditional liberal ethics) then the caring professions must grasp the implications of these developments for the processes of reviewing and revising formal statements of ethics. They cannot be simply grafted onto already hybrid entities. For this reason, a discursive approach to professional ethics would seem to be vital for both the construction and the use of codes of ethics within the caring professions. In conditions of ethical diversity there is an effective choice between seeking an inclusive view of ethics that recognises and responds to different values and a view that tries to remove difference in an assertion of a single statement of what is good and what is right.

Codes of ethics in the caring professions

In order to begin to examine how a discursive approach might relate to codes of ethics I will look at the codes that are current for a representative variety of caring professions in Australia. The points I will draw from this comparison will also be applicable to codes in other countries (see, for example, Johnson *et al.*, 1995; Schmidt, 2000). These professions are medicine (AMA, 2003), nursing (ANC *et al.*, 2001), occupational therapy (OTA, 2001), pharmacy (in hospitals) (SHPA, 1996), physiotherapy (APA, 2003), psychology (APS, 2002), social work (AASW, 2002) and teaching (NSWTF, 2002).

The overall structures and contents of these codes are very similar in three respects. First, with the exception of the code for teachers, they all contain statements about the purpose and application of the code. These are based on notions of 'guiding' the appropriate practices of members of the profession. These statements may be brief, as in the code for hospital pharmacists, or lengthy and detailed, as in the codes for nursing and social work. The idea of guidance in this context refers to the way in which a member of the profession might apply a specific principle or rule, it does not imply that following the requirement of application is optional according to one's own values or preferences. It is clear that these codes are intended to be binding.

Second, all these codes provide detailed statements about what is considered to be 'right action' on the part of members of the different professions. That is, they stipulate in terms of behaviours what would or would not constitute 'good practice' on the part of any individual and in that sense are 'binding'. Examples include restrictions on making public comments about another member of the profession and other forms of 'loyalty', proscriptions on engaging in sexual relationships with service users or other forms of exploitation, maintaining appropriate confidentiality about all service users, ensuring one's own competence and acting honestly.

The third point of commonality, and perhaps that which is most central to the focus of this discussion, is that all these codes are based on a pluralist ethical approach. While only some codes contain statements about the values that underpin the purposes, application and requirements of the codes, in each case these the codes are variations on the 'principlist' synthesis of respect for persons, beneficence, non-maleficence and justice, with particular detailed references to values such as autonomy, honesty, veracity, fairness, dedication to service and so on (see Chapter 1 above). In those instances where explanatory statements or discussions of principles are provided there is clearly a close similarity in the values of good relationships and right action. Where the statements may differ is in the exact way that a principle is applied to the specific role and tasks of any one profession. Nonetheless, there does appear to be a high degree of consensus between the caring professions in Australia about the principles that provide the foundation for ethics. As Gallagher (1999) notes, these are principles that form the foundations of codes of ethics world-wide.

Five of these eight Australian codes of ethics contain an explicit discussion of the philosophy that lies behind principles and their application (medicine, nursing, occupational therapy, physiotherapy and social work). In the instances of medicine, occupational therapy and physiotherapy this is quite brief, taking the form of statements linking the codes to ideas of respect, rights and responsibilities. Nursing and social work each provide a much more extensive explanation of the ideas on which their code is based. In these instances there appears to be a focus on giving an account to members of these professions of the philosophical basis on which the subsequent categorical statements are based. In this context, the nursing code discusses nurses as 'autonomous moral agents' who are responsible and accountable for their actions (ANC *et al.*, 2002, p. 2), while the social work code similarly 'holds [social workers] accountable for practising in accordance with their [ethical] responsibilities' (AASW, 2002, p. 2). In these two codes those who are bound by their imperatives are explicitly engaged in a discursive process within the structure of the documents themselves. This is not to suggest that Australian nurses or social workers are being invited to dispute the requirements of these statements, at least not at the point of individual practice with service users. What is happening here is that the 'rules' of good practice are grounded in an overt presentation of the discursive basis on which they have been established. The members of these professions, and others such as service users or members of different professions, could use these statements to engage discursively with the relevant professional body about the ethics of practice.

The range of codes of ethics considered here thus includes relatively minimal forms, such as those of hospital pharmacists and teachers which are entirely in the form of a list of statements of right conduct, through to those in nursing and social work in which there is a discussion of the philosophy on which the codes are based. What is suggested by this variation is a degree of ambivalence about whether the purpose of such codes is solely to provide binding rules for action or whether it is to engage the members of the profession and others in a wider consideration of what constitutes ethical practice in the profession.

In a review of the codes of ethics of professional associations of social work world-wide, Banks (2001, p. 93) distinguishes between various forms of ethics. Banks notes that for the South African Black Social Workers Association ethics takes the form of an 'oath' similar in concept to the Hippocratic Oath. In contrast, in other countries various degrees of complexity are brought to the development of principles and duties as the way in which codes of ethics are constructed and used. This compares to the quite explicit focus on duties in other professions, such as the Spanish nurses' code, which is actually entitled a 'deonto-logical code' rather than a 'code of ethics' (Rogero-Anaya *et al.*, 1994).

Codes of ethics, in all of their diverse forms, are produced within the profession to which they apply. Furthermore, they tend to be written by groups of members of a profession who have a special inter-est or responsibility in ethical issues, with or without the involvement of moral philosophers or professional ethicists. Thus, as Hussey (1996, p. 253) notes in a discussion of nursing ethics, there is a risk that the special nature of the tasks of caring professions may lead to arguments about ethics that remove the professions from the ordinary moral values of the society in which they are practising. Under such circum-stances the production of codes of ethics may be far from discursive and can lead to a sense that ethics is a source of determination of what is good or right in and of itself, based solely on the formal reasoned statements of a recognised authority in the guise of a professional association (Hussey, 1996, p. 254).

In contrast to the general trends in the production of codes of ethics, the Aotearoa/New Zealand Association of Social Workers code of ethics (NZASW, 1993) was produced through an extensive debate within the association. Of particular concern was the way in which Maori values and the recognition of Maori culture were excluded from the preceding code. Two main points can be seen in the Aotearoa/New Zealand code, namely the way in which an inclusive and discursive process was used to develop the code and the extent to which it has brought together values from different cultural points of reference. In order for a code to bring together differing values in a way that is com-plimentary it was necessary for a much greater number and diversity of groups and individuals to participate than would be the case in most professional associations. The outcome is a code that is able to embrace values from both Maori and non-indigenous cultures.

For Briskman and Noble (1999) the NZASW code of ethics represents a unique attempt to engage with diversity in formal professional ethics. Attention to specifics of Maori culture such as the centrality of the extended family in Maori life, with its implications for liberal ideas of respect for persons and individual autonomy, is incorporated. As we have noted in earlier chapters, this is an issue that faces other countries in which the caring professions must respond to different cultures (compare with: Blackhall *et al.*, 1995; Carrese & Rhodes, 1995). However, the way that this is dealt with in the NZASW code is in the form of separate sections that specify Maori values and the ethical implications that flow from them. So Banks (2001, p. 99) questions the extent to which this way of dealing with diversity actually produces the combination of critical and postmodern ethics that Briskman and Noble suggest it achieves (1999, p. 65). Banks' point that there is still a long way to go before it might be said that a postmodern code had been developed is well made, because Maori and non-indigenous groups are dealt with separately and the NZASW code remains liberal and individualistic in its main structure. Yet, at the same time, the NZASW code goes further than others in seeking to integrate different positions. In this sense, it represents a unique practical step towards a professional ethics that brings together points of difference.

Ethics or standards of practice?

Banks' (2001, p. 99) underlying argument is that all codes of ethics are, by their very nature, both prescriptive (they specify what should be done) and general (they include categories of people rather than individuals, such as 'all social workers' or 'all Maori people'). Consequently Banks repeatedly doubts that ethics based on emotions, care or postmodern perspectives can provide a sound enough foundation for the professions. As we have seen in Chapter 5, this view is shared by Allmark (1995, 1996) in relation to nursing. Yet in both cases these discussions emphasise the point that although formal ethical frameworks must tend towards the specific in terms of content and the universal in terms of who they address they also require core values unless they are to become sets of rules that are grounded only in the authority of dominant perspectives within a given professional association. To return to Hussey's (1996) observations about nursing, if the basis for statements about right action and good purposes rests only in such authority we would no longer be speaking of ethics but of rules and procedures. The alternative position is to recognise that values, while inherent in codes of ethics, are often highly contested and so professions must find ways of promoting a continual discursive process about how codes of ethics are used and how they are modified and developed over time.

Hussey's point stands as a critique of a tendency for many 'ethical' codes to rest on organisational and procedural authority and for this to be seen as positive. For example, basing his analysis on social work in the USA, Reamer (2001) identifies four periods of development in professional ethics. These are:

- the morality period – in which good practice was seen as that which upheld conventional morality;
- the values period – in which social workers debated the underlying values of their profession, such as 'respect for all people', 'justice' and so on;
- the period of ethical theory and decision making – in which conscious exploration of theories was related to the development of skills in applying ethics in practice;
- the period of ethical standards and risk management – in which ethics are prescribed in great detail as standards of conduct and so ethical risks (such as boundary violations and incompetence) are managed effectively.

For Reamer this last period represents a 'dramatic maturation of social workers' understanding of ethical issues' (2001, p. 17). This is because such a construction of ethics permits the profession to specify right conduct in exact and explicit terms, for example in relation to sexual relationships with clients, and enables legal liabilities to be dealt with more precisely. The same concern is event in other professions in the USA (Jordan & Stevens, 1999).

Reamer's main concern in his analysis of 'ethical standards and risk management' is that there are an increasing number of complaints and lawsuits against social workers in the USA (2001, p. 18). He notes that this is a phenomenon shared with other professions but one that is largely seen in the USA compared to other countries. Much of the cause of complaints and legal action is to be found in failures to comply with the professional codes of ethics, such as in inappropriate handling of confidentiality, boundary violations (including sexual and financial), incompetence, failure to obtain informed consent, defamation, and so on. This does not mean that social workers or other caring professions in the USA act in less acceptable ways than elsewhere; it is more likely to be a reflection of the culture of individual rights and litigation as a way of achieving redress that predominates in the USA. Nevertheless, Reamer's discussion raises the question of whether the purpose of professional ethics is to promote good and right practice or to prevent complaints and lawsuits. The former implies an assumption that the moral fabric of the professions is to seek the good of all who are concerned with them (as practitioners, service users or fellow citizens), the latter conveys a sense of being focused on seeking to limit harm in such a way that it gives an emphasis to the protection of the profession. Ethics as the deliberation of what is good and right includes the collective or social aspects of professional ethics while focusing on the prevention of complaints and lawsuits is more individualistic. In that sense a concern with risk management and ethics as 'standards of practice' appears congruent with contemporary neo-liberalism (Hugman, 1998).

The countervailing view of professional ethics, as we have noted above, is that it is not possible to take risk and uncertainty out of professional life. Ethics involves a process in which values are considered through theory and practice, constantly being tested and retested through decision making in action. Allmark's (1995, 1996) and Banks' (2001) objections to relational or situational ethics are not a matter of seeking to produce precise and specific rules of conduct; rather, they both share Hussey's (1996) concern about the reduction of ethics to quasi-legal procedures. What they are rejecting is the opposing possibility that ethics could become the personal and private concern of each individual member of the caring professions acting separately within the specific circumstances of their own situations. In other words, the challenge is how professional ethics might cover all members of a profession, be explicit and public, while at the same time guiding and supporting individual practitioners in making ethical sense of decisions between competing possible actions.

Some codes of ethics in the caring professions refer to statements or codes of 'conduct' or 'standards of practice'. For example, among the Australian professional bodies, the code of the Australian Physiotherapy Association (APA, 2003) is called a 'Code of Conduct'. However, this is prefaced with a preamble and statement of ethical principles and in terms of its structure and content can be seen as a code of ethics in the same way as can the codes of the other professions. Moreover, in contrast to some of the other codes of ethics, the physiotherapy 'code of conduct' states that it is 'a dynamic statement which reflects the changing expectations of physiotherapists and the Australian community at large' and that it 'is subject to regular review to maintain its relevance and merit' (APA, 2003, p. 3). Similarly, many codes contain very clear statements of conduct that are phrased in such a way that they are binding on any individual, repeatedly using forms such as 'Physiotherapists are ...' or 'Social workers shall ...'. Such statements both require the members of the relevant profession to engage in or refrain from particular acts and bind them to specified values. These are, in the terms we have been considering here, ethical statements because although they are categorical they are founded in explicit principles that are capable of being considered and debated by all those to whom these statements apply.

The notion of a 'code of conduct' implies something quite different from that of ethics. Bauman's (1994) criticism of the modern contexts of professional practice, bureaucracy and business, is that they place considerable constraint on engagement with ethics (see Chapter 7 above). Both types of organisations tend to separate professionals from each other and to define their actions in organisational terms. The act of 'whistle-blowing' is a particular example of how this might be understood as a struggle between competing loyalties. In conditions where professionals are defined primarily in terms of their role in an organisation, rather than as members of a distinct occupational group whose identity crosses organisational boundaries, the idea that they should be required, or even just guided, to act in ways that are not within the control of the particular institution or agency is challenging to notions of hierarchical control. Yet, as Johnstone observes (1994, p. 110), the categorical statements of 'codes of conduct' in organisations at best are matters not of ethics but of etiquette and at worst they may be devices by which the moral sensibilities of professional staff are rendered illegitimate.

While 'codes of conduct' may of themselves be useful in so far as they enable practitioners to judge particular actions in a technical sense, they cannot be a substitute for the engagement with values, whether moral or non-moral, that is the substance of ethics. Organisationally based 'codes of conduct' cannot replace the importance of practitioners being able to think through, and so take responsibility for, the values that are integrated with practice and not confined to external considerations of context or the purposes of practice that might be decided separately from the act of practice itself. Technique and values are not separable in this way; claims that distinguish and separate values from practice are mistaken either because they do not recognise the values that are thus imposed from elsewhere or they make values invisible both to practitioners and to their service users.

Pluralism in professional ethics

The conclusion that the actions of professionals concern ethics and not simply technical standards makes the question of competing ethical approaches pressing. Is there a basis on which competing values and ways thinking ethically can be brought to bear on professional practice that responds to diversity but does not fall into the problems of relativism? This is precisely the problem addressed by Kekes (1993) in his discussion of ethical pluralism, which he defines as a middle ground between relativism (that there is no way of deciding between values or approaches in any given situation) and monism (that there is one dominant value and associated ethical approach). For Kekes, ethical pluralism requires that we recognise that there is a plurality of values that may be held by reasonable people, all of which are conditional (as opposed to absolute). Some values are primary (being relatively context independent) while others are secondary (being context dependent). However, because values may be incompatible (not able to be reconciled) or incommensurable (not able to be compared) value conflict is inevitable; the resolution of value conflict is found in a balance between values. Judgement between approaches is based on the extent to which they support the achievement of these characteristics.

Tännsjö (2002) takes a somewhat different view of how competing ethical approaches may be related to professional ethics, arguing that some aspects of relational or situational ethics can be easily combined with other ethical approaches, because they do not contain specific normative criteria. For instance, '[t]he virtues are of importance, no matter what basic moral principle we accept, and among them the tendency to care for others plays a crucial role' (p. 136). Yet the ethics of care itself is rejected precisely because it *has* a normative content, caring defined as a good in itself (Tännsjö, 2002, p. 115). Such a view seems limited in comparison to the pluralist position. It fails to grasp the reasonable way in which ethical approaches may be incompatible with each other, but that a balance may be found between them. It also does not recognise that reconciling conflicting ideas simply by subordinating some leaves absolute conceptions intact without grappling with the implications of doing so.

In the concrete examples of professional ethics that we have considered there is already a plural relationship between rationalist approaches such as deontology and utilitarianism in principlism. Given the widespread acceptance of this way of constructing ethics, it would seem reasonable also to include other approaches, including those which are relational, situational or subjective as part of the ethical discourse of the caring professions. This is especially the case as notions such as compassion, emotion, care, responsibility for the social and physical environment, a concern for life and 'being-for-Other' are connected with the purposes of these professions and so clearly form part of their values.

One of the benefits of recognising such issues in ethics is that in the discursive process the importance of ethics making sense in individual instances of practice can be grasped. The contemporary collapsing of 'ethics' into concepts such as 'standards' or 'conduct' fails to do this because, in seeking to be universal, explicit and precise, recognition of the difficulties of applying different approaches in complex situations is sometimes lost. But, as we have noted, seeing ethics as 'risk management' makes particular sense in the neo-liberal commodification of the work of the caring professions as a product to be consumed (compare with Hugman, 1998). The standardisation of the processes through which health, well-being, learning and spiritual wholeness are produced does not easily accommodate the idea of discretion, contested moral norms or a plurality of values.

In the context of neo-liberalism, reflected both in the socio-economic structures within which the caring professions practise and in the highly individualised culture of rights that leads to complaints and lawsuits, it is reasonable that a profession should not leave a code of ethics open to contradiction in interpretation. For example, all the Australian codes that have been examined in this chapter incorporate the principle that professionals should act with honesty and integrity towards service users and should not exploit service users. As a principle, this is consistent with a duty of respect for autonomous moral agents, with a utilitarian argument about the benefit or harm resulting from particular actions and with the principles of beneficence and non-maleficence. Nor, of course, would any of the relational, situational or subjective approaches to ethics that have been discussed in earlier chapters support an act that could be understood as dishonest or exploitative. At the level of the justification of broad statements of values debates between the different ethical approaches may be fruitful. Choosing what is right for reasons of compassion, care and so on, as opposed to abstract ideas of duty, could be said to expand the range of ethical understanding and provide deeper accounts that are congruent with the purposes of the caring professions. For example, giving regard to matters of honesty, integrity, non-exploitation and so on is not just a question of duty, but their opposites would also be a misrecognition of compassion, care, 'being-for-Other' and so on. However, given the range of possible normative positions held by individual professionals there is also a practical necessity in defining in broad terms what would actually constitute honesty, integrity and not exploiting service users. Thus professional codes of ethics can plausibly provide guidance in great detail and at the same time seek to avoid creating an absolute position out of any one ethical approach.

Conclusion

This chapter has looked at some implications for professional codes of ethics that arise from consideration of the contemporary approaches that have been examined in previous chapters. In particular, the importance of codes of ethics has been highlighted. Codes of ethics have developed as a means of providing a moral framework for individuals who may each draw on very different normative backgrounds but who share a common identity as members of the same profession. As such, codes of ethics provide guidance for practitioners about right conduct and good objectives and at the same time they can also serve as categorical rules governing professional action. Contemporary, relational approaches raise important questions about this latter aspect of codes and serve both as a reminder that ethics must be applied in every specific situation and as ways of thinking afresh about ethical issues in professional practice.

It has been suggested here that ethical pluralism provides a more appropriate way of re-evaluating professional ethics than the tendency towards collapsing ethics into 'standards' or rules of 'conduct'. Pluralism also provides a way of responding to changes in moral philosophy, as in notions such as compassion, care, ecology and postmodern ethics. Because it does not give an absolute position to any one of the more dominant traditions, the plural perspective leaves open the possibility that other ways of defining values may be considered. In this way it points the caring professions towards the important task of conscious reflection and application that constitutes professional ethics.

CHAPTER 10

Discursive Professional Ethics

The conditions for discursive ethics

Finding ways to ensure that ethics is seen as a primary concern in the caring professions (in the contemporary idiom, that it is recognised as 'core business') is as pressing as it has ever been (Balogh *et al.*, 1989). There are pressures to conflate ethics with rules for conduct or defences against complaints and lawsuits, or even to regard ethics as optional. Stevens (2000) notes that attending to ethics can be difficult, challenging and sometimes quite risky. Consequently members of the caring professions may be drawn to rationalisations that explain away the ethical dimensions of practice. The list of possible defences against engaging with ethics includes:

- ethics only matters if you are talking about ethics;
- ethics is what other people think is acceptable;
- ethics is made up by people who do not understand practice;
- ethics only matters if practice is visible to others;
- ethics only concerns people who are unimportant;
- ethics does not matter if you are busy. (Stevens, 2000, p. 177)

As Stevens observes, although such statements may appear frivolous they are encountered in practice and among students preparing to join the caring professions. However, this is not to suggest that the caring professions attract people who particularly regard ethics as irrelevant or irksome. On the contrary, finding such views in the caring professions may even be a surprise. Certainly it reflects that the individual members of professions are part of the wider society, across which such views are at least equally as prevalent. Yet when voiced in the caring professions such rationalisations are inimical to good practice, because by marginalising ethics practitioners reduce what is good and right in practice to matters of technique or expedience.

The tendency among some members of caring professions to treat ethics as a marginal concern reflects a view that ethics is abstract, existing separately from practice, or that it is constituted by formal sets of rules that are alien to the interests and motivations of practitioners. It is against this misapprehension that the ethics of compassion, the ethics of care, the ethics of ecology and postmodern ethics offer alternative ways of thinking that open up a new dialogue. If the discursive development of ethics in the caring professions is to take account of such new approaches we need not only to consider codes of ethics (as discussed in the previous chapter) but also to explore the ways in which ethics can be integrated more explicitly as an element of everyday practice. That is, ethics has to be seen as part of thinking about practice as much as debates about knowledge or skills would be.

The rationalisations that marginalise ethics must be seen in context. There may be many reasons why members of the caring professions see ethics in terms of expedience or who experience ethics as something that contradicts other demands to make choices and act in particular ways. Let us take as an example the members of a multi-disciplinary team working in the care of older people who are given an instruction by the manager of the service to limit the range of options they consider when assessing or reviewing the needs of service users and to restrict their intervention to a maximum of a set number of hours. The members of the team might respond to this situation by accepting that resources are limited and, taking a utilitarian perspective, work out a way of ensuring that those people whom they assess as being in most need will get the most service, working to an average use of resources across all service users rather than setting the same limit for each individual. However, the team members might take a more deontological position by asserting their duty to practise in such a way that each service user is considered in terms of the best possible assessment of their individual needs and given as much service as they are deemed to require, thus challenging the manager's instruction. (They also may look to the codes of ethics from the specific professions to support such a position but, as we have noted, these codes may also contain injunctions to consider justice and fairness, which also support a utilitarian position.)

The introduction of ideas about compassion, care, ecology and 'being-for-the-Other' will all make the situation even more complex, as these approaches tend in different ways towards positions that lie in between relative and absolute stances. For example, the ethics of compassion might suggest the use of criteria such as the subjective meaning of a service user's situation, and the views of the team members about the moral scale of the person's plight. On these grounds professionals might begin to construct an ethos for different responses to different people. However, some aspects of this notion will immediately conflict with the impersonal values of fairness that usually are incorporated in assessment schedules. Moreover, if the idea of making judgements about the moral desert of a service user is included in this process it would be contrary to widely held values within the caring professions. Thus we can see that the ethical approaches that have been explored in this book could be taken seriously in everyday practice but that implications such as these must be addressed.

In a discussion of feminist ethics and the ethics of care, Held (1993) raises the question of whether different ethical approaches are appropriate for different contexts. That is, should the ethics of care be seen as relevant to situations of caring, while more abstract approaches, such as deontology or utilitarianism be seen as relevant to issues such as social policy? Held's answer is that such a view would be implausible, precisely because all ethical theories, whether abstract or relational, make claims to apply to all contexts. Consequently she proposes that abstract ideas and principles can be useful in ethical reasoning if they are embedded in 'patterns of morality arrived at through the course of feminist moral inquiry' (Held, 1993, p. 219). The same, of course, would be arguable in terms of compassion, ecology and those aspects of postmodern ethics that are not totally relativistic.

This argument leaves our multi-disciplinary team caring for older people in no clearer position about one 'correct' way to consider the ethical challenges of their manager's instructions, but it does provide a way of thinking about the competing claims of different ethical approaches. Of course, it cannot be assumed that all the members of the team will favour the same approach. They come from different professional backgrounds and, we may anticipate, will have experienced other influences in their moral development. It may also be the case that they are so busy that they cannot get together to discuss such issues, or that there is a perceived threat to continued employment if they do not comply with the instructions they have been given. What will support them in the process of responding to the ethical demands of their practice context, both individually and collectively, will be the extent to which they are ethically equipped to understand their practice and whether there are wider structures (such as professional associations and trade unions) that can facilitate and support such considerations. Also at issue here is the education in ethics that has been experienced by people entering the caring professions and their subsequent encounter with the wider professional terrain. This includes the social expectations of the caring professions, their own understanding of themselves (including the potential and limits of their knowledge and skills) and the general social circumstances conducive to open reflection and debate. Most crucially, they have to have the capacity to reach a decision about what is the right thing to do.

Unsettling ethics

As Rhodes (1986) has pointed out, particular professional ethics not only presuppose a degree of consensus about the means and ends of practices, but also assume certain values about the social context within which practice occurs. Social context can be taken to include both the wider social, economic and political structures that form the milieu of the caring professions and the more specific relationships within the caring professions, between professions and between professions and other social institutions. Rhodes' (1986) examples include the different political value positions that might affect the context of practice, and differences in religious belief that similarly might have implications for the definition of objectives and of good ways to achieve them. We can add to this other ways of defining 'the good life' that are formed and supported in the social circumstances surrounding each member of the caring professions. Most western ethicists, including Kant ([1785] 1964) and Mill ([1861] 1910), as well as more recent approaches such as Habermas' (1990) concept of discourse ethics, assume a participative democracy in which citizens are sufficiently free to exercise moral responsibility. Alongside formal political freedom we may add a sufficient degree of freedom within social institutions, such as employing agencies, and also freedom from economic necessity.

Assuming that such conditions prevail the approaches to ethics that have been discussed in the previous chapters can enlarge and enrich the ethical vocabularies of caring professions. The 'common sense' adoption of principlism suggests that ethics based on duty or utility, taken as absolute values, are insufficient for the complexities of day-to-day practice. Put simply, there are very few caring professionals who work on the basis of a 'pure' deontological or utilitarian position. Ethics based on consideration of emotions, relationships and communication provides additional ways of thinking about objectives and practices (ends and means) and augments attention to ideas of responsibility, fairness and consequences. Clearly such an assertion is pluralist, in the sense that it does not assume that any one value or approach will be absolute while at the same time rejecting relativism (Kekes, 1993). Compassion, care, sustainability, virtue and 'being-for-Other' are all values that may count as primary, alongside duty, responsibility, fairness, justice and so on, without any one precluding consideration of another. The contribution of the newer approaches is to provide a vocabulary that will enable the caring professions to be more subtle in their attention to the ethical dimensions of practice.

To illustrate this point, let us return to the multi-disciplinary team working in the care of older people.

A member of this team is asked to visit an older man at his home with the aim of assessing for the provision of a residential care placement. In their conversation it becomes clear that the older man does not wish to leave his home, but would accept home care services. At this point a local political leader arrives at the house and joins in the conversation, pressing the older man to choose a residential care placement. The professional asks to speak with the politician separately, with the aim of explaining that the older man must be given the opportunity to express his own views and give informed consent. The politician's response is to threaten the professional with a complaint to the agency director unless the professional 'makes' the older man accept moving to a residential care facility, implying that there is nothing wrong with the use of covert force (for example, by not offering home care services). The politician asserts that the family and neighbours are 'fed up' with providing care and that the older man's rights no longer matter because he is 'a burden' on others.

In this situation the professional has several choices. It would be possible to accept the politician's direction and seek to force the older man to leave his home. However, the values and principles that lie behind such a choice would not be supported by an ethical approach that placed the older man as a central actor in the situation. Indeed, it is only possible to construct an argument to support 'forcing' the older man to accept residential placement on the basis of a very particular interpretation of utilitarian principles. Such an argument would be that the sum of well-being, for the family and neighbours, would exceed the unhappiness of the older man. To this extent, in terms of established ethical theories, the difference between the professional and the politician is the stark contrast of deontology against utilitarianism.

However, more sophisticated interpretations of utilitarianism would also suggest that the use of coercion in this situation ignores the wider costs to the community in terms of trust, respect for all sections of the community. So the grounds for acceding to the politician's argument are insubstantial and the professional would have many good reasons to resist the claims being made to 'force' the older man to enter residential care.

However, at the same time, the older man's claims appear to depend on the involvement of his relatives and neighbours, who can also be understood as being coerced. How then can the professional make ethical sense of these complex circumstances? It is in responding to this question that ethics based on emotions, relationships and communication can provide ways of thinking about the facets of the situation. At an emotional level, older people with needs for assistance face losses and changes that have implications for their identity and perhaps for the immediacy of decline and death. These are 'plights' of great seriousness that come from the common human condition. As such they meet the requirements of the idea of compassion that was discussed in Chapter 4. Thus the professional may find additional reasons to defend the rights of the older man.

But the older man does not exist in isolation. His relationships are a central part of the problem that has to be resolved. From the perspective of an ethics of care (see Chapter 5 above) he must be drawn into a conversation about how he sees this. That is, the way in which he too engages with the rights of others in claiming his own rights forms part of the way of addressing the ethics of the professional response. To do this the professional will need to work through a relationship with the older man that is based both on trust and honesty about the situation. We should not forget that the professional is also part of this relationship, and as such her or his values will also be an explicit part of the interaction, shaping the way in which the older man may be drawn into considering his own wishes in comparison to the needs and rights of others. The social ecology of these circumstances also means that the older man cannot simply continue to assume that existing relationships are sustainable and in considering the needs and rights of the others who are involved here utilitarian ideas may have a role (although they will not be absolute – see Chapter 6 above).

Postmodern ethics, as we have already noted, are more difficult to 'apply'. From the point of 'being-for-Other', the professional would be absolutely committed to the good of the older man, but at the same time prevented from remaining in this 'moral party of two' (see Chapter 7 above). Therefore it would be necessary to make careful and considered judgements about the values on which to proceed, recognising that such values would be related closely to the specific context. For example, what are the primary values of the older person? If independence is the most important value, there may be a different way of proceeding than in the response to a person for whom security and comfort are of greater value. At the same time the professional would seek to ensure that her or his actions were based on self-awareness so that, for example, professional power was used with and not over the older man (such as in the use of language, the way options were explained and so on).

In this illustrative hypothetical situation there is a strong agreement between the various ethical approaches. There is also a clear common ground in the discursive way in which they proceed, in that none assume the abstract and impersonal reasoning of more traditional approaches. Rather, they all assume that the professional engages with other parties (the older man, the politician, perhaps family and neighbours) in the discursive process of establishing good objectives and ways of reaching them. In this situation all the approaches lead to very strong ethical arguments for maintaining the autonomy and dignity of the older man and that he should be actively involved in making decisions about his own life, although they may differ in the weight that they give to other parties. For that reason it may be argued that this is a weak or partial example. However, it has not been my intention here to demonstrate that all such approaches are equally plausible in all situations, nor to argue that there is a single way of relating them. From a pluralist perspective this would not have been a reasonable purpose. How such approaches are integrated with practice will depend on the different primary values that are held by professionals and the contexts in which they are working. We may expect that in the types of situations that have been used as illustrations in previous chapters, such as where young people are in conflict with adult authority, where people appear to be responsible for their own misfortunes, where service users place difficult demands on professionals, where decisions have to be made about life and death, or the quality of life, and so on, we may come to different conclusions about the best ways to think and act.

So the dynamic that has been described in the illustration of the older man and the politician not only applies to our thinking about the care of older people, but to any setting where caring professionals are based in agencies that have accountability in the community. Variations on this event are experienced in other areas of health services, in education, community services, church communities and so on. Of course, the outcome may be influenced by other factors. The politician may or may not actually make a complaint to the agency. The director may or may not support the team member if a complaint is received from the politician. If the community and the agency do not support the professional, then it may be very difficult to hold to a particular ethical position without this having implications for other aspects of that person's work. It is easier to maintain an ethical stance when the circumstances, including significant others, support it. So, when we find ourselves taking a position that is contrary to all those around us, but our own judgement suggests that we are correct, we have to have a clear basis for arguing and acting on our judgement and be prepared to take responsibility for the implications (Bauman, 1994, p. 14).

Banks (2001, p. 156) makes the point that we need to be careful also that members of the caring professions do not confuse what they 'like' or 'prefer' with ethics as such. For example, a social worker may wish that she could give more money to a mother who is on a low income than the agency policies permit, but this does not of itself make the policies 'bad'. A parallel argument would be relevant to questions about the amount of time a nurse or allied health therapist can spend with a patient, or a teacher can spend with a student who needs individual attention. Claims about the ethics of policies and institutional structures require the active focus of members of the caring professions and their 'moral fluency' (Sellman, 1996) in order for ethical arguments to be clear and convincing. As Banks (2001, pp. 156–7) also notes, just as one's wishes do not make a solid case for arguments about ethics, it is also the case that issues of resources are not simply technical matters either: they *do* have profound ethical implications. What is required is the ability to grasp these, as matters of ethics, in reflective practice.

It is the purpose of ethics to pose questions that challenge thought and action, that call our attention to what is good and what is right. In this sense, ethics, whether as an ethos or as codified sets of principles, should be both unsettling and unsettled. Ethics is unsettling because consideration of ethics causes us constantly to examine the values and principles that are embodied in our own practices. This may place demands on us or present us with difficult choices. There are no easy formulae for ethical decision making. Ethics is also unsettled, because it necessarily remains unfinished. As society changes and technologies develop there are new issues and questions to which attention must be given. It is not possible to depend on answers that previously were sufficient; we are faced all the time with having to make ethical sense of new circumstances.

In this book particular attention has been given to recent approaches to ethical theory. In order to develop discursive ethics, which I have argued is the way that the realities of ethical pluralism can be handled, it is necessary for professional ethics to embrace new thinking. It is important to acknowledge two things that this statement does not assert. First, this is not a claim that previously dominant approaches to ethics are redundant and should be jettisoned. Indeed, as has been clear at many points, the traditions of deontology and utilitarianism have informed other recent developments. Second, it is not an assertion of a specific new set of ethical principles for the caring professions. What I have argued is that by exploring recent ethical theories and taking into account the plural nature of contemporary society there is a need for a more discursive way of doing professional ethics. I have considered a range of professions within the notion of 'the caring professions'. In this I agree with Tadd (1998, p. 12) that while the details of practices and the social relationships within which people work may differ, there is also a high level of commonality between the caring professions. Thus each has much to learn from the debates that concern others; all share a common range of values and principles and face similar challenges.

The focus of practitioners is so often on their relationships with service users (whether seen as clients, patients, students, consumers or whatever), on the personal and situated nature of practice and on complex responsibilities that go beyond the individual to include other individuals. Relational approaches in ethics open up new possibilities for thinking about professional ethics, of exploring the creative relationships and tensions 'between moral reasoning, emotion and intuition' (Johnstone, 1994, p. 198). In the conclusions of each chapter that explored substantive approaches I noted that the ethics of compassion seen as an intelligent emotion, the ethics of care, the ethics of ecology and postmodern approaches to ethics each have an important contribution to make to the possibility of a discursive ethics in the caring professions. At the same time I also recognised that none of these developments is in itself sufficient to provide a robust ethics for practice. It this combination of each being necessary but not sufficient as part of the wider ethical vocabulary of the caring professions, in the context of an increasingly plural society, which leads to the argument for ethics as a discursive practice as the most plausible way of thinking about and applying ethical theory.

Coda: the role of ethics education

In order to be able to engage with ethics discursively, not only are wider social and organisational contexts important, as we have already noted, but also it is necessary for members of the caring professions to be prepared for the ethical dimensions of practice. Professional education is widely regarded as the major way in which members of the caring professions can be assisted to develop this capacity (DeMars *et al.*, 1991; Pinnington & Bagshaw, 1992; Weatherall, 1995). Indeed, if ethics is not included in professional education then practitioners learn that it is not important. So in conclusion I want to look briefly at core issues in the implications for ethics teaching of a discursive understanding of ethics in practice.

Schön (1987) describes the caring professions as 'reflective', that is as requiring practitioners to be able to be able to stand back from their own actions and to consider their own actions critically. So Schön advocates the same reflective method for professional education because it is not only congruent with the capacities that are being developed but also teaches by experience as it models the very process that is being learned. In that sense the goal of ethics education is to enable beginning members of the caring professions to develop the capacity to engage in precisely this sort of reflection, rather than to learn and apply one particular ethical approach as such (although some writers on ethics education emphasise particular normative positions). So, looked at in this way, professional education is seeking to enable members of the caring professions to learn an aptitude and an orientation (Nash, 1996). Ethics education is concerned with developing reflective practitioners.

A widely used educational technique is that of the 'case study' or 'case review' in which hypothetical or anonymised examples drawn from direct practice are used as a focus for analysis and discussion among a group of students (Barnitt & Roberts, 2000; Marco, 2002). Gaul (1995) draws parallels between this technique and the ethical approach of 'casuistry', in which ethical reasoning and decision making are derived from the consideration of a series of individual cases. As Gaul notes (1995, p. 49) casuistry provides a very useful structure for developing insights into the moral complexities of situations, but it does not of itself provide a normative content. So it is still necessary for those who are making decisions to be able to reflect on and apply other theories and principles. At the level of individual cases, it models the process of ethical reflection in which practitioners are engaged in their day-to-day work.

Jordan and Stevens (1999) give an example of another technique that has been used in some professional education programs in their description of an exercise in which students 'redesign' a code of ethics for their profession. The objectives of such an exercise are to familiarise students with the relevant code of ethics and the principles that are embodied in them, and at the same time to encourage students to develop a sense that professional ethics is not static but is part of a living tradition. In order to prepare the students for the task, they are first introduced to the code of ethics as it exists, along with accompanying documentation such as practice standards. Working in groups the students then rework or add to the code. So, not only do the students relate the code to their own experiences of practice but they also have to engage in a dialogue in order to produce the changes that they want to see in a code that is relevant to their work.

A third way in which ethics education can be approached it to see it as a form of 'critical thinking' (Plath *et al.*, 1999; Barnitt & Roberts, 2000). This way of looking at ethics education draws most explicitly on a philosophical approach to learning. That is, it focuses on the process of analysing and understanding situations and values by combining tuition in theories and principles with exercises in the application of these ideas to practices (often using a casuistic method in the form of problem-solving exercises). Plath *et al.* (1999) evaluated two ways of teaching 'critical thinking', the first being that of 'immersion', in which theories and values are embedded in the problems to be solved in class exercises, and the second being that of 'infusion', in which theories and values are taught explicitly prior to the problem-solving exercises. They conclude that the 'infusion' method is more effective, as evaluated by students and educators. Theories and values are made explicit and then grounded in the complexities of practice through the use of problem-based learning that accurately models actual practice.

The three strategies that have been described here each provide foundations for ethics to be treated discursively and for members of the caring professions to be prepared to address ethics both as an explicit dimension of their own practice and as part of the wider professional community to which they belong. This capacity to attend to ethics in one's own practice and in a profession more broadly is what Husband (1995) calls that of the 'morally active practitioner' and Sellman (1996) has termed 'moral fluency'. Furthermore, educational approaches that encourage students to develop an active and fluent orientation to professional ethics are also making possible the broadening of the theoretical and value bases which educators and students can explore in the learning process. This is very different from the teaching of abstract theories and principles or the piecemeal inclusion of ethics as an after-thought in the curriculum (Barnitt, 1993; Brockett, 1996).

For example, Kopelman (1995), Weatherall (1995) and Marco (2002) are concerned that medical students should have the opportunity to develop empathy and compassion. Indeed, they take it as a major weakness of medical education that while students will be rigorously taught and assessed on technical knowledge and skills (which are, of course, of considerable importance) in many instances they will not have the same rigour applied to their inter-personal and communication skills, nor to the ethics of their practice (which are also important). Gaul (1995) proposes casuistry as an educational method within the nursing curriculum for a similar reason. She is also concerned to be able to introduce the ethics of care into nursing curricula. This argument can be broadened to take in the ethics of compassion, the ethics of ecology and postmodern ethics. What is less explicitly discussed, but which is just as relevant from the perspective of introducing relational approaches to ethics into professional curricula alongside more traditional rational approaches, is that the methods of ethics education as well as the content can equip students to participate discursively in the ethics of their professions and to contribute to the continuing processes of ethical development. This is also an aspect of modelling that requires attention.

Yet although education in ethics is vital it is not a panacea for maintaining ethical attention in practice. Using a case example, Coulehan and Williams (2001) describe the circumstances in which medical students are effectively 'trained out of' the values that brought them into medicine in the first place. They make the point that it is reasonable to assume that many students enter medical programs because they have a compassionate regard for the needs of others, or a commitment to traditional medical virtues (p. 599). I would argue that the same applies to entrants in all the caring professions. However, the educational process contains 'tacit' as well as overt learning and tacit instruction is often more powerful than the explicit lesson because the tacit is embedded in the routines of 'real' practice, compared to the 'theory' of the overt curriculum. It is the lesson of following what is done and not what is said (p. 600). So, while ethics classes may emphasise principles, values, virtues and so on, a pressured schedule of classes and assessments and implicit modelling on the actions of senior professionals in clinical learning emphasise other values, such as 'detachment' (emotional numbness as a defence, in which cognition and skill become the exclusive focus), 'entitlement' (of professionals to salaries, respect, power and so on) and 'non-reflective professionalism' (in which traditional values are expressed while being at variance with actions) (pp. 600–1). In these ways, by the time students in the caring professions graduate they may have already learned to treat ethics as irrelevant, a nuisance or as a rationalising gloss over expedient decisions. For Coulehan and Williams the solution lies in connecting aspects of the curriculum that may assist students to integrate ethics, including explicit teaching of ethical theories, with the demands of 'real' practice.

This dissonance between ethics and the demands of practice is not confined to professional education. It pervades all aspects of the caring professions. For Johnstone (1994, p. 199), the responsibility for creating and maintaining a milieu that is conducive to open and honest questioning and debate about ethics in practice lies with senior professionals and managers (or administrators). Only under such conditions can more junior professionals and students be held to be fully accountable for the choices that they make. Of course, this argument does not seek to absolve those who are more junior from their own responsibilities. What it is suggesting is that in conditions where those who are more senior establish an ethic of defensiveness, detachment, self-interest, a non-reflective focus on technical competence and so on, these positions will be reinforced in the actions of more junior colleagues who will, in effect, come to be 'trained' to express these values in their practice. Supporting experienced professionals in maintaining and developing their ethical reflexivity is a crucial role for professional bodies. This is a clear example of the necessity for continuing, career-long professional development.

Conclusion

The development of discursive ethics requires both the provision of an 'ethical vocabulary' and of circumstances that are conducive to the exercise of moral responsibility. This chapter began with a restatement of the centrality of ethics to professional practice and the impossibility of one approach being sufficient to grasp the ethical complexity of day-to-day ethics. It then examined ways in which the ethics of compassion, ethics of care, ecological ethics and postmodern ethics may be brought to a consideration of a practice example, noting that each of these approaches offers a way of looking at ethics grounded in emotions, relationships and communication. This, it has been argued, augments and enriches the ethical vocabulary of the caring professions without any one approach being seen as an absolute position. Although discursive ethics may be unsettling the alternative is for the ethos of the caring professions to embody values and principles that are not congruent with their objectives.

This chapter has also briefly considered issues in ethics education as preparation for discursive practice. Particular educational methods have been identified as helpful for thinking about learning for discursive ethics in which discursive practice is itself modelled. Other issues about the 'tacit' curriculum have also been discussed, highlighting challenges to learning about ethics in practice.

In this book I have explored recent thinking about ethics and the implications of new ideas for the caring professions. The more traditional approaches that have defined professional ethics for a long time continue to be relevant. However, as I have argued, the focus of recent developments in ethics on emotion and experience, on relationships between people, on relationships between people and the environment, and on the contingent nature of much of our social experience, contributes to the extension of the ethical vocabulary. Rorty (1999) argues that the function of philosophy is not to provide particular answers to questions but to assist in the process of posing questions and seeking to answer them. Ethics, as a form of practical philosophy, has this purpose. Returning to Hinman's definition of ethics with which we started (2003, p. 5), it enables members of the caring professions to discuss explicitly what is good and what is right in practice and how these can be achieved. The development of discursive ethics, enriched by new ways of thinking about the 'good' and the 'right' as well as by the older traditions, provides a way of openly talking about and applying ethics that enables the caring professions to ensure that their practices are congruent with their values and moral principles.

Glossary of Terms

This brief glossary provides explanations of terms used in this book for readers who are unfamiliar with philosophy and social theory.

Beneficence. The principle of 'doing good'. The application of this principle in the caring professions may relate to the objective of seeking to do 'good' and does not necessarily depend on the actual achievement of a 'good' outcome.

Categorical Imperative. An unconditional requirement that forms the basis of ethics, according to Immanuel Kant (1742–1804). Kant developed several versions of the Categorical Imperative, the most well known of which is that 'I ought never to act except in such a way that I can also will that my maxim should become a universal law' (see *Maxim* below). This means that whatever principle is chosen as the basis for an action should be presumed to apply to everyone.

Compassion. A response of active concern towards the misfortune of another person or creature. Most commentators hold that compassion involves an empathic appreciation of the other's misfortune combined with a positive regard for the well-being of the other. Compassion is also held commonly to differ from 'pity', in that the latter refers to feelings of concern that are not associated with action; in some accounts the concept of pity implies condescension.

Consequentialism. An approach to ethics that considers questions of 'good' and 'right' in relation to the outcomes, that is the consequences, of ideas and actions. Consequentialism may be concerned with the outcomes that are intended, or it may focus on actual outcomes. A major example of consequentialist ethics is *Utilitarianism*.

Constructionism. A theory that explains social phenomena in terms of the processes of human action by which they are produced or 'constructed'. It also incorporates the argument that, as all social phenomena are 'constructed', no social structures or social relationships can be said to be 'natural' but they must all be understood in terms of their cultural context and their history. This theory is also called constructivism.

Critical Realism. A theory that accepts that knowledge is created through human action but argues that such knowledge describes phenomena that are objectively separate from human perception and that such knowledge is capable of being tested systematically (using empirical evidence and theoretical argument).

Deontology.   An approach to ethics that is based on the notion of 'duty' (from the Greek for duty, δεον (deon)). Moral duties are owed to people on the grounds that they are rational subjects and so are capable of exercising their autonomous will. The principle of 'respect for persons' is derived from this approach. Deontology is often associated with Kantian moral philosophy.

Discourse.   This term is used frequently to refer to a way of understanding and speaking about the world, as in the writing of Michel Foucault (1926–84). In a different usage it may also refer to the act of human communication.

Ecology.   Literally, the study of the environment. 'Ecologism' is a philosophical approach that emphasises the central importance of the environment in understanding the world. Ecologism can be combined with the insights of *Feminism* in the distinctive approach of 'ecofeminism'.

Empathy.   The capacity to understand accurately the perceptions and emotions of another person in such a way that this understanding can be used in responding to the other person's situation.

Empiricism.   An approach to knowledge, which claims that only those things that can be grasped by the physical senses can be known.

Enlightenment.   In western philosophy, this term refers to the period of the development of modern thought from approximately the sixteenth to the eighteenth centuries that was characterised by the emergence of empirical science and *Rationalism* in philosophy.

Epistemology.   Literally, the study of knowledge. This is a branch of philosophy that considers the way in which knowledge is formed and operates. It includes the philosophy of scientific methods.

Eudaimonia.   From the Greek ευδαιμονια meaning 'well-being' or 'happiness', this concept describes a primary 'good' or aim of human action.

Feminism.   A social movement, a set of personal and political commitments and a body of social theories that is premised on the critique of patriarchal social relations. That is, society is seen in terms of the dominance of men over women (in public and private life, in art, literature, religion and science, and so on). Feminism argues for an understanding of all aspects of society that fully acknowledges the perspectives of women.

Globalisation.   A theory which argues that a single global society is developing through increasing economic and cultural integration between nation states.

Holism.   Any theory or practice that understands any person or phenomenon as a whole that is more than a sum of its parts. For example, holistic health care would respond to all aspects of a person together rather than focusing on one particular problem or need. This is the opposite of *Reductionism*.

Individualism. In analytical terms, a way of understanding human life in terms of each individual person. As a practical philosophy, seeing the free action of individual people as a primary good. It may be said to form the basis of *Liberalism*.

Justice. The principle that all instances which are alike should be understood and responded to in the same way. It embodies the value of fairness, in that what counts as 'alike' will take into account all matters that are relevant to comparisons between instances.

Liberalism. A philosophical commitment to the maximum possible liberty in human affairs, holding that the chief good is the freedom for each person to pursue their own vision of the good life. Liberalism is usually associated with the minimum possible action of government in the lives of individual citizens and the maximum possible freedom for individuals to exercise their reason and make choices.

Maxim. A subjective rule or 'law' used by a person as the basis for an action. This term is used by Kant in his formulation of the *Categorical Imperative*.

Meta-narrative. A theory that provides a unified and over-arching explanation of the social world. The concept of 'meta-narrative' is used within the philosophy of *Postmodernity* to explain the *Universalism* of *Enlightenment* thought, for example in unitary theories of human nature.

Monism. The view that there is a single over-riding moral value, or set of values, that can always take precedence over all other values in defining what is 'good' and 'right' and that there is one set of principles by which such a value or values can be articulated. It is the opposite of *Relativism*.

Non-maleficence. The principle of 'not doing harm'. This is a separate principle from *Beneficence* as avoidance of harm through one's ideas and actions is distinct from 'doing good'. A well known example of this principle is found in Hippocrates' oath for physicians, in the phrase 'above all seek to do no harm'.

Paternalism. An attitude or set of actions based on an assumption that knowledge and skills which are exercised in an authoritative social role, such as that of a professional, give the right to the person in authority to make decisions on behalf of another person, such as a service user, irrespective of that person's own views or wishes. A more gender neutral term for this is *parentalism*, which conveys the sense of the professional acting like a parent even towards an adult service user.

Phronesis. The capacity of 'practical reason', which Aristotle held was essential for a person to be able to cultivate and practise the virtues in everyday situations.

Pluralism.   The view that there is no one primary moral value that is higher than all other moral values, while holding that there are context independent ways in which the competition between values may be resolved. Pluralism stands between *Monism* and *Relativism*.

Positivism.   An approach to scientific method, which only accepts theories that are derived from formally tested objective evidence.

Postmodernity.   Western philosophy and society after the *Enlightenment* is often referred to as 'modernity' and is marked by *Rationalism, Universalism* and the empirical scientific method. 'Postmodernity' is a term that refers to shifts in philosophy and society marked by a loss of certainty, fragmentation of meaning and by *Relativism*.

Principlism.   An approach to ethics that is based on the use of principles, notably respect for persons, *Beneficence, Non-maleficence* and *Justice*, to evaluate ideas and actions.

Rationalism.   The view that all aspects of the physical and social world, including human experience, can be explained by means of reason.

Reductionism.   Any theory or practice that understands a phenomenon in terms of the different parts of which it is composed. For example, reductionist health care would respond to each aspect of a person's health separately, rather than focusing on problems or needs seen as a whole. This is the opposite of *Holism*.

Relativism.   The view that the meaning of all social phenomena is relative to the standpoint of the person who is making a judgement about it. In ethics relativism supports the notion that judgements about 'right' and 'wrong' or 'good' and 'bad' vary according to a person's social context, personal characteristics and preferences. It is the opposite of *Monism*.

Solipsism.   The belief that only one's own perception of the world can be known.

Supererogatory.   A description of an act that is 'above and beyond the call of duty'. Such acts may be seen as morally virtuous, but because they are 'above and beyond' duty they could not be said to be required of anyone as an indication of virtue.

Universalism.   The view that explanations of social phenomena apply universally to all human life. An example is the idea that there is a core 'human nature' that is shared by all people, irrespective of their sex, age, ethnicity, sexuality or other distinctive characteristics. In ethics universalism supports the notion that judgements about 'right' and 'wrong' or 'good' and 'bad' are independent from a person's social context, personal characteristics and preferences.

Utilitarianism.   An approach to ethics in which what is 'right' and what is 'good' is judged in terms of potential to enhance the sum of human well-being.

This is a form of *Consequentialism* in ethics. There are several forms of utilitarianism, including 'act utilitarianism' in which an idea or action is judged in terms of whether it does contribute to the sum of human well-being and 'rule utilitarianism' in which judgement focuses on whether the idea or action follows a rule that ought to enhance the sum of human well-being. 'Preference utilitarianism' defines well-being in relation to people's preferences. Utilitarianism is usually associated with *Liberalism* in the political and moral philosophies of Jeremy Bentham (1748–1832) and John Stuart Mill (1806–73).

Virtue. A quality of being good, in philosophy usually applied to human characteristics.

Bibliography

Abbot, P. & Meerabeau, L. (1998) 'Professionals, professionalization and the caring professions' in P. Abbott & L. Meerabeau (eds) *The Sociology of the Caring Professions*. 2nd Edition. London: UCL Press, pp. 1–19.

Acker, S. (1995) 'Carry on caring: the work of women teachers' in *British Journal of Sociology of Education*, 16(1), pp. 21–36.

Adams, P. (2002) 'Humour and love: the origination of clown therapy' in *Postgraduate Medical Journal*, 78(922), pp. 447–8.

Allmark, P. (1995) 'Can there be an ethics of care?' in *Journal of Medical Ethics*, 21(1), pp. 19–24.

Allmark, P. (1996) 'Reply to Ann Bradshaw' in *Journal of Medical Ethics*, 22(1), pp. 13–15.

American Medical Association [AMA] (2002) *Code of Ethics*. Chicago: AMA.

Anderson, I. & Brady, M. (1999) 'Performance indicators for Aboriginal health services' in L. Hancock (ed.) *Health Policy in the Market State*. St Leonards, NSW: Allen & Unwin, pp. 187–209.

Apel, K.-O. (1984) *Understanding and Explanation*. (Trans. G. Warnke.) Cambridge, MA: MIT Press.

Australian Association of Occupational Therapists [OTA] (2001) *Code of Ethics*. Fitzroy, VIC: OTA.

Australian Association of Social Workers [AASW] (2002) *Code of Ethics*. Revised Edition. Canberra: AASW.

Australian Medical Association [AMA] (2003) *Position Statement: AMA Code of Ethics*. Sydney: AMA.

Australian Nursing Council [ANC], Royal College of Nursing Australia [RCNA] & Australian Nursing Federation [ANF] (2001) *Code of Ethics for Nurses in Australia*. Canberra: ANC/RCNA/ANF.

Australian Physiotherapy Association [APA] (2003) *Code of Conduct*. Melbourne: APA.

Australian Psychological Society [APS] (2002) *Code of Ethics*. Revised Edition. Melbourne: APS.

Azmi, S. (1997) 'Professionalism and diversity' in R. Hugman, M. Peelo & K. Soothill (eds) *Concepts of Care: Developments in Health and Social Welfare*. London: Arnold, pp. 102–20.

Baartman, H. (1998) 'Compassion and scepticism in child sexual abuse; some historical aspects and explanations' in *International Review of Victimology*, 5(2), pp. 189–202.

Baldwin, S. & Barker, P. J. (1991) 'Putting the service to rights' in P. J. Barker & S. Baldwin (eds) *Ethical Issues in Mental Health*. London: Chapman & Hall, pp. 181–97.

Balogh, R., Beattie, A. & Beckerleg, S. (1989) *Figuring Out Performance*. Sheffield: English National Board for Nursing, Midwifery and Health Visiting.

Banks, S. (2001) *Ethics and Values in Social Work*. 2nd Edition. Basingstoke: Palgrave Macmillan.

Banks, S. (2004) *Ethics, Accountability and the Social Professions*. Basingstoke: Palgrave Macmillan.

Barbalet, J. (2001) *Emotion, Social Theory and Social Structure: a Macrosociological Approach*. Cambridge: Cambridge University Press.

Barnitt, R. (1993) 'What gives you sleepless nights? Ethical practice in occupational therapy' in *British Journal of Occupational Therapy*, 56(6), pp. 207–12.

Barnitt, R. & Partridge, C. (1997) 'Ethical reasoning in physical therapy and occupational therapy' in *Physiotherapy Research International*, 2(3), pp. 178–92.

Barnitt, R. & Roberts, L. (2000) 'Facilitating ethical reasoning in student physical therapists' in *Journal of Physical Therapy Education*, 14(3), pp. 35–41.

Barnitt, R., Warbey, J. & Rawlins, S. (1998) 'Two case discussions of ethics: editing the truth and the right to resources' in *British Journal of Occupational Therapy*, 61(2), pp. 52–6.

Barrowclough, C. & Fleming, I. (1991) 'Ethical issues in work with older people' in P. J. Barker & S. Baldwin (eds) *Ethical Issues in Mental Health*. London: Chapman & Hall, pp. 68–83.

Barry, N. (1998) *Welfare*. 2nd Edition. Buckingham: Open University Press.

Bauman, Z. (1989) *Modernity and the Holocaust*. Ithaca, NY: Cornell University Press.

Bauman, Z. (1993) *Postmodern Ethics*. Oxford: Basil Blackwell.

Bauman, Z. (1994) *Alone Again: Ethics After the Age of Certainty*. London: Demos.

Bauman, Z. (1995) *Life in Fragments*. Oxford: Basil Blackwell.

Bauman, Z. (1998) *Globalization: the Human Consequences*. Cambridge: Polity Press.

Bauman, Z. (2001a) *The Individualized Society*. Cambridge: Polity Press.

Bauman, Z. (2001b) 'Whatever happened to compassion?' in T. Bentley & D. Stedman-Jones (eds) *The Moral Universe*. London: Demos, pp. 51–6.

Beauchamp, T. L. & Childress, J. F. (2001) *Principles of Biomedical Ethics*. 5th Edition. Oxford: Oxford university Press.

Beck, U. (1992) *Risk Society: Towards a New Modernity*. London: Sage.

Beck, U. (1999) *World Risk Society*. Cambridge: Polity Press.

Bentham, J. [1781] (1970) *An Introduction to the Principles of Morals and Legislation*. London: Athlone Press.

Berger, P. & Luckmann, T. (1966) *The Social Construction of Reality*. London: Penguin.

Bersoff, D. N. (ed.) (1999) *Ethical Conflicts in Psychology*. Washington, DC: American Psychological Association.

Bhaskar, R. (1986) *Scientific Realism and Human Emancipation*. London: Verso.

Blackhall, L. J., Murphy, S. T., Frank, G., Michel, V. & Azen, S. (1995) 'Ethnicity and attitudes toward patient autonomy' in *Journal of the American Medical Association*, 274, pp. 820–5.

Blum, L. A. (1994) *Moral Perception and Particularity*. Cambridge: Cambridge University Press.

Boleyn-Fitzgerald, P. (2003) 'Care and the problem of pity' in *Bioethics*, 17(1), pp. 1–20.

Bradshaw, P. (1996) 'Yes! There is an ethics of care: an answer for Peter Allmark' in *Journal of Medical Ethics*, 22(1), pp. 8–12.

Breckenridge, J. (1999) 'Subjugation and silences: the role of the professions in silencing victims of sexual and domestic violence' in J. Breckenridge & L. Laing (eds) *Challenging Silence*. St Leonards, NSW: Allen & Unwin, pp. 6–30.

Briskman, L. & Noble, C. (1999) 'Ethics' in B. Pease & J. Fook (eds) *Transforming Social Work Practice: Critical Postmodern Perspectives*. St Leonards, NSW: Allen & Unwin.

Brockett, M. (1996) 'Ethics, moral reasoning and professional virtue in occupational therapy education' in *Canadian Journal of Occupational Therapy/Revue Canadienne d'Ergothérapie*, 63(3), pp. 197–205.

Brown, R. C. (1999) 'The teacher as contemplative observer' in *Educational Leadership*, 56(4), pp. 70–3.

Browne, A. J. (1995) 'The meaning of respect: a First Nations' perspective' in *The Canadian Journal of Nursing Research*, 27(4), pp. 95–110.

Burnard, P. & Kendrick, K. (1998) *Ethical Counselling: a Workbook for Nurses*. London: Arnold.

Cairns, J. (1998) 'Excessive individualism today threatens liberty tomorrow: sustainable use of the planet' in *Population and Environment: a Journal of Interdisciplinary Studies*, 19(5), pp. 397–409.

Callahan, D. (1990) *What Kind of Life? The Limits of Medical Progress*. New York: Simon & Schuster.

Campbell, A., Gillett, G. & Jones, G. (2001) *Medical Ethics*. 3rd Edition. Melbourne: Oxford University Press.

Carr, D. (2000) *Professionalism and Ethics in Teaching*. London: Routledge.

Carrese, J. A. & Rhodes, L. A. (1995) 'Western bioethics on the Navajo Reservation: benefit or harm?' in *Journal of the American Medical Association*, 274, pp. 826–9.

Cheek, J. & Porter, S. (1997) 'Reviewing Foucault: possibilities and problems for nursing and health care' in *Nursing Inquiry*, 4(2), pp. 108–19.

Cheek, J. & Rudge, T. (1994) 'The panopticon revisited?' in *The International Journal of Nursing Studies*, 31(6), pp. 583–92.

Cherniss, C. (1995) *Beyond Burnout*. New York: Routledge.

Chilton, C. (1998) 'Nurses as health educators: the ethical issues' in W. Tadd (ed.) *Ethical Issues in Nursing and Midwifery Practice*. Basingstoke: Macmillan (now Palgrave Macmillan), pp. 58–79.

Clark, C. (2000) *Social Work Ethics: Politics, Principles and Practice*. Basingstoke: Macmillan (now Palgrave Macmillan).

Clarke, J. (1998) 'Doing the right thing? Managerialism and social welfare' in P. Abbott & L. Meerabeau (eds) *The Sociology of the Caring Professions*. 2nd Edition. London: UCL Press, pp. 234–54.

Collingridge, M., Miller, S. & Bowles, W. (2001) 'Privacy and confidentiality in social work' in *Australian Social Work*, 54(2), pp. 3–13.

Copleston, F. C. (1955) *Aquinas*. Harmondsworth: Penguin.

Corbett, K. (1993) 'Ethics and occupational therapy practice' in *Canadian Journal of Occupational Therapy*, 60(3), pp. 115–17.

Cossins, A. (1999) 'Recovered memories of child sexual abuse: the science and the ideology' in J. Breckenridge & L. Laing (eds) *Challenging Silence*. St Leonards, NSW: Allen & Unwin.

Coulehan, J. & Williams, P. C. (2001) 'Vanquishing virtue: the impact of medical education' in *Academic Medicine*, 76(6), pp. 598–605.

Daniels, N. (1988) *Am I My Parents' Keeper? An Essay on Justice Between the Young and the Old*. New York: Oxford University Press.

Davies, C. (1995) *Gender and the Professional Predicament of Nursing*. Buckingham: Open University Press.

de Botton, A. (2001) *The Consolations of Philosophy*. Melbourne: Penguin.

Delanty, G. (1997) *Social Science: Beyond Constructivism and Realism*. Buckingham: Open University Press.

DeMars, P. A., Fleming, J. D. & Benham, P. A. (1991) 'Ethics across the occupational therapy curriculum' in *The American Journal of Occupational Therapy*, 45(9), pp. 782–7.

Des Jardin, K. E. (2001a) 'Political involvement in nursing – education and empowerment' in *AORN Journal*, 74(4), pp. 468–82.

Des Jardin, K. E. (2001b) 'Political involvement in nursing – politics, ethics and strategic action' in *AORN Journal*, 74(5), pp. 614–30.

Deveaux, M. (1995) 'Shifting paradigms: theorizing care and justice in political theory' in *Hypatia*, 10(2), pp. 115–19.

Dominelli, L. (2002) 'Values in social work: contested entities with enduring qualities' in R. Adams, L. Dominelli & M. Payne (eds) *Critical Social Work*. Basingstoke: Palgrave (now Palgrave Macmillan), pp. 15–27.

Downie, R. S. & Calman, K. C. (1994) *Healthy Respect: Ethics in Health Care*. 2nd Edition. Oxford: Oxford University Press.

Doyal, L. & Gough, I. (1991) *A Theory of Human Need*. Basingstoke, Macmillan (now Palgrave Macmillan).

Etzioni, A. (1969) (ed.) *The Semi-Professions and Their Organization*. Engelwood Cliffs, NJ: Free Press.

Fasching, D. J. & deChant, D. (2001) *Comparative Religious Ethics: a Narrative Approach*. Oxford: Blackwell.

Finch, J. (1989) *Family Obligations and Social Change*. Cambridge: Polity Press.

Fischer, P. C. (2001) 'Putting theory into practice: a psychologist's story' in *Women & Therapy*, 23(1), pp. 101–9.

Flaskas, C. (1997) 'Reclaiming the idea of truth: some thoughts on theory in response to practice' in *Journal of Family Therapy*, 19(1), pp. 1–20.

Foucault, M. (1973) *The Birth of the Clinic*. New York: Pantheon.

Foucault, M. (1980) *Power/Knowledge*. (Trans. C. Gordon.) Brighton: Harvester Wheatsheaf.

Foucault, M. (1997) *Ethics: Subjectivity and Truth – the Essential Works of Foucault 1954–1984, Volume 1*. (Ed. P. Rabinow, trans. R. Hurley *et al.*) Harmondsworth: Penguin.

Francis, R. D. (1999) *Ethics for Psychologists*. Melbourne: ACER Press.

Fraser, N. (2001) 'Recognition without ethics?' in *Theory, Society & Culture*, 18(2), pp. 21–42.

Freeman, S. J. (2000) *Ethics: an Introduction to Philosophy and Practice*. Belmont, CA: Wadsworth.

Freidson, E. (1994) *Professionalism Reborn: Theory, Prophecy and Policy*. Chicago: University of Chicago Press.

Friedman, N. (2002) 'How to make your students cry: lessons in atrocity, pedagogy and heightened emotion' in *Journal of Mundane Behaviour*, 3(3).

Fry, S. T. & Johnstone, M.-J. (2002) *Ethics in Nursing Practice*. 2nd Edition. Oxford: Blackwell.

Fry, S. T. & Veatch, R. M. (2000) *Nursing Ethics – Case Studies*. 2nd Edition. Sudbury, MA: Jones & Bartlett.

Gadamer, H.-G. (1979) *Truth and Method*. 2nd Edition. (Trans. W. Glen-Doepel.) London: Sheed & Ward.

Gaita, R. (1991) *Good and Evil: an Absolute Conception*. Basingstoke: Macmillan (now Palgrave Macmillan).

Gaita, R. (2002) *The Philosopher's Dog*. Melbourne: Text Publishing.

Gallagher, S. M. (1999) 'The ethics of compassion' in *Ostomy Wound Management*, 45(6), pp. 14–16.

Gaul, A. L. (1995) 'Casuistry, care, compassion, and ethics data analysis' in *Advanced Nursing Science*, 17(3), pp. 47–57.

Gibson, D. (1998) *Aged Care: Old Policies, New Problems*. Melbourne: Cambridge University Press.

Giddens, A. (1991) *Modernity and Self-Identity*. Cambridge: Polity Press.

Gilligan, C. (1982) *In a Different Voice*. Cambridge, MA: Harvard University Press.

Gilligan, C. (1995) 'Hearing the difference: theorizing connection' in *Hypatia*, 10(2), pp. 120–7.

Glannon, W. (2002) 'Introduction to the history, theory and methods of biomedical ethics' in W. Glannon (ed.) *Contemporary Readings in Biomedical Ethics*. Fort Worth, TX: Harcourt College Publishers, pp. 1–33.

Goldner, F. H., Ference, T. P. & Ritti, R. R. (1973) 'Priests and laity: a profession in transition' in P. Halmos (ed.) *Professionalization and Social Change*. Keele: University of Keele Press, pp. 119–37.

Gower, B. S. (1992) 'What do we owe future generations?' in D. E. Cooper & J. A. Palmer (eds) *The Environment in Question: Ethics and Global Issues*. London & New York: Routledge, pp. 1–12.

Graham, J. L. (2001) 'Caring from afar: expanding our concept of care in the professions' in *Professional Ethics*, 9(1), pp. 31–60.

Greenwood, E. (1957) 'Attributes of a profession' in *Social Work*, 2(3), pp. 44–55.

Habermas, J. (1990) *Moral Consciousness and Communicative Action*. (Trans. C. Lenhardt & S. W. Nicholsen.) Cambridge, MA: MIT Press.

Hare, R. M. (1991) 'Moral reasoning about the environment' in B. Almond & D. Hill (eds) *Applied Philosophy: Morals and Metaphysics in Contemporary Debate*. London & New York: Routledge, pp. 9–20.

Hathaway, W. L. (2001a) 'Common sense professional ethics: a Christian appraisal' in *Journal of Psychology and Theology*, 29(3), pp. 225–34.

Hathaway, W. L. (2001b) 'Common sense is *not* consensus: professional ethics as marksmanship' in *Journal of Psychology and Theology*, 29(3), pp. 240–5.

Held, V. (1993) *Feminist Morality: Transforming Culture, Society and Politics*. Chicago: University of Chicago Press.

Held, V. (1995) 'The meshing of care and justice' in *Hypatia*, 10(2), pp. 128–32.

Higgs, R. (1998) 'Truth-telling' in H. Kuhse & P. Singer (eds) *A Companion to Bioethics*. Oxford: Blackwell, pp. 432–40.

Hinman, L. M. (2003) *Ethics: a Pluralistic Approach to Moral Theory*. 3rd Edition. Belmont, CA: Wadsworth/Thomson.

Honneth, A. (1995) *The Fragmented World of the Social*. Albany, NY: State University of New York Press.

Honneth, A. (2001) 'Recognition or redistribution? Changing perspectives on the moral order of society' in *Theory, Society & Culture*, 18(2), pp. 43–55.

Howe, D. (1994) 'Modernity, postmodernity and social work' in *British Journal of Social Work*, 24(5), pp. 513–32.

Hugman, R. (1991) *Power in Caring Professions*. Basingstoke: Macmillan (now Palgrave Macmillan).

Hugman, R. (1994) *Ageing and the Care of Older People in Europe*. Basingstoke: Macmillan (now Palgrave Macmillan).

Hugman, R. (1998) *Social Welfare and Social Value*. Basingstoke: Macmillan (now Palgrave Macmillan).

Human Rights and Equal Opportunity Commission [HREOC] (1997) *Bringing Them Home: the 'Stolen Children' Report*. Canberra: HREOC.

Humphrey, M. (1996) *Empty Cradles*. London: Doubleday.

Husband, C. (1995) 'The morally active practitioner' in R. Hugman & D. Smith (eds) *Ethical Issues in Social Work*. London: Routledge, pp. 84–103.

Hussey, T. (1996) 'Nursing ethics and codes of professional conduct' in *Nursing Ethics*, 3(3), pp. 250–8.

Ife, J. (1995) *Community Development*. Melbourne: Longman.

Irving, A. (1999) 'Waiting for Foucault' in A. S. Chambon, A. Irving & L. Epstein (eds) *Reading Foucault for Social Work*. New York: Columbia University Press, pp. 27–50.

Jackson, J. (2002) 'Telling the truth' in W. Glannon (ed.) *Contemporary Readings in Biomedical Ethics*. Fort Worth, TX: Harcourt College Publishers, pp. 61–7.

jagodinski, j. (2002) 'The ethics of the "real" in Lèvinas, Lacan and Buddhism: pedagogical implications' in *Educational Theory*, 52(1), pp. 81–96.

Jecker, N. S. & Self, D. J. (1991) 'Separating care and cure: an analysis of historical and contemporary images of nursing and medicine' in *Journal of Medicine and Philosophy*, 16(3), pp. 285–306.

Johnson, H. C., Cournoyer, D. E. & Bond, B. M. (1995) 'Professional ethics and parents as consumers: how well are we doing?' in *Families in Society: the Journal of Contemporary Human Services*, 76(7), pp. 408–20.

Johnson, T. J. (1972) *Professions and Power*. London: Macmillan (now Palgrave Macmillan).

Johnstone, M.-J. (1994) *Bioethics: a Nursing Perspective*. 2nd Edition. Marrickville, NSW: W. B. Saunders/Baillière Tindall.

Jordan, K. & Stevens, P. (1999) 'Revising the code of ethics of the IAMFC' in *The Family Journal: Counseling and Therapy for Couples and Families*, 7(2), pp. 170–5.

Kant, I. [1785] (1964) *The Moral Law: Groundwork of the Metaphysics of Morals*. (Trans. H. J. Paton.) London/New York: Routledge.

Kekes, J. (1993) *The Morality of Pluralism*. Princeton, NJ: Princeton University Press.

Kidd, R. (2000) *Black Lives, Government Lies*. Sydney: University of New South Wales Press.

Kinnevy, S. (1999) 'Ecological theory as social welfare theory'. Paper presented to the American Sociological Association. Philadelphia, PA: University of Pennsylvania (unpublished).

Koehn, D. (1994) *The Ground of Professional Ethics*. London: Routledge.

Kohlberg, L. (1981) *Essays in Moral Development: Volume 1, The Philosophy of Moral Development*. San Francisco: Harper & Row.

Kohlberg, L. (1984) *Essays in Moral Development: Volume 2, The Psychology of Moral Development*. San Francisco: Harper & Row.

Kopelman, L. M. (1995) 'Philosophy and medical education' in *Academic Medicine*, 70(9), pp. 795–805.

Kuhse, H. (1997) *Caring: Nurses, Women and Ethics*. Oxford: Blackwell.

Kushner, T. K. & Thomasma, D. C. (2001) *Ward Ethics: Dilemmas for Medical Students and Doctors in Training*. Cambridge: Cambridge University Press.

Lamont, J. (2001) 'The ethics of doctor supply restriction in Australia' in *Australian Journal of Professional and Applied Ethics*, 3(1), pp. 22–39.

Lane, R. E. (2001) 'Self-reliance and empathy: the enemies of poverty – and the poor' in *Political Psychology*, 22(3), pp. 473–92.

Leonard, P. (1997) *Postmodern Welfare*. London: Sage.

Lèvinas, E. (1981) *Otherwise than Being or Beyond Essence*. (Trans. A. Lingis.) The Hague: Martinus Nijhoff.

Lèvinas, E. (1985) *Ethics and Infinity*. (Trans. Richard A. Cohen.) Pittsburgh, PA: Duquesne University Press.

Lèvinas, E. (1987) *Collected Philosophical Papers*. (Trans. A. Lingis.) The Hague: Martinus Nijhoff.

Lewins, F. (1996) *Bioethics for Health Professionals: an Introduction and Critical Approach*. South Melbourne: Macmillan (now Palgrave Macmillan).

Lichtenberg, J. (1996) 'What are codes of ethics for?' in M. Coady & S. Bloch (eds) *Codes of Ethics and the Professions*. Melbourne: Melbourne University Press, pp. 13–27.

Lindsay, R. (2002) *Recognizing Spirituality*. Perth: University of Western Australia Press.

Lynch, J. W. (2002) 'A lesson in empathy: what our patients are most likely to remember is our compassion' in *Saturday Evening Post*, 274(1), pp. 30–1.

Lyon, D. (1999) *Postmodernity*. 2nd Edition. Buckingham: Open University Press.

Macdonald, K. (1995) *The Sociology of the Professions*. London: Sage.

MacIntyre, A. (1985) *After Virtue*. 2nd Edition. London: Duckworth.

MacLeod, R. D. (2001) 'On reflection: doctors learning to care for people who are dying' in *Social Science & Medicine*, 52(11), pp. 1719–27.

Manthorpe, J. & Stanley, N. (1999) 'Shifting the focus from "bad apples" to users' rights' in N. Stanley, J. Manthorpe & B. Penhale (eds) *Institutional Abuse*. London: Routledge, pp. 223–40.

Marco, C. A. (2002) 'Teaching ethics to problem residents' in *Academic Emergency Medicine*, 9(10), pp. 1001–6.

Maslow, A. (1970) *Motivation and Personality*. 2nd Edition. New York: Harper & Row.

Mayer, J. D. & Salovey, P. (1993) 'The intelligence of emotional intelligence' in *Intelligence*, 17(4), pp. 433–42.

McCallum, J. & Geiselhart, K. (1996) *Australia's New Old*. St Leonards, NSW: Allen & Unwin.

McDonald, C. (1999) 'Human service professionals in the community services industry' in *Australian Social Work*, 52(1), pp. 17–25.

Midgely, M. (2001) 'Individualism and the concept of Gaia' in T. Bentley & D. Stedman-Jones (eds) *The Moral Universe*. London: Demos, pp. 93–8.

Mies, M. & Shiva, V. (1993) *Ecofeminism*. Halifax/London: Fernwood Publications/Zed Books.

Mill, J. S. ([1861] 1910) *Utilitarianism, Liberty & Representative Government*. London/New York: J. M. Dent & Sons/E. P. Dutton.

Morgan, L. M. (2002) ' "Properly disposed of": a history of embryo disposal and the changing claims of fetal remains' in *Medical Anthropology*, 21(3–4), pp. 247–74.

Mujawamariya, D. (2001) 'Associate teachers facing integration of visible minorities into the teaching profession in Francophone Ontario' in *Canadian Ethnic Studies*, 33(2), pp. 78–87.

Murdoch, I. (1993) *Metaphysics as a Guide to Morals*. Harmondsworth: Penguin.

Nash, R. J. (1996) *'Real World' Ethics*. New York: Teachers' College Press.

New South Wales Teachers' Federation [NSWTF] (2002) *Ethics of the New South Wales Teachers Federation*. Sydney: NSWTF (downloaded from www.nswwtf.org.au/about/ethics2.html on 8 May 2004).

New Zealand Association of Social Workers [NZASW] (1993) *Code of Ethics*. Dunedin: NZASW.

Noddings, N. (1984) *Caring: a Feminine Approach to Ethics and Moral Education*. Berkeley, CA: University of California Press.

Nussbaum, M. (1996) 'Compassion: the basic social emotion' in *Social Philosophy and Policy*, 13(1), pp. 27–58.

Nussbaum, M. (2001) *Upheavals of Thought: the Intelligence of Emotions*. New York: Cambridge University Press.

Olsen, D. P. (2001) 'Empathic maturity: theory of moral point of view in clinical relations' in *Advanced Nursing Science*, 24(1), pp. 36–46.

Park, K. M. (1996) 'The personal is ecological: environmentalism of social work' in *Social Work*, 41(3), pp. 320–3.

Parsons, E. C. (2001) 'Using power and caring to mediate white male privilege, equality and equity in an urban elementary classroom' in *The Urban Review*, 33(4), pp. 321–38.

Parton, N. (1985) *The Politics of Child Abuse*. London: Macmillan (now Palgrave Macmillan).

Parton, N. (1994) ' "Problematics of government", (post)modernity and social work' in *British Journal of Social Work*, 24(1), pp. 9–32.

Parton, N. (2003) 'Rethinking *professional* practice: the contributions of social constructionism and the feminist "ethics of care" ' in *British Journal of Social Work*, 33(1), pp. 1–16.

Payne, H. & Littlechild, B. (eds) (2000) *Ethical Practice and the Abuse of Power in Social Responsibility*. London: Jessica Kingsley.

Pellegrino, E. D. & Thomasma, D. C. (1993) *The Virtues in Medical Practice*. New York: Oxford University Press.

Penhale, B. (1999) 'Introduction' in N. Stanley, J. Manthorpe & B. Penhale (eds) *Institutional Abuse: Perspectives Across the Life Course*. London: Routledge, pp. 1–15.

Perkin, H. (1989) *The Rise of Professional Society: England Since 1880*. London: Routledge.

Pink, G. (1994) 'The price of truth' in *British Medical Journal*, 309, pp. 1700–5.

Pinnington, L. & Bagshaw, A. (1992) 'The requirement for ethical reasoning in occupational therapy education' in *British Journal of Occupational Therapy*, 55(11), pp. 419–22.

Pizarro, D. (2000) 'Nothing more than feelings? The role of emotion in moral judgement' in *Journal for the Theory of Social Behaviour*, 30(4), pp. 355–75.

Plath, D., English, B., Connors, L. & Beveridge, A. (1999) 'Evaluating the outcomes of intensive critical thinking instruction for social work students' in *Social Work Education*, 18(2), pp. 207–17.

Plumwood, V. (1993) *Feminism and the Mastery of Nature*. London: Routledge.

Plumwood, V. (2002) *Environmental Culture: the Ecological Crisis of Reason*. London: Routledge.

Potgieter, C. & de la Ray, C. (1997) 'Gender and race: where to psychology in South Africa?' in *Feminism & Psychology*, 7(1), pp. 139–42.

Preece, G. (2002) 'The unthinkable and unlivable Singer' in G. Preece (ed.) *Rethinking Peter Singer*. Downers Grove, IL: IVP, pp. 23–67.

Rachels, J. (1986) 'Active and passive euthanasia' in P. Singer (ed.) *Applied Ethics*. New York: Oxford University Press, pp. 29–35.

Rachels, J. (1998) 'Ethical theory and bioethics' in H. Kuhse & P. Singer (eds) *A Companion to Bioethics*. Oxford: Blackwell, pp. 15–23.

Reamer, F. G. (2001) *Ethics Education in Social Work*. Alexandria, VA: Council on Social Work Education.

Redfern, M. (Chair) (2001) *The Royal Liverpool Children's Inquiry Report*. London: The Stationery Office.

Regan, T. (1984) *The Case for Animal Rights*. London: Routledge.

Rhodes, M. (1986) *Ethical Dilemmas in Social Work Practice*. Boston, MA: Routledge & Kegan Paul.

Roberts, G. W. (1999) 'Values in the spiritual context of occupational therapy' in *British Journal of Occupational Therapy*, 62(2), p. 51.

Robinson, D. (1999) *Nietzsche and Postmodernism*. Cambridge/New York: Icon Books/Totem Books.

Rogero-Anaya, P., Carpintero-Avellaneda, J. L. & Vila-Blasco, B. (1994) 'Ethics and research in nursing' in *Nursing Ethics*, 1(4), pp. 216–23.

Rorty, R. (1999) *Philosophy and Social Hope*. London: Penguin.

Sarason, S. B. (1985) *Caring and Compassion in Clinical Practice*. San Francisco: Jossey-Bass.

Scarry, E. (1999) 'The difficulty of imagining other persons' in C. Hesse & R. Post (eds) *Human Rights in Political Transitions: Gettysburg to Bosnia*. New York: Zone Books, pp. 277–309.

Schmidt, K. W. (2000) 'The concealed and the revealed: bioethical issues in Europe at the end of the Second Millenium' in *Journal of Medicine and Philosophy*, 25(2), pp. 123–32.

Schön, D. (1987) *Educating the Reflective Practitioner*. San Francisco: Jossey-Bass.

Scott, P. A. (2000) 'Emotion, moral perception, and nursing practice' in *Nursing Philosophy*, 1(2), pp. 123–33.

Sellman, D. (1996) 'Why teach ethics to nurses?' in *Nurse Education Today*, 16(1), pp. 44–8.

Sen, A. (2001) 'East and west: the reach of reason' in T. Bentley & D. Stedman-Jones (eds) *The Moral Universe*. London: Demos, pp. 19–34.

Sevenhuijsen, S. (1998) *Citizenship and the Ethics of Care: Feminist Considerations on Justice, Morality and Politics*. London: Routledge.

Silverman, P. & Maxwell, R. J. (1982) 'Cross-cultural variation in the status of old people' in P. Stearns (ed.) *Old Age in Pre-industrial Society*. New York: Holmes & Maier, pp. 46–69.

Sim, J. (1996) 'Client confidentiality: ethical issues in occupational therapy' in *British Journal of Occupational Therapy*, 59(2), pp. 56–61.

Sim, S. (1999) *Derrida and the End of History*, Cambridge/New York: Icon Books/Totem Books.

Singer, P. (1975) *Animal Liberation: a New Ethics for Our Treatment of Animals*. London: Jonathan Cape.

Singer, P. (1986) 'All animals are equal' in P. Singer (ed.) *Applied Ethics*. New York: Oxford University Press, pp. 215–28.

Singer, P. (1993a) *Practical Ethics*. 2nd Edition. Melbourne: Cambridge University Press.

Singer, P. (1993b) *How Are We to Live? Ethics in an Age of Self-Interest*. Melbourne: Text Publishing.

Singer, P. (2002) *One World: the Ethics of Globalisation*. Melbourne: Text Publishing.

Smith, D. (1999) *Zygmunt Bauman: Prophet of Postmodernity*. Cambridge/Oxford: Polity Press/Blackwell.

Smith, M. J. (1998) *Ecologism: Towards Ecological Citizenship*. Buckingham: Open University Press.

Society of Hospital Pharmacists of Australia [SHPA] (1996) *Code of Ethics*. South Melbourne: SHPA.

Stanley, L. & Wise, S. (eds) (1993) *Breaking Out Again*. London: Routledge.

Stanley, N., Manthorpe, J. & Penhale, B. (eds) (1999) *Institutional Abuse: Perspectives Across the Life Course*. London: Routledge.

Stephan, W. G. & Finaly, K. (1999) 'The role of empathy in improving intergroup relations' in *Journal of Social Issues*, 55(4), pp. 729–43.

Stevens, P. (2000) 'The ethics of being ethical' in *The Family Journal: Counseling and Therapy for Couples and Families*, 8(2), pp. 177–8.

Stevenson, A. C. T. (2002) 'Compassion and patient centred care' in *Australian Family Physician*, 31(12), pp. 1103–6.

Strasburger, L. H., Jurgensen, L. & Randles, R. (1995) 'Criminalization of psychotherapist–patient sex' in D. N. Bersoff (ed.) *Ethical Conflicts in Psychology*. Washington, DC: American Psychological Association, pp. 229–33.

Sumison, J. (2000) 'Caring and empowerment: a teacher educator's reflection on an ethical dilemma' in *Teaching in Higher Education*, 5(2), pp. 167–79.

Sumner, L. W. (1996) *Welfare, Happiness and Ethics*. Oxford: Oxford University Press.

Szasz, T. (1991) 'Psychiatry and social control' in *The Humanist*, 51(1), pp. 24–5, 34.

Sznaider, N. & Talmud, I. (1998) 'Moral sentiments and the social organization of public compassion: the case of child abuse in Israel' in *International Journal of Contemporary Sociology*, 35(1), pp. 14–27.

Tadd, W. (1998) 'Ethics in nursing' in W. Tadd (ed.) *Ethical Issues in Nursing and Midwifery Practice*. Basingstoke: Macmillan (now Palgrave Macmillan), pp. 10–41.

Tallon, A. (1997) *Head and Heart: Affection, Cognition, Volition as Triune Consciousness*. New York: Fordham University Press.

Tännsjö, T. (2002) *Understanding Ethics: an Introduction to Moral Theory*. Edinburgh: Edinburgh University Press.

Tawney, R. H. (1938) *Religion and the Rise of Capitalism*. Harmondsworth: Penguin.

Taylor, J. (1995) 'In a different voice in occupational therapy' in *British Journal of Occupational Therapy*, 58(4), pp. 170–4.

Tjelveit, A. C. (1999) *Ethics and Values in Psychotherapy*. London; Routledge.

Tjelveit, A. C. (2001) 'Natural moral sense as basis for professional ethics: an important proposal but unlikely to produce excellence' in *Journal of Psychology and Theology*, 29(3), pp. 235–9.

Tope, R. & Smail, J. (1998) 'Community nursing: the ethical issues' in W. Tadd (ed.) *Ethical Issues in Nursing and Midwifery Practice*. Basingstoke: Macmillan (now Palgrave Macmillan), pp. 80–102.

Tronto, J. (1993) *Moral Boundaries: a Political Argument for an Ethic of Care*. New York: Routledge.

Tschudin, V. (1998) 'Nursing ethic at the end of life' in W. Tadd (ed.) *Ethical Issues in Nursing and Midwifery Practice*. Basingstoke: Macmillan (now Palgrave Macmillan), pp. 233–54.

Tuckett, A. G. (1998) 'An ethic of the fitting: a conceptual framework for nursing practice' in *Nursing Inquiry*, 5(4), pp. 220–7.

Ungerson, C. (1987) *Policy is Personal*. London: Tavistock.

Ungerson, C. (1990) 'The language of care' in C. Ungerson (ed.) *Gender and Caring*. Hemel Hempstead: Harvester Wheatsheaf, pp. 8–33.

van Hooft, S. (1995) *Caring: an Essay in the Philosophy of Ethics*. Niwot, CO: University Press of Colorado.

Veatch, R. (1997) *Medical Ethics*. 2nd Edition. Sudbury, MA: Jones & Bartlett.

Veatch, R. M. (2002) 'When should the patient know? The death of the therapeutic privilege' in W. Glannon (ed.) *Contemporary Readings in Biomedical Ethics*. Fort Worth, TX: Harcourt College Publishers, pp. 54–61.

von Dietze, E. & Orb, A. (2000) 'Compassionate care: a moral dimension of nursing' in *Nursing Inquiry*, 7(3), pp. 166–74.

Warnke, G. (1995) 'Discoures ethics and feminist dilemmas of difference' in J. Meehan (ed.) *Feminists Read Habermas: Gendering the Subject of Discourse*. New York & London: Routledge, pp. 247–61.

Watson, W. H. (1999) *Against the Odds: Blacks in the Profession of Medicine in the United States*. New Brunswick, NJ: Transaction.

Weatherall, D. J. (1995) 'Teaching ethics to medical students' in *Journal of Medical Ethics*, 21(3), pp. 133–4.

Whitebrook, M. (2002) 'Compassions as a political virtue' in *Political Studies*, 50(3), pp. 529–44.

Whiteford, G. & St Clair, V. W. (2002) 'Being prepared for diversity in practice' in *British Journal of Occupational Therapy*, 65(3), pp. 129–37.

Wilding, P. (1982) *Social Welfare and Professional Power*. London: Macmillan (now Palgrave Macmillan).

Williams, C., Soothill, K. & Barry, J. (1992) 'Nursing wastage from the nurses' perspective' in K. Soothill, C. Henry & K. Kendrick (eds) *Themes and Perspectives in Nursing*. London: Chapman & Hall, pp. 214–30.

Wise, S. (1988) *Doing Feminist Social Work*. Studies in Sexual Politics 21. Manchester: Department of Sociology, University of Manchester.

Wise, S. (1995) 'Feminist ethics in practice' in R. Hugman & D. Smith (eds) *Ethical Issues in Social Work*. London: Routledge, pp. 104–19.

Witz, A. (1992) *Professions and Patriarchy*. London: Routledge.

Yerxa, E. J. (1991) 'Seeking an relevant ethical and realistic way of knowing for occupational therapy' in *American Journal of Occupational Therapy*, 45(3), pp. 199–204.

Index